MW00609460

Harnessing the UEFI Shell

Moving the platform beyond DOS

Michael Rothman
Tim Lewis
Vincent Zimmer
Robert Hale

Intel
PRESS

Copyright © 2009 Intel Corporation. All rights reserved.
ISBN 978-1-934053-14-0
No part of this publication may be reproduced, stored in a retrieval system or transmitted in any form or by any means, electronic, mechanical, photocopying, recording, scanning or otherwise, except as permitted under Sections 107 or 108 of the 1976 United States Copyright Act, without either the prior written permission of the Publisher, or authorization through payment of the appropriate per-copy fee to the Copyright Clearance Center, 222 Rosewood Drive, Danvers, MA 01923, (978) 750-8400, fax (978) 750-4744. Requests to the Publisher for permission should be addressed to the Publisher, Intel Press, Intel Corporation, 2111 NE 25th Avenue, JF3-330, Hillsboro, OR 97124-5961. E-Mail: intelpress@intel.com.

This publication is designed to provide accurate and authoritative information in regard to the subject matter covered. It is sold with the understanding that the publisher is not engaged in professional services. If professional advice or other expert assistance is required, the services of a competent professional person should be sought.

Intel Corporation may have patents or pending patent applications, trademarks, copyrights, or other intellectual property rights that relate to the presented subject matter. The furnishing of documents and other materials and information does not provide any license, express or implied, by estoppel or otherwise, to any such patents, trademarks, copyrights, or other intellectual property rights.

Intel may make changes to specifications, product descriptions, and plans at any time, without notice. Fictitious names of companies, products, people, characters, and/or data mentioned herein are not intended to represent any real individual, company, product, or event.

Intel products are not intended for use in medical, life saving, life sustaining, critical control or safety systems, or in nuclear facility applications.

Intel and the Intel logo are trademarks or registered trademarks of Intel Corporation or its subsidiaries in the United States and other countries.

† Other names and brands may be claimed as the property of others.

This book is printed on acid-free paper.

Publisher: Richard Bowles
Editor: David J. Clark
Program Manger: Stuart Douglas
Text Design & Composition: STI
Graphic Art: Matt Statton (illustrations), Ron Bohart (cover)

Library of Congress Cataloging in Publication Data:

Printed in China

10 9 8 7 6 5 4 3 2 1

First printing August 2009

IMPORTANT

You can access the companion Web site for this book on the Internet at:

www.intel.com/intelpress/eshl

Use the serial number located in the upper-right hand corner of the last page to register your book and access additional material, including the Digital Edition of the book.

To my wife Sandi, for having infinite patience in allowing me to find the "spare" time for this endeavor, and to my sons Ryan and Aaron, who keep me grounded in what life is really about. Also to my grandfather Joseph, who instilled the love of learning and set an example I strive to promote for the next generation.

—Mike Rothman

To my wife Helen, always bright and beautiful, and to my kids, curious Shannon, caring Brahms, and courageous Miriam, always the joy of my life.

—Tim Lewis

To the three beautiful women in my life: my wife Jan, and my daughters Ally and Zoe.

—Vincent J. Zimmer

To my father, Erik, Alex, and Prinz, thank you. Thank you to my co-workers who keep me grounded and inspired.

—Robert Hale

Contents

Chapter 11 - Managing UEFI Drivers Using the Shell   235

Appendix A - Security Considerations   253

Appendix B - Command Reference   265

Foreword

A little more than two and half years ago, I helped introduced the book Beyond BIOS. In 2008, the industry has seen significant movements in this direction for the x64 systems. Microsoft shipped both the Windows Vista SP1 and Windows Server 2008 with the support of the UEFI boot process. System vendors are beginning to include the option to boot UEFI applications (including operating systems). For example, HP has made the transition for all its newly-designed Elitebook and Compaq commercial notebooks. MSI also enabled the option with the UEFI-based motherboards and netbooks. This trend will continue. As we estimate that 50 percent of the PCs shipping by the beginning of 2010 would be based on UEFI technology, we expect more and more of these systems would include this option. Eventually, the traditional BIOS boot process would become an after-market option. However, before removing its support, we need to enable the industry to move beyond DOS.

DOS was a dominant operating system for the x86 market before 1995. With the introduction of Windows and Linux, the role of DOS has significantly diminished as an operating system. Its single-user, single-task, non-reentrant environment makes it no longer viable. Its memory addressability and hard disk access limitations also plague its use. However, its ability for shell scripting and hardware access, its simplicity, and its familiarity, still make it an attractive pre-OS environment for manufacturing and diagnostics.

With the ubiquitous availability of the x64 processors, the viability of DOS as a pre-OS environment for diagnostics is challenged. DOS-based diagnostics cannot perform memory testing for memory not accessible in the DOS environment. DOS is also heavily dependent on the BIOS interfaces. As we move beyond BIOS, we will need a 64-bit pre-OS environment that takes advantage of the UEFI environment while offering shell scripting ability, hardware access, simplicity and familiarity.

Let me introduce the UEFI Shell. Actually, a shell environment was provided in the original EFI Sample Implementation and later on the TianoCore.org open source project from Intel. Intel designed the shell to support the features that are normally available in DOS or the UNIX shells such as Bourne, Korn, or C shells, but made it distinguishable from these other shells. That shell has in fact been found very useful. HP Integrity† Servers and MSI Click BIOS motherboards, for example, embedded this shell in the ROM. Others such as the HP commercial notebooks and Apple† iMacs do not include the shell in the ROM, but these systems can launch the shell from other storage space. Intel left it out of the EFI Specification originally thinking this pre-OS environment would likely be a vendor value differentiation. Although it is true that the vendors are likely to differentiate, the UEFI Forum collectively decided that we need a baseline that is standardized so we can expect interoperability. Then came the UEFI Shell Specification 2.0, published in October last year. Standardizing the shell also gives us the anchor to run the UEFI Self-Certified Test.

This book is a perfect sequel to the Beyond BIOS book. If you are still using or shipping DOS-based solutions, this book is definitely a must-read for you. It provides an important bridge between the normative specifications and the informative details of the development and the insights.

We are fortunate to have the same authors to offer their insights again: Michael Rothman chairs the UEFI Shell Subteam that owns the standardization of the UEFI Shell. He also chairs the Configuration Subteam that owns the Human Interface Infrastructure (HII) that the shell can use for configuration purposes. Vincent Zimmer chairs the Networking Subteam owning the UEFI network stack and the IPv6 support. He has also been very involved in the Trusted Computing Group, defining security related extensions for UEFI. Robert Hale has been working in many of these areas for a long time and is a driving force behind many of the shell and HII development. This time we also have Tim Lewis, the Chief BIOS Architect from Phoenix, covering the batch scripting and shell application programming. Tim chairs the UEFI Security Subteam and is one of the leading contributors in the UEFI Shell and Configuration Subteams. I cannot think of any better dream team to teach on this subject matter.

Using this book along with the code on the TianoCore.org open source Shell project would be the excellent tutorial for the engineers to develop UEFI Shell based solutions to move beyond DOS. I am very pleased to recommend this new book.

Dong Wei

Vice President and Chief Executive, the Unified Forum

HP Distinguished Technologist

Granite Bay, California

January 18, 2009

Preface

A man is rich in proportion to the number of things he can afford to let alone.

—Henry David Thoreau

This is a book about a computer program that was never intended to be what it is. The first version of what is now the UEFI Shell was created to facilitate debug of early parts of EFI. It was never intended to see a customer. It was a simple expedient tool to speed up an EFI developer's job. Its escape to the rest of the world was, in retrospect, inevitable because it was more valuable than we realized. It became popular enough that, in the eyes of many, it was EFI. It was not, and it is not. EFI (now UEFI) is a commonly agreed upon set of interfaces between operating systems, BIOS, and option ROMs. The shell is, in many ways, simply another operating system that sits on top of EFI.

In the next few years of "add what we need" the shell became more and more valuable. Badly suffering from too many hands and not enough guidance, it became complex enough to warrant serious effort, a seriously out of control adolescent if there ever was one. In the end, it has become valuable enough to warrant the creation of an industry specification and adoption throughout the industry. It is becoming a basis of computer component validation, computer validation, and manufacturing, system testing, and applications. Pretty good for something originally intended as a throwaway piece of code to test some EFI drivers.

The Shell started its life started in 1999 or 2000 (we don't exactly remember) so it is comparatively a newcomer. Yet, it is in many ways a throwback to (at least what now) seems a much simpler time, say 1970 or so. It doesn't run protected code, have a swap file or a registry, or even a GUI. As far as we know, it doesn't even have a virus scanner.

We've discovered there is still a place for a small simple developer's environment that provides enough resources and support for complex programs without getting in the way of applications that need to (or at least think they need to) "own the system".

The Book

The first part of this book introduces the basic concepts: history (Chapter 1), UEFI, the underlying operating environment (Chapter 2), basics of the shell (Chapter 3), and basic benefits of a pre-OS shell (Chapter 4). The second part of the book reviews some of the ways the UEFI Shell is used today ranging from manufacturing (Chapter 5), provisioning (Chapter 6), configuration management (Chapters 7), and diagnostics (Chapter 8). The third part of the book reviews useful tips for batch script programming (Chapter 9) and application programming (Chapter 10). Chapter 11 discusses how the shell can be useful to debug UEFI drivers, ironically the shell's original purpose. Appendixes cover security considerations, UEFI Shell library descriptions, and provide brief descriptions of the shells commands and APIs.

Acknowledgements

From Intel (at least once upon a time), we'd like to thank Mark Doran, Andrew Fish, Mike Richmond, Mike Kinney, Don Cisar, Sam Wu, Lu Ju, Harry Hsuing, Laurie Jarlstrom, and the large number of developers of the Shell before UEFI.

We'd like to thank the other members of the UEFI Shell Subteam, particularly Paul Maia and Mark Young of Dell as well as Dong Wei of HP but also, we fear, several others that our failing memories have unintentionally lost. Imagine: Various competing industry members working together for the betterment of all.

We want (honestly) to thank our managers Jeff Griffen and Doug Fisher for finding the funding and support. Thank you to the editors whose patience seems to border on the infinite.

Chapter 1

Introduction

Less but better.

—Dieter Rams

To most users, an operating system is a computer program that takes a long time to boot, draws windows on the screen, has a bunch of confusing options (POP 3 server?), and generally interferes with users getting things done.

In fact, the operating system is a much more complex collection of programs, drivers, kernels, and such that accomplishes its subtle tasks of resource sharing and the like behind the scenes. What the end user sees is in fact only the outside shell of the operating system. Much of the real value is invisible.

Still, this shell is what the user interacts with. Much of the perceived value of the underlying operating system is attributed to the shell. It is the skin for the body that is the operating system.

The UEFI Shell provides a predictable, specified shell for UEFI. UEFI is not an operating system per se. Instead, it is intended as a set of defined interfaces to provide defined interfaces between the system firmware (BIOS), Option ROMs, and operating systems. The richness of the interfaces required for this main purpose secondarily provide the interfaces that can support a rich command line environment.

What Do We Mean by *Shell?*

A shell is the operating system's way of providing the user a mechanism of interacting with the operating system. It is the operating system's user interface.

Taken to an extreme, a windowing GUI with pull downs and pop-ups is a shell. So is a command line interface (CLI). Just in case we've got you're hopes up, if you are looking for GUIs here, you're going to be disappointed. Could you implement one? If you have the time, patience, and competence, sure, but why? There are several good ones that boot using UEFI.

The relationship between the shell and the operating system is loose but not completely orthogonal. Bits of the operating system seep through: what a file name looks like, how files reside on devices, etc.

A command line interpreter is usually treated by the operating system as just another application. UEFI was never really intended to be an operating system but then again the UEFI Shell was never initially intended to be a shell.

A Short and Rambling History of Shells

To understand why the UEFI Shell is the way it is, we need to start back in the depths of ancient (for computers anyway) history, say 1955 or so.

Organic Evolution

There was no single designer of shells. No one sat down at a desk one afternoon in say 1963 and fully described what we have today. Instead, those who went before us made it up as they went along. Operating systems evolved and adapted to meet new needs and take advantage of new technology. And if we had to start from scratch, we'd undoubtedly do it differently and make new and different errors. In the end, the conflicting goals and requirements would probably make something very similar to what we have today.

Before we start wandering down memory lane, a few important points seem in order. The UEFI Shell is a command interpreter, not an operating system. As such, we've focused on the history of that aspect of operating systems. That said, particularly in the early days, no one really made this distinction as crisply as we do today.

Command interpreters have had to answer the same basic questions throughout history: Where do I get data from (input)? Where do I put data (output)? What do I do if there's an error? How do I run a program? What appears are thus variations on a theme.

Cards and Batch

The first tentative steps towards today's shells started primitively. As with the primitive nature of the computers they ran on, almost all of the technology looks different but the basics were there.

We start with cards. Each card represented one line of text or data. These were stacked into "*decks*" and shoved into the card reader. The cards had to do all of the activities an interactive session does today: log-in, enter programs, enter data, get data from elsewhere, use operating system utilities to copy or rename files, and run applications and the like. These commands and data were *batched* together to create a *job*. Some operating systems and many older programmers still call shell scripts *batch files*.

The early designers were presented with an interesting issue. The same cards and characters had to represent both data and commands so to tell the difference between the two. The common solution was to require non-data (command) cards to start with a special sequence that couldn't appear in the data, usually "//". The end of input also had a terminator with "/*" being the most common. For modern programmers and users, this can seem strange. It was a little like being always programming from a text editor with escape commands to compile and run programs.

Some issues with operating systems are with us today. Each programming language has a slightly different model for doing input and output and most are at least a little different from the model the operating system has. The solution created in the batch days seems at first very different from what we do today but, under several layers of syntax and libraries, isn't really all that different.

Initially programs were written with intimate knowledge of a target system's peripherals and configuration. As programs began to be used in multiple installations with different configurations, programs could no longer count on known configurations. The devices interfaces had to be abstracted from program I/O. This first occurred as libraries but didn't take long to become system calls. The first operating systems had been born although the name *operating system* took many more years to become universal.

For many years the abstractions, although useful, were extremely awkward. Programs read or wrote to abstract I/O streams (identified by small integers usually) called (by FORTRAN at least) *units*. It was up to the developer or batch script author to associate units with devices (and later files). There was no way, other than the program's documentation and local convention, to determine what unit any program was going to use for what. On the other hand, abstracting I/O from devices was an important step. Given the memory constraints (32 kilobytes was a mainframe memory size at the time), remarkably advanced. Although generated differently, the modern analogy would be file handles in the C standard I/O library.

Many systems didn't even have disks (or their close counterparts, drums) and, if they were available, they were much too valuable for intermediate storage to store programs. Disks and drums were typically managed by sector or track rather than files. Space had to be reserved in advance. Common practice meant programs were mostly loaded from tape. It wasn't that uncommon to have to compile a tape to tape copy program before copying the tapes.

JCL and Its Kin

The most commonly used batch file was known as JCL, for Job Control Language. It was (and still is) used on IBM Mainframes starting with the operating systems that ran on the IBM 360, shown in Figure 1.1. It provides an interesting insight as to the state in the early to mid 1960s of what would become shell scripts over time. The following sorts three equal size sets of data (source: http://www.isc.ucsb.edu/tsg/jcl.html.)

Figure 1.1 IBM 360—First Home to JCL

```
//S3       EXEC ISOSORT,SORTSPA='8560,35'
//SORTIN   DD DSN=*.S2.DETAIL,DISP=(OLD,DELETE)
//SORTOUT  DD DISP=(NEW,PASS),UNIT=SYSDA,SPACE=(8560,(80,20)),
//            DCB=(RECFM=FB,LRECL=80,BLKSIZE=8560)
//S1       EXEC DBSTDS,MBR=ISS1527,LIB=PR15,REGION=260K,DB=A,

//            DISP=SHR,PSB=PSB215,SORTSPA='8560,35'
//SORTIN   DD UNIT=SYSDA,SPACE=(8560,(80,20)),
//            DCB=(RECFM=FB,LRECL=80,BLKSIZE=8560)
//SORTOUT  DD UNIT=SYSDA,SPACE=(8560,(80,20)),
//            DCB=(RECFM=FB,LRECL=80,BLKSIZE=8560)

//SORTWK01 DD UNIT=SYSDA,SPACE=(8560,(35,10))
//SORTWK02 DD UNIT=SYSDA,SPACE=(8560,(35,10))
//SORTWK03 DD UNIT=SYSDA,SPACE=(8560,(35,10))
```

JCL is famous (infamous) for taking the design tack that defaults are not a good idea, leading to incredible complexity for comparatively simple tasks. Batch scripts for other operating systems of the time were much cleaner but were still not programmable.

The next significant innovation started down the path by allowing programs to return status as positive integers. In common use, the higher number the more critical the error. In the earliest versions, errors that were high enough would simply cause the batch interpreter to cease execution of the batch file. This was primitive but permitted complex actions like:

```
compile my program
if there are errors quit
link my program
if there are errors quit
run my program
```

When computer time cost hundreds of dollars an hour and builds possibly taking many hours, this was a real saving of money. Later, statements were added that could affect which subsequent programs were run based on status. The conditional statements could only skip parts of the subsequent batch file. While there still was no looping and no variables, the path to programmable batch files had started.

Some programs needed to affect the execution of subsequent programs in batch files and did so using the expedient of returning a fake error. The problem was that it was impossible to tell a fake error from a real one. That problem is still with us although the UEFI Shell makes progress in that regard.

Inevitably programmers started to see batch files (not yet shell scripts) as programs themselves. They certainly had gained a level of complexity equivalent to programs. So, they asked, why can't a batch file invoke another batch file? The short answer is that a batch file could jump to another batch file but not call a batch file. There was no call stack in the batch language interpreters. There was no parameter passing as well although this sort of script-as-procedure thinking did motivate that as well.

At about the same time, the 1960s, recursion was the subject of considerable study. With the ability to error out of batch files, if you could get a call stack, you could do recursion and error out to exit to the caller. The world of scripts was primed for the next big leap.

Interactive

In the early 1960s, terminals started their conquest of cards. The word *terminal* covered a wide range of devices from teletypes to interfaced electric typewriters to the later CRTs with keyboards. Rather than revolutionize the nascent shells, terminals were simply integrated as just other additional devices. Most were initially used for system administration and high end assignments. Odd tidbits filter through due to this initial integration: standard CRT terminals are 80 characters wide because cards had 80 columns.

While not immediate, the more and more interactive nature of terminals over cards was to have important impacts on the development of shells.

CTSS, RunCom, and Linux

In retrospect, the idea of viewing commands like procedure calls and treating the command line script like a programming language seems obvious. Yet, until the mid-1960s, this doesn't seem to have been clear at all. The concept had to be invented, and it probably was several times. One of the first and most influential was Louis Pouzin, who wrote a program called RunCom for IBM's CTSS, which allowed for simple iteration and parameter substitution (as in the Unix '$2' and DOS '%2' constructs).

Pouzin later worked for a while on the highly influential Multics project, which ran on computers like the GE-600 series shown in Figure 1.2, and drove similar concepts into the Multics project. Other influential results from Multics include the directory tree structure, file as array of bytes (rather than sectors programs had to muck with) and use of a high level language (PL/1 in Multic's case) to write the operating system.

Figure 1.2 The Type of Computer Multics Ran On: The GE-600 series, the type of computer Multics ran on.

Multics, Unix, and Redirection

Multics invoked commands as what they called subroutines but which are really more similar to DLLs today. Unix invokes commands in separate (logical) address spaces so they can't (unintentionally or intentionally) attack each other and the system.

Multics persisted in the preexisting "assign printer to 5" kind of I/O setup. Unix replaced this with the common angle bracket I/O redirection most shells use today. The concept is identical. What a difference a little syntactic sugar can perform. The implementation is similar, except in the details shell folks like to argue about but which bores the rest of us silly.

Multics used ">" to separate files in a path, Unix uses "/". The slash is easier to type since it is not a shifted key like the greater-than symbol. Both used "-" to initiate commands. This sort of thought may seem simple and arcane but it is what shell designers report that they were thinking about (or should think about) at that time.

In a fit of perhaps overzealous typing simplification, many of the Unix commands were abbreviated, sometimes to the point that their original meaning is all but lost. Commands like ls, tar, and awk have been compared to digestive noises as opposed to commands, although all are Unix commands.

Unix did have a use for ">" (and "<" and "|" for that matter) however. Unix calls it redirection. I/O redirection was nothing very new although the syntax was. We went from something like

```
ASSIGN 5 DK1:INPUT
ASSIGN 6 DK1:OUTPUT /C
PROG
```

to

```
prog <input >output
```

The functionality is identical. The syntax is so different as to obscure that fact. This syntax drove a fundamental change into the way the early Unix developers started to think about writing new commands and programs. The idea was that most commands could be designed to have a single input and a single output and could then get strung together with pipes to create applications. Applications designed with single input and single output are known as *filters*.

In reality, most programs are really more complex than simple filters. For example, a compiler theoretically has one input (the source) and one output (the object). Which is all well and good until the source has a syntax error. It's very confusing to get error reports interspersed in the object text. So we see constructs like "2>" to redirect standard error. And we aren't all that far from FORTRAN after all.

Still, the concept was compelling enough that filters proliferated. Simple filters (`tee` and `more`, for example) showed up first. The first source code control systems showed up. Proto-languages (like `sed`) and languages (notably `awk`) were eventually created to simplify creation of these building block script file elements. (Unix seems to have been the environment that popularized scripts or shell scripts over batch files and shell over command line interpreter.)

Unix then popularized the concepts of software tools, programs that were created to help build programs. Many of these had existed before, such as compilers and linkers, but were not viewed as such. The concept of a software builder needing tools just like a home builder would held sway. Editors, search utilities, compiler compliers and the like proliferated. Only with windowing environments did we start the migration back to more thoroughly integrated development environments. Even so, many of these programs are sophisticated front ends that transparently invoke batch tools to accomplish tasks ranging from searching to compiling to archiving.

Proliferation of Unix Shells and Posix

The first shells were invented by the developers of Unix themselves. The first one was known as the Thompson Shell starting the style of naming the shell after one of its inventors.

Unix proved particularly inviting or easy to write shells for. Others got in the fray, each with their own ideas. If one shell is good, why not have several? So we got the C-shell, Bourne shell, and the like. Today, there are a number of popular (and despised) shells in the Unix/Linux community.

The proliferation of shells frustrated many of the customers of Unix. They'd here about a new program for Unix, buy it, and then discover that the program wouldn't work on their Unix because the program was targeted at a different shell. A major customer, the United States Department of Defense, at the time the largest purchaser of software in the world, got irritated with this one-program one-computer scenario that they defined a set of interfaces, known as Posix, which Unix applications they purchased were to comply with. The UEFI Shell does not comply with Posix due to its size and complexity but the same interoperability requirements drove the Shell design too.

DEC RT-11, CP/M, and DOS—Shells for the Single User

Card-based systems and the Multics/Unix tradition focused on multiple users. With the advent of minicomputers, operating system designers were presented with computers that again only had enough resources to support a single user.

One important lineage of single user operating system syntax emerged from Digital Equipment Corporation. It is exemplified by the RT-11 (Run-Time for the PDP-11) operating system of around 1970. The operating system offered foreground and background processing but neither complex threads nor protection between users and programs.

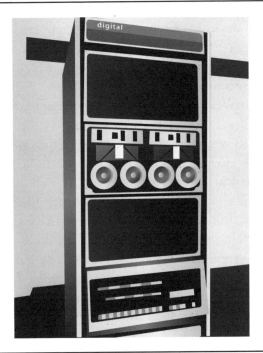

Figure 1.3 Small Operating Systems for Small Computers: The DEC PDP 11/40—From Many Cases to a Single Rack

The operating system was designed to be interactive from the start. It is from the RT-11 lineage that we get commands such as DIR and FORMAT (to format disks, not documents), as well as the .BAT extension for shell scripts. DEC did use a separate program called PIP for what would today be seen as COPY, RENAME, and the like. Given the small memory targets for the operating system (32 kilobytes), pushing such less used utilities to a single disk-based utility made sense. Tradeoffs between the size of the shell and the amount of space left for end users are less important today. The issue hasn't disappeared completely. Flexibility in managing UEFI Shell size is still important because, in some applications, it may end up residing in costly NOR flash memory.

RT-11 and its brethren at other companies had a simple view of the world of devices. The unit concept reappeared, this time with an important distinction made explicit. Each device had a name like LP01 or CR04. Some of the devices had files on them, which could be named. There were no subdirectories. So we see file "path" names like MC04:FRED.DAT. Device names were given the title *physical units* (PUNs). FORTRAN's units became *logical units* (LUNs).

LUNs were now an explicit part of the operating system and functioned as pointers to files and devices. LUNs continued to serve to abstract batch files from physical system configuration. A batch file that contained `MC04:FRED.DAT` would only work in systems where FRED.DAT existed on Medium Capacity disk number 04. If instead, LUN QQ was assigned to the right drive before invoking the batch file, invoking QQ:FRED.DAT would work correctly regardless of configuration. The current directory was treated as another LUN so the concept lives on today. In more modern shells, LUNs have been replaced by variable text substitution and paths, although it has to be said that it is far easier to type `qq:xyz..dat` than `%myvar%/xyz.dat`.

CP/M and MS/DOS

The most influential early operating system for personal computers was CP/M. CP/M stands for Control Program for Microcomputers, Control Program being another term for operating system. Gary Kildall invented CP/M while using an RT-11 system so the command names and the like migrated.

IBM asked Microsoft for a CP/M-like system so the CP/M (ex RT-11) commands migrated once more, along with the "/" for options in MS-DOS 1.0. When Microsoft introduced a directory tree structure to DOS in version 2.0 of the operating system and CLI, they realized that using "/" as a separator would be ambiguous since they'd used it as the prefix character for options. The closest lower case character on the PC keyboard was "\", so that got used instead. To retain backward compatibility, rather than using Unix's idea integrating all of the devices under a single directory tree structure, the MS-DOS designers retained the drive designator (the famous "c:"). Unix's solution is known as the tree method since there is a single all-encompassing tree. MS-DOS is known as the forest method since there are several trees, one per drive letter.

Subsequent versions of DOS included a richer and richer scripting environment with shell variables, FOR statements, labels, GOTO, ECHO, and other commands that don't have much use outside of batch files (shell scripts). The syntax has been, in the main, preserved to the CMD.EXE command processor that is a part of recent Windows systems. DOS also imposed versions of the Unix-style I/O redirection and piping, although piping hasn't been as commonly used in DOS as in Unix.

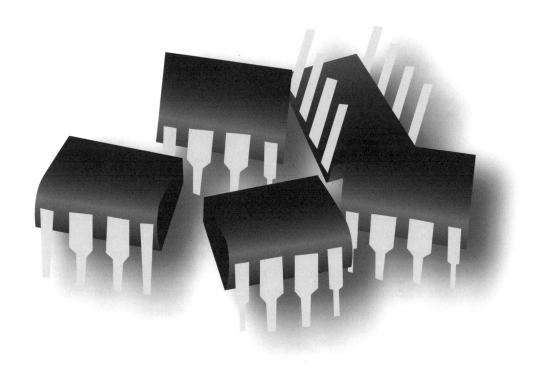

Figure 1.4   Example Flash Parts: The Shell's Most Common Home

The UEFI Shell carries on the tradition of command line shells of Unix (now Linux), RT-11, and MS-DOS, augmented this time to live in the even smaller home of a flash part. What with the changes in technology and experience, the UEFI Shell is in many ways easier to use and more flexible than the mainframes or minicomputers that are its precursors.

The Underlying Operating System and the Shell

We can also see how the underlying operating system affects the CLI in another way. In Unix, the devices are kept as part of the file system, traditionally as /dev, making all available data map into a single tree. In DOS (and CP/M and RT-11), each device had a unique name, separated from the tree (if the device is file oriented) by a colon. There seems to always have been confusion as to whether the colon was a separator or a part of the device name. You can see this in the DOS construct

```
COPY CON MYFILE.TXT
Line 1
Line 2
^Z
```

Is CON a file called CON or a device (the console)? Since MS-DOS treated the colon as a separator rather than a part of the device name, CON is treated as the console even though it looks like a file. Shell designers spend much of their time working around compatibilities established in previous versions.

Internal Interfaces ("The Guts")

This short history has focused mainly on the evolution of the user interface and batch functionality while giving short shrift to internal interfaces. There are a couple of reasons for that. First, the internal interfaces are not as readily documented or technically easy. Second, there is not always a strong distinction between the interfaces that are part of the operating system and those that are part of the shell.

Suffice it to say that there has been an evolution in the internal interfaces that parallels that in the aspects of shells visible to the user. In fact it can be argued that the user interfaces drove the internals.

When disks appeared, users needed a way to determine what was on them. The necessity to implement DIR or ls drove internal mechanisms to scan directories.

When users wanted to run programs from a shell, it required some sort of "go invoke that command over there" command or set of commands. In some cases, that involved invoking a LOAD function that copied the command into memory, doing relocation as required. A further EXEC command caused execution to begin, either synchronously (like a subroutine) or asynchronously (like starting a new thread). Unix provided `fork`, which duplicated the current command and re-invoked it.

Invocation itself has taken many forms. Some operating systems, for example, loaded different versions of the command interpreter in each memory map. Programs were then loaded in the same maps and called more or less as subroutines or dynamic libraries. In cases like this, you could have one map crash due to an errant application. The only recourse was to ask the operator to kill the job. In others implementations, each invocation involved another map. Each had different effects, some of which were user visible.

DOS Internals

The closest internal model for the UEFI Shell is MS-DOS and its relatives. While MS-DOS supported add-in drivers, many of its basic information flows ran back through the hardware abstractions provided by the BIOS. Similarly, the UEFI Shell uses the firmware abstractions upon which it is based (UEFI) for its access to peripherals and the like. UEFI provides a ready driver abstraction that the UEFI Shell uses, making a separate one (as in MS-DOS case) unnecessary.

Interactive Systems

The first timesharing system worked at the same time as the first BASIC interpreter. They were one and the same. The language, editor, and what amounted to operating system commands, were all part of a single command interpreter. The interpreter then shifted between different sets of memory chunks, each representing a user.

This concept moved another step forward with Forth, a stack-based language. Forth programming involves adding what amount to additional op-codes to the Forth interpreter. The operating system op-codes look like user op-codes, which in turn look like the intrinsic op-codes. The interpreter and the operating system and the language are merged. The concept has been applied to firmware and is known as Open Firmware.

Scripting Languages: AWK, TCL, Rexx, Perl, Python, ...

The major impact interpreted languages have had on programming ways would surprise and astonish a programmer time traveler from even as recently as 1975 or 1980. Back then there was a large argument over what were known as fourth generation languages. Had they known where to look, they would have found what they were looking for, or at least the seeds of these supposedly very high level languages. Most wouldn't have recognized the new little languages for the revolutions they were about to cause.

After many years of quietly gaining popularity, the programming public has discovered this "new" class of language has developed, generally known as scripting languages.

The first of these languages, AWK (named after the first letter of the last name of the three Bell Lab authors and pronounced like the first syllable in awkward) was intended to assist development of very short throw away filters, halfway between `grep` and C. In fact, the first AWK was built using code from the script editor `sed` and `grep`. The language was designed to make it easy to write comparatively powerful programs in only a few lines.

AWK set the standard for this class of language although today it is regarded as the most primitive of the bunch. AWK's features, which continue to appear in most of the class, include:

- Built-in pattern matching primitives
- Call-like invocations for other programs with the ability to simply consume output
- Dynamic typing
- Little or no variable declaration
- Tables: Arrays whose indexes are strings. Originated in SNOBOL, this construct can also be called a *hash* (Perl) or *dictionary* (Python) and provides what amounts to free symbol tables.
- Focus on strings as a major data type
- Invisible memory management (no need to call `malloc` or `free`)

AWK's syntax is like C, with curly braces as block delimiters, `while`, `for`, `if` and the like. It does vary considerably in its execution, treating the main program as a set of filters, which are provided lines of input text one at a time.

While people do use AWK for its intended purpose, the authors were surprised to discover that people found the language (particularly in its second version) to be rich enough that it became their main language, particularly for prototyping. This even surprised the inventors, who had invented the language to simplify small scripts. This origin accounts for these languages being called scripting languages. They can do scripting but they can do a lot more.

Rexx is IBM's entry into the fray. Although it is a rich general-purpose language, it has features that make it particularly useful to manage complex intercommunication between programs. Rexx is notable for having greatly diminished the use of JCL in IBM mainframe shops.

While these languages and their more modern progeny are still able to invoke programs, they are mainly used for general purpose programming at a higher level than the traditional C++, Pascal, and similar languages.

Perl and Python both have advocates and strong bases. Both are available with generous licenses from Web sites so they can be ported to any operating system environment. Recent versions of Python have been ported to the UEFI Shell.

While these are called scripting languages, they are not languages normally supported by the shell any more than C or Java would be. They are run by interpreters that the shell sees as programs like any other.

A Short History of the UEFI Shell

The UEFI Shell had very humble beginnings. It was developed along with the EFI interfaces in 1999 and 2000. The first program along the lineage that became the UEFI Shell was a small test environment to run the modules that EFI supports. The program was designed to run with a minimum amount of support so additional modules could be debugged one at a time.

Developers found the program useful and an underground after-hours effort formed to add to the shell. Scripts were added and some scripting commands (`if` and `for`) along with commands for general shell use (`copy`) and a rich if not entirely organized set of applications useful in debugging the underlying UEFI applications. This included memory dump routines, handle tracing routines, variable access routines and so on.

Initially marketing and management didn't see the shell at all. It was a programmer's tool and the programmers liked it that way. It rapidly escaped its internal bounds, however, proliferating within the small group of organizations working on the first versions of EFI.

Soon the developers at these organizations started using EFI as well. When they demonstrated the new BIOS interfaces, they naturally used the EFI Shell to do the demos. The executives walked away from the demos thinking that the EFI Shell was EFI. Marketing and management became very concerned and initially tried to squelch the EFI Shell. They were too late.

Finally, it was decide that the EFI Shell should be treated like a project. This sounded easier than it proved to be. Thorny issues popped up quickly.

First, which previously existing command line interface would the shell should look like? There were two major candidates: Unix and MS-DOS. Should it be `ls` or `dir`, `cat` or `copy`? In the end, we came up with a mix of both, introducing the concept of synonyms, where two differently named commands invoke the same code. Note that the command line options are unlikely to be like their precursors.

Second, which commands should be part of the shell and which should be distributed as separate programs? The server folks wanted everything in the shell itself because they had flash to fit it in. The client folks wanted everything out of the shell and stored on the EFI boot partition on the hard drive because they didn't have flash space to spare. Several alternatives were tried. They've ended in the shell level concept in the current UEFI Shell.

Third, what do we do about all of the very similar commands that have appeared in the UEFI Shell? By the time these discussions were going on, a large library of script files had appeared and many would have needed to be changed if commands were coalesced. Several manufacturing organizations had already started using the UEFI Shell. We didn't want to disrupt manufacturing and we didn't want to change the definition of the UEFI Shell enough to make manufacturing decide it wasn't stable enough to use. Validation organizations shared the same concerns. In the end, the only solution has proved to be to limit the amount of change over time.

Fourth, will the UEFI Shell be seen as an operating system in competition with the operating systems we're trying to boot? The developers were incredulous that the little UEFI Shell could be seen as competition to Linux or Windows. Over time, all parties came to realize that the UEFI

Shell could be used in cooperation with the big operating systems, rather than as competition. Manufacturing doesn't like reboots and particularly doesn't like long reboots. The UEFI Shell reboots quickly so it can be used effectively particularly for the early stages of manufacturing, removing stress on the operating system vendors to provide quick booting versions for manufacturing.

With the success of EFI, it was agreed that an industry forum was needed to manage its future path. The UEFI Forum was founded in 2005. The first version of its UEFI Specification was 2.0, to avoid confusion with the pre-forum versions. UEFI created another working group a year or so later to manage the Platform Initialization (PI) specifications, which address the firmware between the reset vector and UEFI.

In 2006, UEFI agreed that it should own the specification for the Shell, which then became the UEFI Shell. Throughout 2007, the UEFI Shell Sub-Team (USHT) of the UEFI Specification Working Group (USWG) developed the UEFI Shell specification, taking the existing EFI Shell specification as a start. The new version is known as UEFI Shell 2.0 and is what this book is about.

UEFI Shell Goals

The program that was to become the UEFI Shell wasn't initially designed to be a shell. It was designed to be a way to run unit tests to test what were to become the UEFI interfaces. It was a debugging and quality tool. While we've added and modified the shell beyond comprehension, it is still intended to be a good debugging and quality tool.

The UEFI Shell is designed to be useful to different sorts of programmers. To do so, it provides the traditional commands common to any operating system. It does so in many cases in the words that the programmers speak, even if they at times speak different languages. Rather than decide whether we should punish the part of the world that uses `ls` or the part that uses `dir`, we made them synonyms (not aliases but both a part of the shell).

Much of the way the UEFI Shell has been used so far is to automate processes. While the processes may vary from hardware validation to software testing to manufacturing, the basics of automation are the same. They are the basics of programming as well: data and control flow.

The data side of the equation is addressed via specified output from many of the shell commands in a way that is hard for humans to understand but intended to be easy for programs to parse. The format is extensible and rich enough to express the types of output we foresee. It is well enough defined so that other UEFI Shell programs (including yours) can use the same format.

The code side of automation includes the well known looping and conditional structures most programming languages have. Some of these are less structured than we'd expect to see in a language today. This is due to legacy requirements but also due to the interpreted nature of scripts.

The shell addresses the requirements of I/O redirection, wild carding, and the like while still allowing any input to be entered. The overrides are well defined, if not exactly the ones everyone uses. To support both camps, both "/" and "\" are allowed in file paths. This made "\" unavailable for what it's become known for in the C and Linux camps, override. Instead, the override function is assumed by "^". This makes a few commands (the traditional `grep` in particular) somewhat confusing since "^" already had meaning in the command lines for those commands.

Shells have been around for a comparatively long time. The designers tried to use from that experience without being constrained by any existing environment. The UEFI Shell is not a direct copy of any other shell including the one you most commonly use.

One thing that was *not* a goal of the UEFI Shell specification was a rigorous definition of the syntax of all commands. Not only was this thought to be impractical but also to be somewhat pointless. Instead, the specification defines the syntax of certain options in some of the commands whose output is expressly intended for use by other programs. This format is not easy to read by humans but is easy to parse and consume by programs and is extensible. If you are writing programs that consume the output of commands, use the script options where possible. If you are creating new programs for the UEFI Shell, consider creating options that provide useful data in a similar format.

Brief Overview of UEFI Shell

The shell consists of two parts, a set of APIs and a command line interface.

UEFI Shell APIs

The set of APIs abstract the command line and file I/O aspects of the system. The command line APIs allow UEFI Shell programs to read the command line, for example.

The File I/O aspects allow reading and writing files from languages like C just as in any language. The APIs resolve several issues that don't arise in the layers below the UEFI Shell and so should be used where possible. The basic issue is that different APIs are provided in the firmware layers for each volume whereas a single API is provided for all volumes in the UEFI Shell. To do this, the UEFI Shell has an algorithm for mapping devices onto short device names. The shell then takes care of mapping the names back to the devices.

Command Line Interface Features

The command line interface can be defined into several parts.

Like all operating systems, the UEFI Shell has a consistent command line format. The command appears first, followed by options (initiated by hyphens) and parameters (with no hyphens) all separated by spaces. Wild cards are supported as is I/O redirection. As noted, overrides and quoted strings (such as file names with spaces in them) are also supported. Note that some of this support is only available to programs that use the UEFI Shell APIs. All utilities (programs provided as a part of the UEFI Shell) do use this interface.

The UEFI Shell uses the same executable program format as does its underlying software layers: PE/COFF. PE/COFF is not a pure binary image. Instead, it is a series of variable length data structures that allow the UEFI Shell to load programs at arbitrary addresses in memory via a process known as relocation. PE/COFF was chosen because it is well known in the industry and produced by a wide variety of compiler/linker sets across the operating systems most developers use.

The UEFI Shell defines a scripting language. This language is similar to programming languages but operates at a higher level. The language allows for looping, conditional execution, and data storage and retrieval via environment variables. The scripting language is unique to the UEFI Shell but similar enough to other shells that learning it shouldn't be difficult.

The UEFI Shell is designed for a variety of environments. To meet all of the requirements, different levels of command support are specified. In the most minimal, there is space for one user application. The shell is simply used to kick that application off. In richer versions, you'll find batch commands to control automation. Again, the user may never interact with the UEFI Shell. Instead, the shell is useful to manage the order of execution of programs. In the most full featured versions of the UEFI Shell, like the ones you might be developing applications on and for, you'll find the standard commands like dir (ls), copy, a minimal full screen editor, and the like.

Why Has It Persisted?

The UEFI Shell has persisted for one simple reason: because it is useful. The programs that run below the shell reach all the way back to the reset vector. Those programs must be tested. The question is what environment makes debugging these programs easiest. The alternative environments to the UEFI Shell cause most of the evidence of the infrastructure created during the boot process to disappear by the time these other operating systems are booted to the point most users can debug. The UEFI Shell, on the other hand, uses the same boot interfaces as these boot programs and so does not destroy them. Debugging drivers and applications using print statements and the like is a lot easier.

The UEFI Shell is useful for automation. Examples from real life, which are also described in this book, include specialized memory tests for chip and board validation and manufacturing validation tests. Many of these take advantage of the lack of memory management and protection in the UEFI Shell. A memory test can simply allocate an area of memory and test it, avoiding the gyrations required in a system like Linux.

The UEFI Shell requires no platform-level customization. It requires no drivers beyond those included in the shipping system. This means as the UEFI Shell is used it becomes less and less likely to be the culprit of bugs introduced as a part of the system. It becomes an island of consistency in an ocean of variability.

The UEFI Shell is, in the end, useful because it is small and not intrusive, just as its cousins are useful because they are large and all-encompassing.

Chapter 2

Under the UEFI Shell

Without the wind, the grass does not move. Without software, hardware is useless.

—Geoffrey James

The ability to run programs can be viewed as a method to customize the operating system to perform specific tasks. Similarly, the UEFI Shell is itself a customized application of the programs that run below it. The attributes of the programs that the shell uses to perform its tasks are important to understand and take advantage of when programming for and using the UEFI Shell.

The UEFI Shell lives on top of a series of interfaces known as UEFI. The programs that manifest these interfaces reach all the way back to the reset vector. In fact, their main purpose is to initialize the computer and hand control off to much more grandiose programs, operating systems like Linux and Microsoft[†] Windows. Whereas these systems replace most of the boot environment after finishing with it early in their boot processes, the shell simply uses the boot environment as its underlying operating system. The complexity of the large operating system is replaced by a much more modest environment that is simpler to understand.

That is not to say that the environment is either simple or modest in its capabilities. It just has different requirements and a different focus. Performance is given less priority and code size more. Reliability and simplicity of interface are given higher focus and expansive functionality less.

Shell and UEFI

The UEFI Shell sits between UEFI and applications. Applications may then use the UEFI Shell APIs and UEFI's other APIs to accomplish their tasks. Generally, simple command line tasks can be accomplished using only UEFI Shell APIs whereas complex tasks will probably require UEFI support.

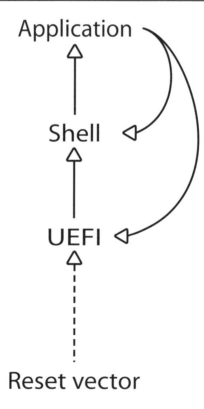

Figure 2.1 Execution order and interaction

Evolution and Revolution

To understand the rationale for the difference in focus from a large and complex operating system, we must examine the motivations behind the design of UEFI. Most of these had to do with the experiences with the set of interfaces UEFI replaced, the legacy BIOS.

The Basic Input/Output System (BIOS) was designed in an era when personal computers had a maximum of 640 kilobytes of RAM and hard disks, when available, had capacities in the 10 to 20 megabyte range. The entire BIOS was designed to fit into 64 KB and was written in assembly code.

The interfaces the BIOS provided to the operating system were of necessity extremely primitive. Graphical interfaces were limited to 640 by 480 pixels and 24 by 80 characters. Disk interfaces were block-oriented as described by cylinder, head, and sector location. Maximum cylinder, head, and sector had to be entered by the user and were limited to an unimaginable 540MB.

Booting was simply a matter of loading a sector (512 bytes) off the boot media and jumping to it. The operating system then made calls back into the BIOS to load parts of itself until it was able to take over.

Extensibility for add-in cards was provided via option ROMs, which added small parts to the BIOS in non-standard and, by today's standard, dangerous methods such as intercepting interrupt vectors. This was not because the option ROM developers were bad programmers. There was simply no other means provided to them, nor was there any means to do even basic services like memory allocation or timing.

This set of minimalist interfaces quickly proved inadequate to support rapidly evolving technology. BIOS developers became experts at squeezing new content into old interfaces. They supported higher display resolutions, larger drives, more memory, network booting, manageability (to describe the system to administrators), and the like. They were made to support 32-bit operating systems. By the advent of 64-bit processors in PCs, it was becoming clear that the old interfaces were at the end of their lifespan and had to be replaced.

The new design, which became UEFI, sought to learn from this past as well as to take advantage of the technology and innovations in software engineering that had occurred in the intervening 20 years.

The most fundamental change is that UEFI is an operating environment. It manages memory, can read and write files, has priorities, and has most of the other features of a small non-preemptive operating system. Extensibility mechanisms are now built in and option ROMs are treated as full parts of the firmware. The one thing that really hasn't changed is that people still call the code that implements UEFI the BIOS.

Using the UEFI Specifications

UEFI is technically a set of interfaces. It is however common to talk about the code that implements the interfaces using the same name so we'll do that throughout this book. The specification is owned by the UEFI Forum. The latest version of the specification at the time of this writing is 2.2.

UEFI is specified in a somewhat unusual way that can catch first time developers. The specification makes a distinction between two types of requirements. The first set of requirements is necessary to be compliant with the specification. The second (and larger) set is optional, but if implemented must meet the specification to be compliant. When using this second set of interfaces, it is important that the program test for presence and fail gracefully if the relevant interfaces are unavailable.

UEFI Basics

UEFI provides a set of services. Two types of programs can use those services: applications and drivers. The two are very similar. *Drivers* have a slightly higher priority and stay resident. *Applications* are expected to do their job and exit. The environment presented to both types of programs is an unprotected flat memory model.

The services define fundamental interfaces like memory allocation, time, and date in ways that most programmers would be quite familiar withrecognize. The services are defined in a exist off of a table known as the bBoot sServices table. A pointer to the Boot Services table is provided to each driver or application when invoked. A similar table, much less commonly used, known as the Run-Time table is also available.

Protocols

Arguably the most important set of services UEFI provides are those that enable inter-program communication known in UEFI-speak as *protocols*. Most of the more complex services your program accesses to do its job are via protocol. It is important to separate UEFI protocols from other types of protocols such as LAN protocols in your mind. The two are similar but distinct.

The basis of protocols is a data structure: think C `struct`. This is the payload of the protocol and is interface-specific. Most entries in these structures tend to be pointers to functions, making a protocol a sort of primitive cross between a C++ class and a dynamic link library (DLL).

Associated with this structure is a name in the form of a Globally Unique Identifier (GUID, also known as a UUID). A GUID is a 16-byte value that is unique to a particular type of protocol. The format of GUIDs is standard. GUIDs may be generated using a number of different methods, a common one being to concatenate a system's LAN MAC address with the date and time.

In UEFI, the name GUID implies a contract. If you see a protocol with a particular name, you know its associated structure. If you change the elements in the structure, you must change the GUID.

UEFI manages protocols by associating them together into groups associated with automatically generated *handles* (similar in usage to file handles in Unix). The semantics of which protocols are associated with a handle are up to the designers. For example, the protocols associated with a disk (attributes, block, file, and so on) might all end up on the same handle. The one major rule is that only one protocol with a particular name may be installed on a handle.

UEFI provides services to create, locate, and delete handles. For example, a service allows your program to find all of the handles that contain protocols with a particular GUID. Another service allows your program to find a protocol on a handle with a particular GUID. A further service allows programs to be notified when new protocols having a certain name are created. This service is important because it alleviates many ordering problems. A driver may be loaded at any time and still know about all of the protocols it is interested in without polling.

This set of services may seem quite primitive, and indeed the amount of code required to implement them is quite small. On the other hand, this allows for complex interactions between cooperating drivers and programs written by different organizations and companies. These naturally (or through a lot of hard work and design) form driver stacks as in the big operating systems. For example, here are the stacks for IP support in UEFI 2.2.

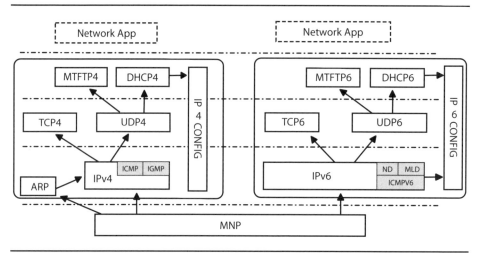

Figure 2.2   IP Support in UEFI 2.2

The connections between each of the major elements are a specified protocol. Implementers may choose to use other protocols to implement their drivers that support the defined interfaces. Due to the non-published nature of the GUIDs, those interfaces are kept private.

Control Flow: Interrupts, Call-backs, Priorities

UEFI is generally non-preemptive: programs run until they exit, or give up control by, for example, calling another program via a protocol or invoking a system service. There is only one exception. The only interrupt supported by UEFI is the timer. As such, most I/O that would be interrupt-driven in richer environments is polled in UEFI.

Services allow programs to sign up to be called after a given amount of time. The usual issues of very short duration timing apply to UEFI as well. Requesting a delay very close to the timer granularity of UEFI tends to result in poor response and poor behavior. UEFI offers simple delay services, which are a better choice in these cases.

When invoked during a timer, several services are unavailable (more precisely, they may be called but with unpredictable results). The only data provided to the code when invoked is a pointer, usually to some context that was previously set up. The call order is important as well. The programs are called in highest to lowest priority order. For a given priority (there are 32), the order is from longest waiting to shortest. Priorities are managed by system services.

Persistent Storage

UEFI has two types of persistent storage. First is the familiar persistent storage that is on a disk or other media. This type is managed via partitions, file systems, files, and the interfaces that access them. The shell has a full set of calls to read and write files, for example. The second type of persistent storage is smaller, is stored on the system itself, and is managed differently. To see why, we need to understand how this storage is used.

Most of the interfaces in the system are recreated during each reboot. A few cannot be, mainly having to do with system configuration and consistency between the firmware and the operating system. One of the most important among these interfaces is the interface that controls boot order: which devices should be examined in what order to determine from which device the the operating system should be loaded. Other consistency items include the default language to be used and paths to the equivalent of the standard input, output, and error devices. These parameters must also be accessible from the operating system as well as the firmware so that consistency is maintained between the two.

The UEFI solution to this issue is derived from the shell technology known as environment variables. In UEFI, they are almost always known simply as *variables*. Variables are named using a GUID and a Unicode (UCS-2) text string. Services are provided to find, read, write, and delete variables. The UEFI specification reserves a GUID for its own use and distinguishes variables by their names.

The most important thing to remember when using UEFI persistent storage is that it is extremely limited. Assume that the whole storage (not just your applications) may be only 16 kilobytes. Larger amounts of persistent information should be saved on disk.

One word of caution: a program should not delete variables unless it has written them. Different drivers may store their configuration in driver defined variables. Simply deleting unknown variables will almost undoubtedly lead to trouble down the road.

UEFI also supports non-persistent variables. In fact, the UEFI Shell environment variables are typically implemented as UEFI variables with a single GUID and the name of the UEFI Shell variable as the name of the UEFI variable.

Transition from Boot Services to Runtime

Complex operating systems use UEFI to solve an apparent paradox. When first given control, the operating system doesn't have enough of itself loaded to load the drivers that talk to the boot device. It needs drivers to load the drivers. UEFI provides those drivers. During this phase, the OS acts very much like the UEFI Shell, using UEFI for its services.

Soon enough, however, the operating system does load enough drivers for the OS to take over. The operating system is then almost done with UEFI. To signal the end of this phase, it calls the `ExitBootServices` UEFI service. This tells UEFI to limit further functionality to the UEFI Runtime. For this reason, unless you are using the UEFI Shell to debug a boot loader, calling `ExitBootServices` is a sure way to crash your UEFI Shell.

Output Tables

Callable runtime interfaces between the firmware and OS can be fraught with complexity. The major culprit in making the interfaces difficult is the wide variability in the OS memory model of which the firmware is not, and really cannot, be aware. Complex operating systems operate in paged virtual memory systems where there is only an indirect relationship between physical and logical memory. Some of the pages may in fact reside on the disk. UEFI (and the UEFI Shell), on the other hand, operate on a pure one-to-one relationship between address and memory and support nothing as complex as swapping.

UEFI has a few runtime callable functions, including the variable services mentioned above. To continue to function at runtime, these must go through a sort of relocation process in order to work in the runtime. The operating system must then take special care of the memory these functions use. In the UEFI Shell, we avoid all this.

Given the complexity surrounding runtime callable interfaces, UEFI takes a different method to provide most of its data to the operating system: tables generated during UEFI that are available to the operating system. In the case of the shell, these tables are also available to UEFI Shell applications.

The largest table provided by UEFI is known as the *System Table*. This table consists of a list of GUID and pointer pairs. The GUID indicates what the pointer points at. There is no required order to the list. You must search the GUIDs to find your table.

UEFI supports two useful tables left over from BIOS. The first of these is the SMBIOS (System Management/BIOS) table, which is accessible via the system table. SMBIOS is a complex data structure composed of variable length data structures. The structures describe aspects of the system ranging from the manufacturer to the types of memory the system supports to the number of PCIe slots to where PXE is. The SMBUS specification is managed by the Desktop Management Task Force and can be found at dmtf.org

Also accessible via the system table is the Advanced Configuration and Power Interface (ACPI) table. ACPI is a standard specification that enables UEFI to describe methods to manage system devices. The interface abstracts the hardware implementation while leaving the functionality required by the operating system consistent. It does so via a variable length byte code set of operations known as ACPI Machine Language (AML). AML implements a set of tables and a functional language that can substitute methods and tables more or less arbitrarily. The OS then uses known methods with known parameters as interfaces to assign resources to on-system devices, manage the system power (including the sleep states), and other items such as (limited) thermal control. You can find more information about ACPI at acpi.org.

Useful UEFI Protocols

The following sections describe a few of the protocol stacks developers of UEFI Shell applications have found useful and some ways you might need or want to use them in your applications. Large operating systems typically have similar services. It is important to note that there can be important differences between the levels of support and the models behind that support.

At times there may seem to be overlap between UEFI protocols and UEFI Shell services and, indeed, between different UEFI protocols themselves. The general rule for which service to use is to use the service closest to your application but below it. So, for example, if you are writing a UEFI Shell application, use UEFI Shell services first, then UEFI services. If you are writing a UEFI driver and using the UEFI Shell to debug it, use UEFI services. You cannot assume that the UEFI Shell will be there during driver operation.

Before you plunge headlong into using the UEFI calls, a word of warning regarding the way UEFI manages requirements is in order. UEFI divides its interfaces into two sets: those that are required for all implementations and those that are required if the corresponding feature is supported in the platform. In the former category are interfaces like memory management and protocols and the other basics that make the whole thing hold together. In the latter category are the protocol stacks that are the equivalent of driver stacks in operating systems. These are typically more variable and more complex than the basics. They also are more likely to appear and disappear as hardware changes. For example, there's quite extensive support for PCI. If history is any judge, someday PCI will disappear in favor of a newer faster bus. As such, the UEFI specification categorized the PCI interfaces in the second category roughly saying "If you've got PCI, you've got to support the PCI interfaces." For lack of a better term, we'll call these *advanced* protocols, to distinguish them from the basic required protocols.

What does this mean to the shell application author? You can count on the basics being there without testing for them. You must check to see if the other APIs are there before using them. This is usually fairly simple, however, since the protocol search routines are quite good at returning "not found." Your application must adapt to the protocols not being there. If for example, you're writing a PCI dump application (first, go look for one that's already written—there are a lot out there) search for the PCI protocols. If they aren't there, report a message to that effect and return to the shell.

One solution to missing protocols is to carry your own. Many advanced protocols sit atop existing hardware abstractions. If those abstractions are there, it doesn't much matter where the protocols come from. One word of warning, however: the "cleanliness" rule is to check for the system's already loaded protocols and use them first. The most important rationale for this approach is that the protocols may already be in use by other parts of the shell. If you simply write over them or add a parallel implementation besides them, you could cause instability by disrupting synchronization solutions. If the protocols aren't there, you can load your own.

Devices

Devices in UEFI are managed at their lowest levels by device drivers. These communicate to the next level via protocols that are bus-specific. For example, USB host controllers communicate to general purpose USB drivers via specified protocols. Similar drivers exist for PCI, PCIe, and PCIx, as well as for networking, SCSI, and firmware.

Host controllers, such as USB and SCSI, make other devices visible. These devices are treated by device type. You can find device types for media (hard drives, USB "thumb" drives, CDs), keyboards, and mice, each making themselves visible for use via their protocols.

Layering on top of media devices are what are known as block level protocols. They treat the storage one the device as a linear array of fixed sized blocks. The File Allocation Table (FAT) file system drivers then reside on top of the block devices protocols. This means that it is common to find a fairly long chain of devices starting with a FAT partition, which knows about the FAT driver, which knows about the Block driver, which knows about the USB device driver, which then knows about the USB host controller. In some cases, depending on bus idiosyncrasies, there may even be a few more protocols mixed in.

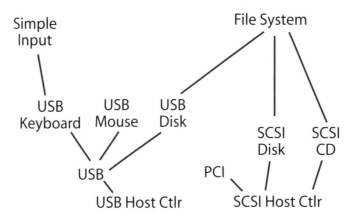

The protocols are the lines between the drivers

Figure 2.3 Example Device and Protocol Hierarchy

Actual devices have associated with them *device paths,* variable-length data structures that describe paths like the one just mentioned in a compressed form. There's an optional protocol to turn paths into printable form.

Why would a UEFI Shell developer need to know about devices and device paths? If you're doing something like porting a SNOBOL interpreter to the UEFI Shell, you probably don't.

If you're wondering how to test your company's new USB headphones on a manufacturing line using the UEFI Shell, you definitely do need to know about devices. There is no standard audio support in UEFI or in the UEFI Shell. Several people over the years have, however, implemented audio players in UEFI. MP3 interpreters have been ported to UEFI and are probably available via some searching. You will have to write the USB driver for your headphones yourself. You do want to write the driver using the existing USB driver protocols so that your USB keyboard and mouse still work, and so that if the USB host controllers change, your program won't have to. The easiest way to get started on writing drivers is to look at the publicly available code others have done for the standard devices. Yes, headphones aren't keyboards but both are configured using the same type of USB packets. Having the UEFI specification and a running example makes things much clearer.

User Interface and Localization

UEFI supports user interfaces via the Human Interface Infrastructure (HII). HII is a cooperating group of five main protocols. Four of the protocols handle different aspects of human/computer interaction while a fifth provides a way to process encapsulations containing some or all of the other types.

HII is important for UEFI Shell developers for two main reasons. The more obvious is that it greatly assists developers in creating and managing localized applications. Even if you are writing a manufacturing line tool, this facility is likely to become important as your tool becomes used in many locations around the world. Making the tool speak the language of its users makes it easier to learn and use.

The less obvious use for the UEFI Shell is that you can use the system's setup as a form-based user interface. This means you can do all of your menu construction via existing applications and have less to do yourself. The interfaces allow for immediate response or, if you can design it that way, can hand off your HII forms and get a response back. You do have to use the HII form browser (of unpredictable quality) implemented on the system. You have to decide whether you can do a better enough job to sacrifice consistency with all of the other shell applications and the local setup.

Although HII seems to manage fonts, strings, forms, and graphical images separately, it is often useful to envision HII as a database. The various components are fed into the database and later the database is queried for information.

Much of this discussion may make it sound like HII provides localization as rich as a large operating system. It does provide a comparatively rich infrastructure however implementations are only required to carry what they need and very little more. Another reason to understand HII is to understand what it doesn't require. It does support ways to add extra support you might need but you'll need to do work to carry that data.

Characters

HII is based on Unicode. Unicode is a set of standards that assign numerical values to alphabetic and symbolic characters. In many ways, you can think of Unicode as an extended ASCII. There are a number of Unicode encodings. HII uses two. First, it uses the same 16 bits per character version of Unicode as the rest of UEFI and XML, UCS-2. To achieve greater compression, HII uses UTF-8, an 8-bit progressive encoding in compressed strings to comply with a Unicode standard. The Unicode versions supported by HII encode for all of the characters you're likely to need for your user interfaces.

Fonts

A font is defined to be a set of character images (*glyphs*) corresponding to Unicode values ("weights"). The system (including the UEFI Shell) is only required to support the set of weights corresponding to the Latin-1 (common Western European) languages. You must supply characters beyond this set. To enable this, HII defines the characteristics of each glyph. Narrow characters are 8 x 19 pixels and wide characters (as are common in logographic languages such as Japanese, Chinese, and Korean) are 16 x 19 pixels. This size supports 25 x 80 narrow glyphs on a 640 x 480 screen and 31 x 100 on a 600 x 800 screen. If you plan on using an even higher resolution, you will probably want your own font.

This method of support would make it inefficient to support a text editor supporting all characters since this would require around 37000 characters, which requires about 24 megabytes (uncompressed) of font images. Instead, this mechanism is focused on support for the presentation of known or mostly known strings. This is more common in the target environment for UEFI, that of booting systems. As well, most programs require few characters outside the ones they print. In many cases this is limited to numbers, punctuation, and the already present Latin-1 narrow characters.

Other fonts can be supported. Each font is named via a GUID. All characters (including Latin-1) that are used must be supplied.

The main customer of the font support in UEFI is the Simple Text Output (STO) protocol. This protocol is the basis for most textual display to the user. While not part of HII itself, STO is the most common way programs interact with the HII. STO manages the screen as if it were a remote text terminal (although all local video output is in fact graphical). It supports cursor positioning as well as the equivalent of `printf`.

Keyboard input is handled via the Simple Text Input protocol. The protocol provides character by character input as well as string input. The protocol defines mechanisms to detect function keys and other meta-character input.

HII supports Simple Text Input by providing simple keyboard remapping. This remapping basically takes the form of a table. Each entry maps a key press and meta-key (Shift, Control) state to a Unicode weight. The upshot of this is that you can create a Norwegian or Russian keyboard mapping. This simple solution does not do as good a job when it comes to ideographic languages such as Japanese and Chinese. In Japanese, however, a good mapping of keys to the common Kana characters is possible. There is no support for Input Method Editors (IMEs). In addition to common keyboard-based input, UEFI supports a pointer protocol which provides rudimentary mouse support.

The Simple Text Input and Simple Text Output protocols can abstract not only the common USB keyboards, mouse pointer devices, and graphics displays, but can also communicate with character-based terminals directly via serial ports or as abstracted via LAN protocols. The fewer assumptions you make about your output devices, the more likely they'll work in all cases. This is one reason it's much better to use Simple Text Output's cursor positioning controls rather than diving directly to Graphics Output Protocol (GOP). GOP graphics don't make it across serial ports, cursor positioning controls do.

Strings

Encoded with Unicode, fonts are not language-specific. Strings are.

Strings are null-terminated arrays of UCS-2 (CHAR16) Unicode weights. Strings are referred to by string IDs. Most of these are generated during the build process to simplify localization. The IDs are "local" to a particular program. The alternative would have been to refer to each string by a GUID, which would be inefficient in terms of size. As such, each program has a handle that defines which set of local string IDs to refer to. The handles are created dynamically.

A string ID and a handle are not enough to uniquely identify a string. The third item required is the language. This is the key to localization. The program deals with abstract string tokens and doesn't have to manage different languages. That's all taken care of by HII and the data structures. UEFI has a variable that defines the current language. If that language isn't one of the translations available for a string, HII has a back off algorithm.

The string protocol supports dynamic creation of new strings, removal of old strings, and replacement of an old string with a new one.

Why would you want to replace an old string with a new one? Consider the case of determining the contents of a string while the program is running. For example, you might want to display how long a particular piece of music is. Until you know which piece of music you are going to display, you can't fill in that string. A simple way to solve this problem is to get your localization tools to create what amounts to a dummy string. This causes the identifier to be generated and costs at most a byte or two. At runtime, you can replace that string with the actual string. All users of the string simply know it by its ID and so can simply extract or print the string.

The string protocol and font protocol work together. You can ask the string protocol if the string is printable using the font characters available. If not, your program can choose how to back off if you don't like HII's solution. Applications can also submit strings and have returned the bitmap image of the characters. This is useful when creating picture editing software and is, in fact, the way Simple Text Output usually gets implemented. This and similar routines are also a way to know how wide a string is when it's printed. Simply counting the number of characters in the string is not safe when you might have some narrow and some wide.

The string protocol is intelligent in one other rather subtle way. It's quite common for a 50-character (narrow) string to be printed in a column on the screen that only supports 30 characters. Where can we break the string? Unicode defines a subset of 'breaking' characters, such as spaces, commas, or periods. The string protocol can be used to break the string into acceptable pieces.

Images

UEFI supports rendering both bitmap (BMP) and Joint Photographic Experts Group (JPEG or JPG) style still images. It does not have any support for creating or editing such images. JPEG is a group of over 20 different image formats. UEFI only supports the common early formats.

The image routine also optionally supports animated images as a sequence of still images. This functionality is useful for routine animation like rotating an hourglass to indicate a long wait. It is not designed to be efficient enough to show a long movie or even full screen events.

The image display routines sit on top of the Graphics Output Protocol (GOP), which provides display reconfiguration and bitmap displays along with basic Bit BLT functions. To avoid interaction with the rest of the system, avoid using low level functionality like the GOP unless you are sure yours is the only application using the screen.

Forms

UEFI does not support HTML or XML natively. It does have its own forms and its own form language, Internal Forms Representation (IFR). IFR is a binary form, as opposed to XML and HTML, which are in (Unicode and ASCII) text. Several high-level language versions of IFR are available along with their compilers. VFR is the most common.

IFR fills much the same niche as HTML Forms does for the (early) Web. In fact there are programs that translate between IFR and HTML. Both are ways to present pages to users and allow them to respond via questions with a menu-driven interface (like buying an airline ticket on the Web). Basic IFR statements perform many of the same tasks. There are IFR items corresponding to basic input types including radio buttons, check boxes, numbers, and strings.

IFR manifests itself as a contiguous set of variable-length byte encoded operations. Its expressions are stored in "prefix" form. So for example 4+5×6 would be encoded as (+ 4 (* 5 6)). This form was chosen because it supports the short circuit logical operators (&& and || in C). VFR hides all this of course. IFR does not allow escape to other languages such as JavaScript since these are not possible to support in the size-constrained spaces for which UEFI is targeted.

IFR mitigates this by supporting a richer set of computational features than does HTML, including string and arithmetic operators and conditionals.

IFR also provides operators to control display and user access, which must be implemented in HTML. For example, there is a "Suppress If" operator enclosing form entries if an expression evaluates to true. This is useful in cases where it doesn't make sense to present one question depending on another question's value. For example:

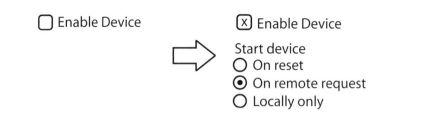

Figure 2.4 Sample Before/After use of Suppress capability.

This would be implemented by doing (in pseudocode at a lower level than VFR to emphasize structure):

```
(Checkbox On=1 Off=0 Storage=Enable String=EnStr)
(SupressIf (Equal Enable 0)
   (OneOf Storage=Start String=StartStr Help=StartHelp
      (OneOfEnt Value=0 String=ResetStr)
      (OneOfEnt Value=7 String=RemoteStr)
      (OneOfEnt Value=1 String=LocalStr)
   )
)
```

If all else fails, IFR supports the use of callbacks: calls from the browser back into the driver that submitted the IFR in the first place. While callbacks are useful, there are reasons not to use them. First, they make it more difficult to debug. Second, they limit how your form can be used. To understand why, we need some knowledge about how forms and strings are managed as a whole.

Database

We mentioned earlier that it is helpful to think of the parts of HII as contributing to a dynamically created database. HII makes a distinction between driver-specific information, application information, and general information. Forms and strings provided by drivers are kept separate from the same types of data used by applications. Keyboards and fonts are considered general information since they aren't specific to any application or device. HII allows all of the driver-specific data submitted to it to be extracted into a single blob. By the time the shell is loaded, that blob is stored in the system table. It can then be used in a pre-boot setup or, more importantly for the shell, be sent say via a LAN to a remote system for configuration. That remote system cannot perform the callbacks to the drivers, which means only non-callback IFR commands are supported remotely.

Output

The IFR device has an output format that has surprised some first time users: UCS-2 ampersand-separated name=value pairs a la the CGI network format: "george=4&fred=6&ron=0". The storage and value pairs mentioned in the "SuppressIf" example above would constitute name and value pairs. An interesting special case of name value pairs enables the names to be indexes into an array rather than pure text. Routines in the output management protocol allow for easy translation.

Networking

How do we get those forms across the net? Use the UEFI provided networking stacks of course.

At the highest level, the application could use the File Transfer Protocol (FTP) to write the data to a file on a remote device and poll for the results. The application could use the TCP/IP stacks to send the request as an Internet message and receive a message like a little (or big) Internet browser. At the lowest level, the application could define its own local network protocol (in both the LAN and UEFI senses) using the protocols MNP or UDP. If security is required to trust the results, use IPSec.

The UEFI Shell provides IPCONFIG and PING commands but the transfer application could implement them internally as well.

UEFI also supports boot protocols like BIS and network management protocols including EAP, VLAN, and ARP.

As with any security-related feature, it is important to understand not just the technology but its implementation. Given its lack of required user authentication and its lack of support for hardware memory protection, it should be clear that the UEFI Shell is not intended to be a secure environment.

Internet browsers of various levels of complexity have been ported to the UEFI Shell. A limited text-only browser is made easier to port if you use the existing HII and I/O protocols.

Decompression

Decompression is a basic interface because it is required to support option ROMs on add-in cards. The compression scheme used is an implementation of the one of the powerful LZMA series of dictionary lookup algorithms.

The code for the compression program is publicly available (the code is in the specification). The compressor is comparatively large and the compressor is, itself, not available as a required protocol in UEFI since 1) it's quite large and 2) it's not required to boot the system. The `Compress` UEFI Shell command does implement this standard compression scheme. The decompress algorithm is by contrast small and fast. The protocol is fairly easy to use: feed in a compressed image and, if it's in the right format, out comes a decompressed image.

Image Loading and Disk Formats

It is sometimes necessary for one program to load another. An install program may wish to install and run a driver, for example. UEFI provides two methods to do so.

The simpler method is known as the Load File Protocol and its expanded version, the Load File2 Protocol. These load files off of disks and the like. These protocols are allowed to assume that the format of the drive is FAT. Unlike older operating systems, UEFI uses a new highly extensible partition scheme, known as the GUIDed Partition Table.

The second method for loading images (programs) allows digitally signed images to be loaded but is hidden in the security part of the specification.

Security

UEFI defines a wide range of security protocols using many of the more common security standards and schemes. The protocols are focused on three areas: secure boot, driver signing, and general hashing.

We can divide security into two types: signed images and encrypted images. The contents of signed images are not secret whereas those of encrypted images are. The goal of signed images is to gain assurance that the signed data is from whom it's supposed to be from and hasn't been corrupted or tampered with along the way. The goal of encrypted images is to keep the data secret from unintended viewers.

The goals of UEFI Secure Boot are to be able to know that the firmware that booted the system was "secure." However, this is "secure" in a very technical sense. It roughly means that all of the pieces that were used to boot the system were from trusted sources and hadn't been corrupted. It generally isn't possible to require the system to trust all firmware (there has to be a root you trust at the start of the chain) so Secure Boot really means that you trust all of the firmware that's not part of the system firmware: the option ROMs.

Secure boot focuses on the first of these technologies using methods already a part of the PE/Coff load image format. UEFI Secure Boot uses a subset of the PE/Coff by limiting the types of signatures to well-known methods, namely X.509 certificates and digital signatures using RSA 2048 and SHA-256.

Secure boot is important if you plan to exit the shell and continue on to boot a large operating system that requires secure boot. It is important not to, for example, use Load Image. Instead, your program must use the secure load image protocol.

Security makes use of some basic building blocks that can be useful for non-security tasks. One of these is hashing. A hash is a mapping from a large amount of data (say 16000 bytes) to a small value. So a checksum is a hash. The kinds of hashes security people use have two important characteristics. First, they're larger. The most common today, SHA (Security Hash Algorithm)-256 is 256 bits (32 bytes) long and second, there is no known method of figuring out how to generate the same hash value from two different sets of input data. These cryptographic hashes involve some fairly complex algorithms but are well known: a SHA-256 hash calculated on one system can be verified on any other.

If you are sending data around upon which you would normally perform a checksum, you should at least consider hashing it instead. The hash is stronger and well defined around the computing industry. Checksums are comparatively weak and vary widely.

Platform Initialization (PI)

Just as the UEFI Shell is written using the UEFI interfaces, so UEFI can be written using interfaces below it. The most popular set of interfaces to use is the Platform Initialization (PI) interfaces. These interfaces are also specified by the UEFI Forum. At this writing, the PI 1.2 specification is under development.

The largest part of the PI consists of two cooperating phases known as the Driver Execution Environment (DXE) and Boot Device Selection (BDS) phases. These cooperate together to create the UEFI interfaces. In doing so, they use a limited version of the UEFI themselves. Much of this internal infrastructure survives the transfer to UEFI, particularly in the area of protocols and persistent storage.

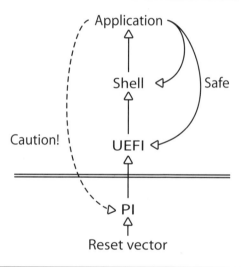

Figure 2.5 Boot Flow and Safe Calling Practices

The presence of PI can manifest itself in some unexpected ways. Using UEFI Shell commands, you can browse variables. On a PI-based system, you're likely to notice several that are not documented by the UEFI specification or anywhere else you can find. It is important not to delete these although you might be tempted to in order to free up space for your application. It is likely that the PI firmware you're relying on is relying on those variables to store the system's setup configuration, perhaps some S3 (suspend) data, and other data vital to system operation. On many systems, you simply won't be allowed to delete the PI data. General rule: unless you know what a variable does, leave it alone.

Similarly, using the UEFI Shell program to browse protocols, you'll see a lot more than you might otherwise expect. You'll be tempted to call them at times. Consider this decision carefully. It is quite acceptable to implement UEFI on top of a completely different structure than PI, in which case your program won't work if you call PI protocols. On the other hand, if you're debugging a PI driver, have at it. That's one of the ways the shell is useful. The same rules apply: 1) Use the highest level interface you can and 2) Use interfaces below your own level.

-

Chapter 3

What Is the UEFI Shell?

Try to be like the turtle—at ease in your own shell.

—Bill Copeland

With the advent of an environment like UEFI, it would stand to reason that a common concept like a shell would arise. Conceptually, a shell is built "around" some aspect of a rather complex system and provides simplified abstractions for users to gain access to the underlying infrastructure. These users could be pieces of software (such as scripts and applications) or they could be humans interacting with the shell in an interactive manner.

A platform running a BIOS that is UEFI compliant is what might be characterized as the "rather complex item" that a UEFI Shell is built around. The UEFI standards organization (www.uefi.org) publishes the UEFI and PI specifications, which drive the underlying architecture of the BIOS that runs in many of today's platforms. This same organization has published a UEFI Shell Specification intended to guide what one can expect from a compliant UEFI Shell environment.

This chapter talks about various concepts such as how the UEFI Shell is abstracting the underlying UEFI compatible BIOS infrastructure, how certain concepts such as localization are accomplished within the shell, and the various manners in which a user can interact with the shell. It should also be noted that one of the most common uses of a shell today is to launch programs and/or scripts to enable some automated processing to occur. In many cases, DOS was a very common base for such types of activity.

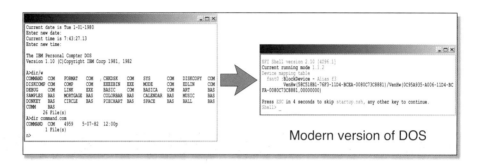

Modern version of DOS

Figure 3.1   The program launching and script support of the UEFI Shell is providing an alternative to what users of DOS and other shells have been using for a very long time.

The UEFI Shell is unusual in that it is not a shell that is a client of an operating system, but is actually considered a BIOS extension. This puts the shell on par with components that traditionally would be launched prior to an operating system such as an add-in device's option ROM. Where the UEFI Shell is launched from is largely irrelevant, but for many platform vendors, the underlying feature set and size are important considerations since in some cases the shell may actually be contained in the platform's FLASH device.

What Is Contained in the UEFI Shell?

With the consideration that size and features are important to the platform vendor, the features that are provided by a UEFI Shell are likely even more important to the users of the shell. With this in mind, the concept of having varying levels of UEFI Shell support became very important along with the ability for a client of the UEFI Shell to determine what support was being provided.

What Kind of Shell Do You Have?

The concept that a UEFI Shell can vary its support can be worrisome to some, but suffice it to say that this support is both predictable and easily dealt with. The shell is composed of two primary classes of contents:

- *Programmatic Shell Environment.* This environment is guaranteed to remain available regardless of what underlying Shell level is supported by a platform that purports to support the UEFI Shell. It is composed of the calling interfaces that shell applications can use.

- *Script Shell Environment.* This environment is the one that supports the launching and interpreting of shell scripts. The biggest variation that one might witness between shell support levels is the enumeration of commands that are supported in a given support level.

    The shell contains an environment variable known as the *shellsupport* variable. This variable can be used by shell applications as well as shell scripts to determine what the underlying UEFI Shell's function support is.

    In Table 3.1, the various levels of shell support are listed. This illustrates how at its simplest, the shell may be used strictly for purposes of shell applications to be launched (no scripting services). At level 1 basic scripting support is introduced, while level 2 simply adds a few more commands and functionality as well. In level 3, the concept of being "interactive" is introduced. For people who are familiar with the "C:" prompt from DOS, this interactive mode is similar in concept. Whereas in level 2 when a script was finished processing, the shell would terminate, in level 3 the shell provides a mode that allows the user to type at the UEFI Shell prompt.

Table 3.1   UEFI Shell Levels of Support

Level	Name	Execute()/ Scripting/ startup.nsh	PATH?	ALIAS?	Interactive?	Commands
0	Minimal	No	No	No	No	None
1	Scripting	Yes	Yes	No	No	for, endfor, goto, if, else, endif, shift, exit
2	Basic	Yes	Yes	Yes	No	attrib, cd, cp, date*, time*, del, load, ls, map, mkdir, mv, rm, reset, set, timezone*
3	Interactive	Yes	Yes	Yes	Yes	alias, date, echo, help, pause, time, touch, type, ver, cls, timezone

Note:* Noninteractive form only

- *Execute()/Scripting/startup.nsh.* Support indicates whether the Execute() function is supported by the EFI_SHELL_PROTOCOL, whether or not batch scripts are supported and whether the default startup script startup.nsh is supported.

- *PATH.* Support determines whether the PATH environment variable will be used to determine the location of executables.

- *ALIAS.* Support determines whether the ALIAS environment variable will be used to determine alternate names for shell commands.

- *Interactive.* Support determines whether or not an interactive session can be started.

What!? No Shell? No Problem!

In many usage cases, bootable media is used to launch scripts or other utilities. Historically, the common components for bootable (removable) media were a floppy disk with DOS on it, some scripts, and possibly some executable utilities. DOS itself had some inherent limitations associated with a relatively weak API set compared to more modern environments, limited access to certain memory ranges, and other miscellaneous issues with more modern hardware environments. With the advent of UEFI systems, the same infrastructure can be launched as was done before (a DOS bootable image), but with relatively no discernable advantage—it simply preserves what was previously working. However, many users of bootable media (such as manufacturing operations. diagnostics, and so on) are actively porting their DOS solutions so that they can leverage the underlying UEFI BIOS environments.

Coupling UEFI-based BIOS with the UEFI Shell, a user can achieve a true advancement in what was done in prior solutions since any of the prior limitations associated with the DOS environment have been eliminated. In fact, since the infrastructure within which the UEFI Shell runs is robust, the utilities that are launched can fully leverage all of the UEFI BIOS APIs as well as the UEFI Shell infrastructure APIs in addition to running various sets of UEFI Shell scripts.

In some situations a user's shell requirements are not compatible with what the platform currently supports. For those who are trying to provide solutions (utilities, scripts, and so on) that leverage the UEFI Shell and its environment, there are three situations to consider:

■ *When the built-in UEFI Shell does not meet the solution's requirements.* If the UEFI Shell's *shellsupport* level is insufficient for the solution provider's needs, a copy of a UEFI She-ll might need to be carried with the solution itself.

■ *When there is no built-in UEFI Shell.* There may be cases where the platform does not have a UEFI Shell built in as part of its feature set. With this in mind, the solution provider will want to carry a copy of a UEFI Shell along with its solutions carried on the provider's media.

■ *When the platform is not compatible with UEFI.* Even though UEFI BIOS is being adopted in a rapid manner in the industry, some platforms will have no underlying UEFI support. To address this situation, Intel has provided to the open source community something known as the Developer's UEFI Emulation (DUET). DUET is designed to provide a UEFI environment on a non-UEFI pre-boot system. This is achieved by creating an UEFI file image for a bootable device, and then 'booting" that image as a legacy boot. On this same bootable device/media a solution provider can, in addition to providing UEFI emulation, provide a copy of the shell environment as well as any other material the solution provider desires.

■ This DUET infrastructure is made available for download on the companion Web site associated with this book as well as being made available on the open source Web site www.tianocore.org.

Figure 3.2 illustrates three common usage scenarios for the UEFI Shell. The first is when the platform contains all the needed support for the script/utility solution, the second is when the underlying platform shell support is insufficient, and the third is when the platform is not UEFI compatible.

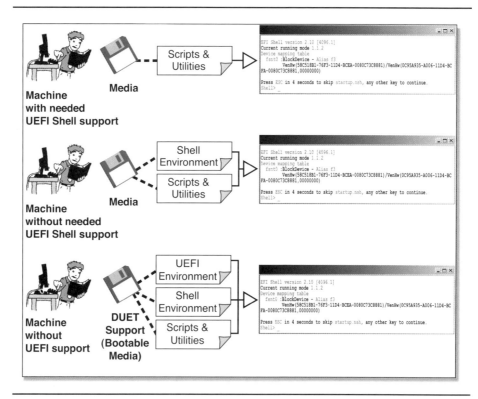

Figure 3.2 Different UEFI Shell usage models. One built within the platform, and the others provided by a bootable target.

Programmatic Shell Environment

Interfaces that are callable from binary programs are what form the UEFI Shell services. These services are what provide simplified access to various shell features and also simplify the interactions that shell clients would have with the underlying UEFI infrastructure. Figure 3.3 provides a high level view of what the interactions would be between the UEFI infrastructure, Shell interfaces, and Shell clients.

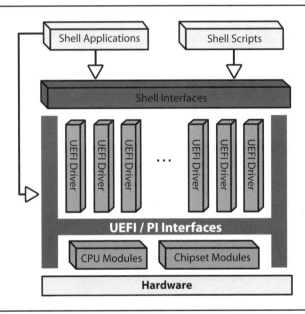

Figure 3.3 The architectural view of the UEFI Shell and the underlying platform infrastructure.

Even though Appendix B has an exhaustive enumeration of the UEFI Shell script commands, and Appendix C has an exhaustive enumeration of the UEFI Shell environment interfaces, this chapter covers the basic programmatic capabilities, their relationship with the underlying infrastructure, and how they are practically used.

Using UEFI Shell Commands

Two classes of operations occur within the UEFI Shell environment. One class of operations runs a script file that uses built-in shell commands (such as DIR and COPY) and the other class of operations are binary programs that when launched can use a variety of underlying services.

An example of this interaction would be when a script executes a DIR shell command. When doing this, the following steps occur:

- DIR command in a script file is interpreted by the Shell Interpreter.
- Shell Interpreter then calls a Shell Protocol function such as `Open-Root()`.
- The Shell Protocol would then call a UEFI service such as the UEFI Simple File System Protocol's `OpenVolume()` routine.
- The UEFI Simple File System Protocol would then call other routines, which would ultimately interact directly with the hardware and return the requested information.

Figure 3.4 shows how a script that uses a UEFI Shell command will in turn interact with both the UEFI Shell interfaces and UEFI BIOS interfaces to achieve what is requested. It also shows that Shell applications would also interact with the underlying UEFI Shell and UEFI BIOS interfaces.

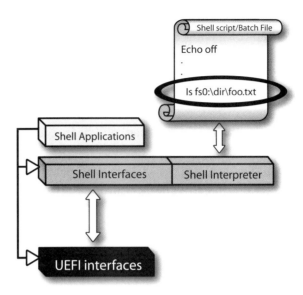

Figure 3.4   UEFI Shell interpreter processing a script file

Localization Support

Some of the inherent capabilities that were introduced into UEFI 2.1 were the ability to easily construct applications that can seamlessly support multiple languages. It should be noted that the primary difference between what someone might call a standard UEFI driver/application and a UEFI Shell application would be that the latter has knowledge of the programmatic components of the UEFI Shell infrastructure. That being said, UEFI Shell applications can leverage the underlying localization support in the same manner as any other BIOS component, such a. UEFI Drivers and Option ROMs.

Interactive Shell Environment

The concept of having a shell that is interactive is almost always assumed. The stereotypical scenario is the command prompt where a user might type a command and the results are printed to the screen (either locally or through a remote connection). With the advent of the *shellsupport* environment variable and the concept that a shell might have varying levels of support, it should not always be assumed that a shell will be interactive. In fact, it might be very common, based on the type of shell shipped with a given platform, that a script would launch and the shell environment would be closed as soon as the script were terminated (whether through a user initiated event or the script completing).

In the interactive shell environment, the usage model for the UEFI Shell is similar to what would traditionally be thought of with most shells. Some of the basics that will be discussed are the launching external binary applications, launching UEFI Shell scripts, and how the various UEFI Shell commands would ultimately resolve into programmatic interaction with the underlying UEFI Shell infrastructure as well as potentially interacting with the underlying UEFI firmware and hardware itself.

Scripting

Depending on the reader's background, three common terms might be used to represent this definition, "a list of commands that can be executed without requiring user interaction." These terms are *scripts, macros,* or *batch files,* and to simplify things, this book will try to settle on the term *scripts* when referring to the aforementioned definition.

The UEFI Shell environment is responsible for parsing the script file and interpreting the contents sufficiently to understand what type of action it is being requested to proxy. Some of the basic operations that this environment would need to accomplish would be:

- Execute UEFI Shell commands
- Chaining of UEFI Shell scripts
- Launch UEFI Shell applications
- Launch UEFI applications/drivers

Basic Overview of Commands and How They Interact with Shell Environment

Figure 3.5 illustrates the various components that the UEFI Shell interpreter would interact with when processing a script file. In this illustration we see an example of a script-based command being parsed by the interpreter itself. Ultimately the interpreter (depending on the command being parsed) would potentially end up calling some underlying UEFI firmware interfaces. In an example where a UEFI Shell application was launched, it in turn may end up calling programmatic UEFI Shell interfaces, which would then potentially interact with some underlying UEFI firmware interfaces.

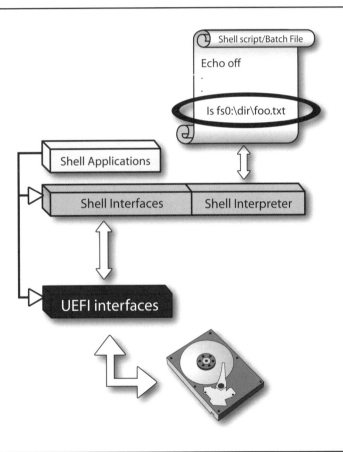

Figure 3.5 UEFI script interacting with the shell environment

1. Shell Script Interpreter parses each line of the script.

2. LS command is recognized and passed to Shell's LS handler.

3. The programmatic handler of the LS command reads the command-line parameters that were passed to it.

4. Using the UEFI Shell infrastructure, the parameters are associated with a particular set of UEFI firmware interfaces and the UEFI Shell calls these firmware interfaces.

5. The UEFI compatible firmware processes the request and in turn communicates with the underlying hardware that was ultimately referenced by the script.

6. This data request is fulfilled and eventually returned back to the UEFI Shell interpreter and the results are processed by the LS handler.

7. The script/user is then made aware of the results of the command having been processed.

Chaining of Script Commands

It is common practice for script files to execute shell commands, which for purposes of the script, are considered part of the shell environment. However it is also common practice to launch commands or other scripts in shell environments. The UEFI Shell environment is no exception. The concept of one script launching another is often termed *chaining,* and as long as the target script is accessible, a script can choose to launch any other script it has been programmed to launch.

However, there are some definite distinctions between launching a text-based script and launching a binary program. Most of these distinctions have to do with how arguments are passed and what is or isn't accessible to a particular target program. Luckily enough, for most scripts, these distinctions are completely invisible and immaterial. Since many users who are creating binary programs will launch these programs with the UEFI Shell, they may want to understand how some of these interactions would work (for example, getting command-line arguments). The following section talks a bit more about the launching of binary programs and covers some of these underlying interactions.

Program Launch

It should be understood that the UEFI Shell is running within the scope of a UEFI-based firmware environment. This means that the shell itself is a UEFI-based component that complies with the descriptions that are laid out in the UEFI specification. That being said, binary programs launched by the shell will also be UEFI compatible. Since we are introducing the topic of launching UEFI programs, it should be noted that three distinct types of programs that would typically launched by the UEFI Shell:

- *UEFI Driver* – This is a UEFI compliant binary program that would follow the UEFI specification driver model. Upon launch, this program may remain in memory and install protocols or services that also remain resident in the system.

- *UEFI Application* – This is a UEFI compliant binary program. Upon exit, this application will be unloaded from memory.

- *Shell Application* – This is a UEFI compliant binary program. This program has the same primary characteristics as a typical UEFI application with the addition of having knowledge of how to interact with the underlying UEFI Shell environment.

Even though all of these programs are compliant with the UEFI specification, several characteristics may be unique to UEFI Shell applications.

Argument Passing and Return Codes

When launching a shell application, there is an assumption that parameters would be able to be passed to the application in some fashion. Unlike many conventions where an argument count and array of argument values are directly passed to an application, in a UEFI environment the standard entry point does not consist directly of this kind of data.

When an application is launched in UEFI, sufficient data is passed to the application for it to gain access to the essential components of the UEFI environment. Figure 3.6 shows this standard entry point and how the data contained within this will also provide access to other essential material in the UEFI environment.

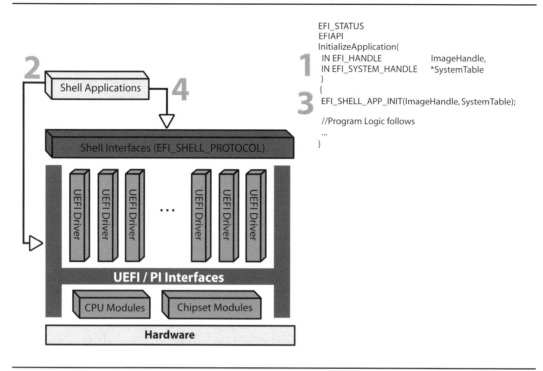

Figure 3.6   Anatomy of an application launch

1. This item illustrates what the standard entry point for any UEFI compatible binary application or driver looks like. This is the fundamental starting point for all UEFI compatible programs which exposes the underlying UEFI firmware services.

2. During the initialization of a UEFI program, the standard entry point would be used to access the standard runtime and boot services that the UEFI compatible firmware provides.

3. In most shell-aware applications, there would be either a library or macro which would be used to provide access to the underlying shell protocol interfaces. This library/macro isn't required by the UEFI shell specification, but would commonly be found in many of the available shell-aware programs.

4. In shell-aware applications, the availability of the functions defined in the EFI_SHELL_PROTOCOL can be leveraged.

Figure 3.7 shows three main components:

- *Standard Entry Point* – This is the fundamental starting point for all UEFI compatible programs that exposes the underlying UEFI firmware services.
  - Image Handle – When an application is loaded into memory for execution, this value will be the unique identifier for the application.
  - System Table – The table that contains a variety of required data and also provides a means to acquire access to the runtime and boot services that UEFI provides.
- *Runtime and Boot Services* – These are the callable interfaces that can be used to interact with the UEFI environment. These interfaces encompass several general classifications:
  - Task Priority Services
  - Memory Services
  - Event/Timer Services
  - Protocol Services
  - Image Services
  - Time Services
  - Variable Services
  - Miscellaneous Services
- *Shell Parameters Protocol* – This is the protocol that is used in a shell environment to describe all of the command-line parameter data as well as standard handles for output, input, and error. An instance of this protocol is installed on the Image Handle of the application.

```
//
// Standard Entry description for UEFI app or driver
//
EFI_STATUS
InitializeApp (
  IN EFI_HANDLE         ImageHandle,
  IN EFI_SYSTEM_TABLE   *SystemTable
  )
```

```
//
// Excerpt of the above-referenced UEFI System Table
//
typedef struct _EFI_SYSTEM_TABLE {
  EFI_TABLE_HEADER              Hdr;

  .
  .
  .

  //
  // Gain access to UEFI Runtime services
  //
  EFI_RUNTIME_SERVICES          *RuntimeServices;

  //
  // Gain access to UEFI Boot services
  //
  EFI_BOOT_SERVICES             *BootServices;
  .
  .
  .

} EFI_SYSTEM_TABLE;

//
// This protocol is installed on the application's
// ImageHandle.
//
typedef struct _EFI_SHELL_PARAMETERS_PROTOCOL {
  CHAR16           **Argv;  // Array of arguments
  UINTN            Argc;    // Argument Count
  EFI_FILE_HANDLE  StdIn;   // Standard Input
  EFI_FILE_HANDLE  StdOut;  // Standard Output
  EFI_FILE_HANDLE  StdErr;  // Standard Error
} EFI_SHELL_PARAMETERS_PROTOCOL;
```

Figure 3.7   Standard UEFI Entry point

Figure 3.8 is an example of how one might leverage the standard entry point data to acquire information like the passed in command-line parameters:

```
//
// Standard Entry description for UEFI app or driver
//
EFI_STATUS
InitializeApp (
  IN EFI_HANDLE         ImageHandle,
  IN EFI_SYSTEM_TABLE   *SystemTable
  )
{
  EFI_STATUS                      Status;
  EFI_SHELL_PARAMETERS_PROTOCOL   ShellParameters;
  CHAR16                          *FilePathName;

  //
  // Search for the Shell Parameters Protocol which was
  // installed on the application's ImageHandle.
  //
  Status = SystemTable->BootServices->HandleProtocol (
          ImageHandle,
          &ShellParametersProtocolGuid,
          &ShellParameters
          );

  //
  // The first parameter is the executable file path
  // name. Subsequent parameters reflect the processed
  // command-line parameters
  //
  FilePathName = &ShellParameters->Argv[0];

  .
  .
  .

  //
  // When exiting an application, there will be a status
  // returned. The UEFI Shell environment will reflect
  // this status in the LastError environment variable so
  // that scripts can see what the last error was
  // produced by a given application or shell command.
  //
  return Status;
}
```

Figure 3.8   Retrieving command-line data

Since many underlying functions such as acquisition of command-line data are normally abstracted by library services, the example in Figure 3.8 is good for showing how some of these fundamental pieces of data are inter-related. This is especially true since the ability to acquire the entry point for protocol services is key to creating a UEFI-aware application; and knowing how to acquire such data from solely the commonly passed-in data from the entry point will help not only for UEFI Shell programming but for any UEFI programming.

When programs are launched, they will have their returned status codes analyzed by the UEFI Shell environment and have an internal copy of the LastError environment variable updated with this result. Figure 3.8 shows that when a program exits (thus returning a status), the UEFI Shell environment will automatically be updated so that when a script checks %LastError%, it will automatically be reflected with this returned status.

File-System Abstractions

In a traditional operating system where scripting is prevalent, a simple abstraction for file systems are usually available (such as. "C:"or "D:"). The UEFI Shell environment is no different than these traditional operating systems. In fact, it goes one step further in that it provides clear abstractions for LBA-based (sector-based) accesses through a block I/O interface, and it provides abstractions for file-system based accesses through disk I/O interface. Figure 3.9 introduces two common UEFI protocols that have to do with abstracting storage devices.

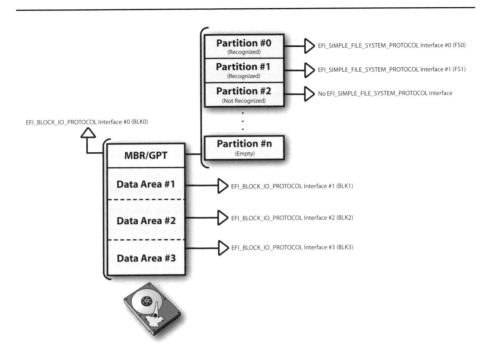

Figure 3.9   File System Abstractions in the UEFI Shell

In Figure 3.9, references to BLK and FS are used to note a block and file-system interface. These interfaces are constructed during the UEFI Shell environment's initialization. These text-based references are used as simply text notations for various aspects of storage devices. When the UEFI Shell (and especially the MAP command) analyzes the UEFI environment, it searches for instances of EFI_BLOCK_IO_PROTOCOL. This is a UEFI protocol that provides an LBA-based abstraction for a storage device. Upon discovery, it will tag each discovered instance with a unique name. These interfaces are a logical abstraction, which means that they abstract a range of physical sectors on some media, and are not necessarily providing access to the entire media.

In the example of BLK0, this is an abstraction used to designate the entire disk. That simply means that when a command references BLK0, the first sector is the real first sector of that disk, while the last sector is the real last sector of the disk. This would contrast with the usage model of a partition's BLK instance such as BLK1.

In the example, BLK1 is associated with the data range for a particular partition entry. That simply means that when a command references BLK1, the first sector is the first data sector of that partition (not the disk), while the last sector is the last sector of the partition.

In addition to the discovery of block devices during the UEFI Shell initialization, the UEFI Shell will analyze the UEFI environment looking for instances of `EFI_SIMPLE_FILE_SYSTEM_PROTOCOL`. This is a UEFI protocol that provides abstractions for recognized file-systems. Upon discovery, it will tag each discovered instance with a unique name. It should be noted that this protocol will not be established if the formatting of the media or partition is not recognized. For instance, if a media is formatted as a FAT32 file-system, a UEFI system will layer an `EFI_SIMPLE_FILE_SYSTEM_PROTOCOL` instance.

Shell Script Resolves into a UEFI Firmware Action

When the UEFI Shell is executing a script, a lot of data needs to be interpreted. Figure 3.10 shows a very common example where a statement such as

```
COPY FS0:\Source.txt FS0:\Destination.txt
```

is interpreted by the UEFI Shell environment. The UEFI Shell initiates several steps during this interpretation:

1. Determine what command the UEFI Shell needs to pass this data to. In this case, the COPY command is recognized and used.

2. Prior to launching the COPY command, install the `EFI_SHELL_PARAM-ETERS_PROTOCOL` on the target command's image handle. (Recall that this is used for understanding the command-line parameters)

3. Launch the COPY command.

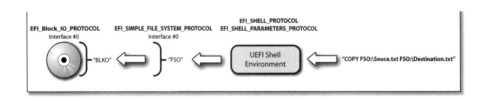

Figure 3.10 From script to hardware interaction

The target command will then be responsible for several actions to complete the requested process.

1. The called command (such as. COPY) will retrieve the command-line parameters to determine what it is being asked to do.

2. Since the COPY command is a shell-enabled command, it will use the appropriate shell interface commands to accomplish its action. For instance, to read/write a particular file (for example: FS0:\Source.txt) it will likely use the EFI_SHELL_PROTOCOL.OpenByFileName() function to obtain a file handle.

3. Once a file handle is obtained, the same protocol has worker functions to read or write to that file (ReadFile/WriteFile).

4. Various other miscellaneous activities would occur.

The UEFI Shell environment is ultimately responsible to handling the underlying functions associated with EFI_SHELL_PROTOCOL. When calls are made to the functions in this protocol, several actions end up taking place.

1. When a command (such as. COPY) calls the OpenByFileName() function to obtain a file handle, one of the key things is to determine where the file physically resides. This is determined by interpreting the passed-in data (for example, FS0:\Source.txt)

2. The UEFI Shell environment will have an internal mapping of the file systems that have been recognized (for example, FS0) and it can in turn call the protocol EFI_SIMPLE_FILE_SYSTEM_PROTOCOL associated with that text-based shortcut.

3. When calling the aforementioned simple file-system protocol, it would pass in the path and file name (such as \Source.txt) and see if the file can be discovered.

4. If found, the UEFI Shell would have an assigned handle for this opened file. This handle would later be used by subsequent calls to the UEFI Shell and easily associated with the physical file. When asked to read or write to such a handle, the appropriate UEFI interfaces can then be called to complete the request.

Chapter 4

Why We Need an Execution Environment before the OS

In every phenomenon the beginning remains always the most notable moment.

—Thomas Carlyle

As mentioned in Chapter 3, quite a number of software components on the platform execute prior to the operating system taking control. The state of the machine prior to the operating system runtime is generally referred to as the pre-OS state and can be broken down into many details. Why is the pre-OS state such a rich environment, what are all of the software components on the machine, and what do they do? These are some of the questions this chapter answers. This chapter provides a review of the states of a platform and the activities that occur therein. This review provides a foundation for successive chapters and their deeper treatment of the items discussed.

Evolution of a Machine

To begin with, the machine restarts in a nascent state. At this point of the machine evolution, there is no memory of I/O devices available. There is just a flash read-only memory (ROM) device on the system board from which the initial code is fetched. This code contains various modules that configure the I/O devices, memory, and system fabric. Figure 4.1 shows an example platform and its flash ROM container.

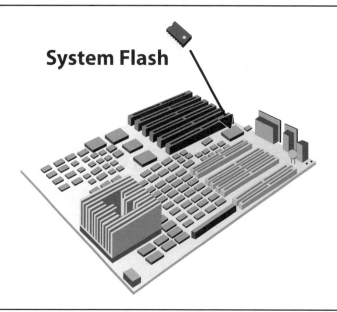

Figure 4.1   System Board with Flash

The flash ROM is manufactured as part of the system board. The executable modules within this device have a priori knowledge of the platform and its various components. The flash ROM contents are not intended to be third-party extensible; they are created and updated under the authority of the equipment manufacturer.

The Platform Initialization Flow

A series of executable modules and data files are organized in the flash; these elements abstract basic capabilities and the initialization functions listed above. Figure 4.2 shows the relationship between the types of elements that are board- and module-specific. The important distinction is that a series of modules initially execute in what is referred to as the Pre-EFI Initialization or PEI phase of execution.

The bulk of PEI executes in place (XIP) and uses some temporary memory store on the platform as a call-stack and heap. This store can include but is not limited to one a portion of the processor cache used in such a way that the accesses are not evicted. This use of the cache as RAM (CAR) allows for running PEI modules built from C code using standard compilers. But the limitations on this uncompressed XIP PEI code and paucity of CAR means that the minimum amount of activity needs to occur in PEI, namely "initialize useable main memory, discover the DXE core file, and invoke DXE."

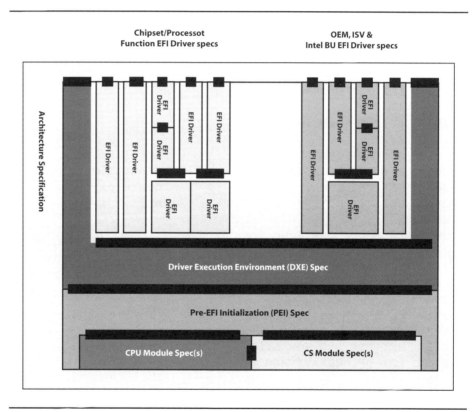

Figure 4.2   Layered Modules in Flash

PEI is the lowest level of elements shown in Figure 4.2 and runs first. Once PEI has enabled a sufficient amount of memory, though, the Driver Execution Environment (DXE) is invoked from the flash ROM. The DXE elements are richer in capability and do not suffer from the space/performance constraints of PEI since they have ample system memory. Figure 4.2 shows discrete, separable components. This separation is accomplished by having the modules communicate with the PEI core via the PEI core services, such as memory allocation and service registration/discovery. The executables themselves are referred to as PEI Modules (PEIMs) and can invoke the PEI core services, publish interfaces for another PEIM to leverage, namely a PEIM-to-PEIM interface (PPI), or bind to other PPIs. The PPIs are named by a Globally Unique Identifier (GUID) such that APIs and data associated with a PPI can evolve as new technology, buses, and capabilities evolve.

The PEI Services table is shown in Figure 4.3.

```
256 typedef struct _EFI_PEI_SERVICES {
257    EFI_TABLE_HEADER              Hdr;
258    //
259    // PPI Functions
260    //
261    EFI_PEI_INSTALL_PPI           InstallPpi;
262    EFI_PEI_REINSTALL_PPI         ReInstallPpi;
263    EFI_PEI_LOCATE_PPI            LocatePpi;
264    EFI_PEI_NOTIFY_PPI            NotifyPpi;
265    //
266    // Boot Mode Functions
267    //
268    EFI_PEI_GET_BOOT_MODE         GetBootMode;
269    EFI_PEI_SET_BOOT_MODE         SetBootMode;
270    //
271    // HOB Functions
272    //
273    EFI_PEI_GET_HOB_LIST          GetHobList;
274    EFI_PEI_CREATE_HOB            CreateHob;
275    //
276    // Firmware Volume Functions
277    //
278    EFI_PEI_FFS_FIND_NEXT_VOLUME2 FfsFindNextVolume;
279    EFI_PEI_FFS_FIND_NEXT_FILE2   FfsFindNextFile;
280    EFI_PEI_FFS_FIND_SECTION_DATA2 FfsFindSectionData;
281    //
282    // PEI Memory Functions
283    //
```

```
284    EFI_PEI_INSTALL_PEI_MEMORY        InstallPeiMemory;
285    EFI_PEI_ALLOCATE_PAGES            AllocatePages;
286    EFI_PEI_ALLOCATE_POOL             AllocatePool;
287    EFI_PEI_COPY_MEM                  CopyMem;
288    EFI_PEI_SET_MEM                   SetMem;
289    //
290    // Status Code
291    //
292    EFI_PEI_REPORT_STATUS_CODE        PeiReportStatusCode;
293    //
294    // Reset
295    //
296    EFI_PEI_RESET_SYSTEM              PeiResetSystem;
297    //
298    // Pointer to PPI interface
299    //
300    EFI_PEI_CPU_IO_PPI                *CpuIo;
301    EFI_PEI_PCI_CFG2_PPI              *PciCfg;
302    EFI_PEI_FFS_FIND_BY_NAME          FfsFindFileByName;
303    EFI_PEI_FFS_GET_FILE_INFO         FfsGetFileInfo;
304    EFI_PEI_FFS_GET_VOLUME_INFO       FfsGetVolumeInfo;
305    EFI_PEI_REGISTER_FOR_SHADOW       RegisterForShadow;
306  } EFI_PEI_SERVICES;
307
308 //
309 // PEI PPI Services
310 //
311 typedef
312 EFI_STATUS
313 (EFIAPI *EFI_PEI_INSTALL_PPI) (
314   IN CONST EFI_PEI_SERVICES           **PeiServices,
315   IN CONST EFI_PEI_PPI_DESCRIPTOR     * PpiList
316   );
317
318
```

Figure 4.3   PEI Services Table and Example Function Declaration of One of the PEI Services

In Figure 4.3, lines 257–307, show the full PEI Services table. Lines 310–317 show one function declaration from the PEI Services table, namely the EFI_PEI_INSTALL_PPI service. This latter API is used by a PEIM to publish an interface from its PEIM so that other PEIMs can discover and bind to the interface, respectively.

UEFI Transitions

Figure 4.4 shows the boot flow when PEI hands off into DXE. The early portion of diagram shows the time evolution of the PEI, which then passes control into the DXE phase. The DXE phase invokes a series of drivers that orchestrate the possible testing of memory not covered by PEI, discover and allocate resources for I/O buses like PCI, initiate other buses like USB, and so on. Once the system fabric has been initialized and basic platform capabilities are available, the DXE infrastructure provides a set of interfaces that conform to the UEFI specification. This is shown by the line in Figure 4.4 that reads *UEFI APIs*. At this point, DXE passes control to the Boot Device Selection (BDS) interface of the platform firmware and the boot manager capability of the UEFI specification takes control.

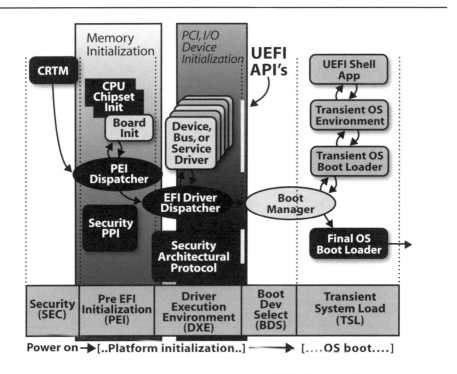

Figure 4.4   Time-based View of Boot

All of the activity up until this point has been orchestrated by components that are under the authority of the system board or platform supplier (PS). The PEI and DXE components should be installed by the PS authority with suitable protections on the flash part and should not be extensible by third parties. In other words, all of the code running in PEI and DXE should come from the PS. Once BDS has been invoked and the UEFI API's area is available, though, code from third parties, such as UEFI drivers in option ROMs and operating system loaders or applications from the UEFI system partition may be invoked.

Within this flash part are a series of components that successively initialize more of the platform state. The flash ROM with the boot UEFI code is only one portion of the platform, though. There are several other components on the system board, whether soldered down or attached via cables. These include block devices, consoles, and networking devices.

The state of these platforms, especially the block devices that have things like the UEFI system partition with the operating system loader, can be installed at various points. The various states of the platform and its configuration will be briefly reviewed here but treated with more detail in subsequent chapters.

States of a Platform

Within this flash part are a series of components that successively initialize more of the platform state, as shown in Figure 4.5. State1 in shown in Figure 4.6 can include the raw system board with just the boot flash ROM and no attached peripherals.

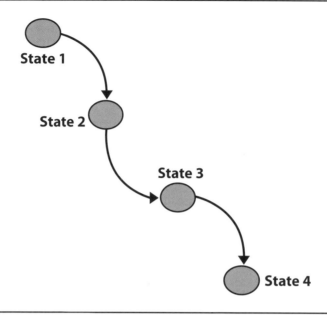

Figure 4.5   Various States of a Platform's Configuration and How They Evolve

In state1, the platform will not be configured with platform firmware or the operating system. We refer to this as *raw,* composed of just the CPU, chipset, RAM, and flash part. The latter will not be programmed with any of the binary code content, nor would other reprogrammable elements on the platform, such as EEPROM's or device flash components.

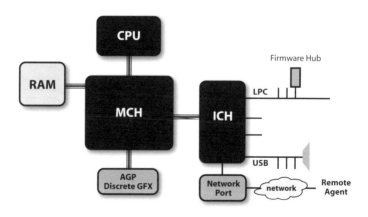

Figure 4.6   State1: Raw Platform

From this raw system board, it is typically put into a box or integrated into a chassis by a vendor, during which time the peripherals may be added. We refer to this as state2, shown in Figure 4.7. At this point, there is typically no information on the added hard disk.

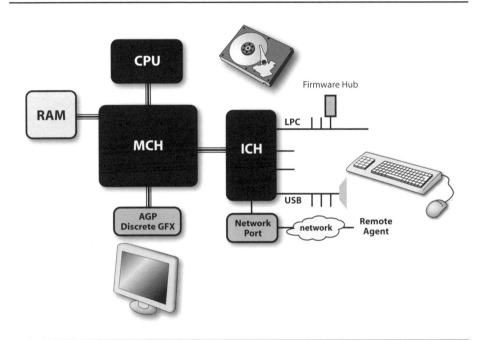

Figure 4.7   State2: System Board with Peripherals

State2 may evolve in the vendor factory (for a fully integrated system) or at a value-added reseller into state3. State3 entails installing the operating system on the machine. During state2 some vendor tests may be run in order to ensure the physical integrity of the system.

Also, this type of deployment isn't limited to a single system board. A blade server in a rack can also be the target of the states of configuration described herein, as shown in Figure 4.8.

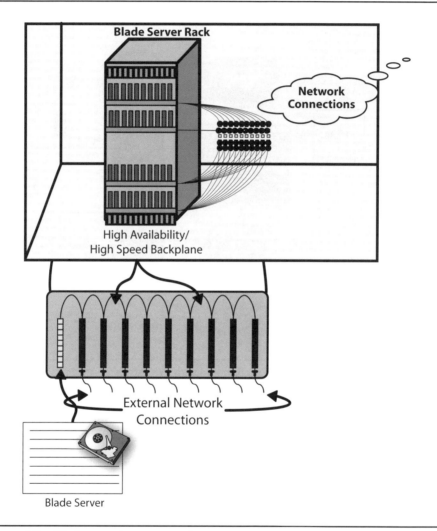

Figure 4.8   Blade server in a server rack

Readiness of UEFI

At this point UEFI and the PI firmware have discovered the hardware complex, but there is still no an operating system. State3 entails "imaging" an operating system onto the hard disk via a locally attached device, such as a CD-ROM drive, or via a network boot, as shown in Figure 4.9. The act of imaging an OS is to write it directly to the logical block addresses of the storage media with a file system intermediary.

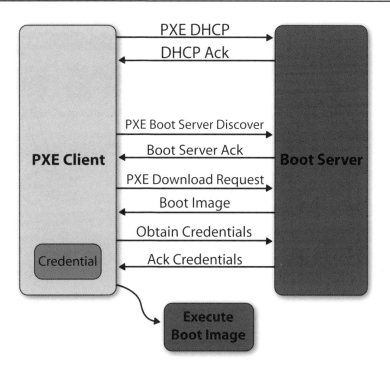

Figure 4.9   Network Boot

The network boot case is important for both manufacturing flow, when the final disk image is sent onto the newly built machine, and also for live deployment. In the latter case, a diskless client machine that boots an IT-authorized OS image each day or a blade server that only has memory and CPU elements but requires loading the runtime OS image from the server area network (SAN) both entail the use of the platform networking capabilities.

The manufacturing case of network boot is valuable since the build-to-order machine may have the user select one from various operating system options, including Microsoft Windows or Linux. This final stage of manufacturing when the OS image is transferred onto the disk via UEFI networking allows for a no-touch, remote configuration of the product.

As noted above, the UEFI interactions occur once the PEI and DXE have executed. The rich set of UEFI drivers and applications occur in the flow as shown in Figure 4.10.

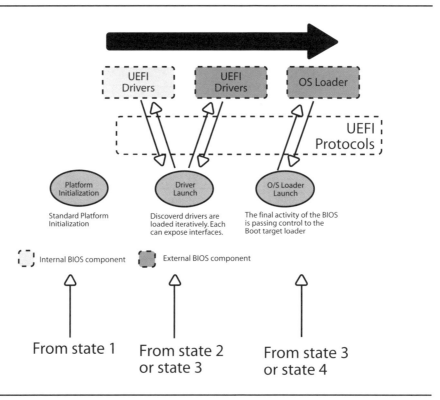

Figure 4.10 Flow of the System

The UEFI drivers can be loaded from the UEFI system partition or from a host-bus adapter (HBA), such as a PCI SCSI or NIC. The UEFI applications can include executables integrated into the flash ROM, on the UEFI system partition, or loaded across the network. These applications include diagnostics, operating system loaders, and the UEFI Shell.

The most important activity in state3 is to install the operating system on the disk. Recall from state2 that the disk was attached, but at this point it contained blank logical block addresses.

During state3, the platform manufacturer is still in control of the system. An operating system installer can run from the factory environment in order to deposit the OS loader, kernel, and support files on the disk, as shown in Figure 4.11.

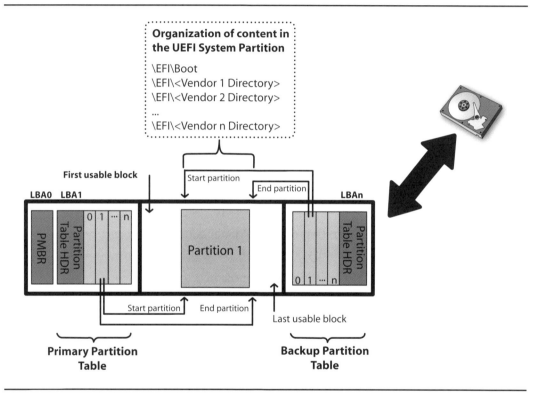

Figure 4.11   Disk with OS Installation

At this point, a complete system, such as server or laptop would ship to an end user. We refer to the end user as the owner of the platform. The owned platform, in our state diagram, now refers to state4. The owner can choose to run diagnostics, install additional operating systems, or reinstall the former OS as a repair or upgrade operation.

At state4 the ability to run the UEFI Shell, including diagnostics such as reading the SMBIOS tables or other asset information is still valuable. The

UEFI Shell exposes all system memory and hardware resources. An end user may choose to boot into the UEFI Shell during the life of his or her platform in order to run some memory test or disk diagnostics. Such exhaustive testing cannot easily occur during the OS runtime since a failure in memory or I/O surfaces in unpredictable ways during an OS crash. Also, attempting to run such diagnostics *in situ* during OS runtime can lead to various *Heisenbugs* (bugs where the observing agent and system under observation interact, named after Heisenberg's Uncertainty Principle, which noted that momentum and position of an electron could not be precisely measured at the same time because the act of observing the electron would perturb it).

Migration Using the UEFI Shell

Another important application of the UEFI Shell is to facilitate the migration of one machine to another. The scenario is as follows:

■ A single machine is configured manually or via UEFI Shell script by IT per their requirements

– This is referred to as the "golden" machine

– The configuration of the golden machine is sent to a central network or rack repository, such as a Chassis Management Module (CMM)

■ The golden machine is then attached to the network

– Imagine the scenario below where the golden machine is a blade server in a rack

■ The rack of blades is activated and a UEFI application runs on each of the unconfigured blades.

– Each blade talks to the well known network authority, such as CMM, to get the configuration

– The UEFI Shell application on each blade applies the golden configuration

■ The act of collecting the configuration or each of the blade's configuration application actions will apply generic settings, such as OS boot targets, language codes, and other UEFI-defined specification options, but it will elide certain blade-specific options, such as the local blade MAC address

■ Once the configuration of all of the blades has occurred in the pre-OS state, the rack can be restarted and the successive blades booted to their locally attached storage or a network-based boot target via a PXE or ISCSI boot

This golden machine cloning or migration of the machine personality is something that must occur prior to the OS launch, and entails a state3 to state3 migration or state4 to state4 migration across the different computation units, as shown in Figure 4.12.

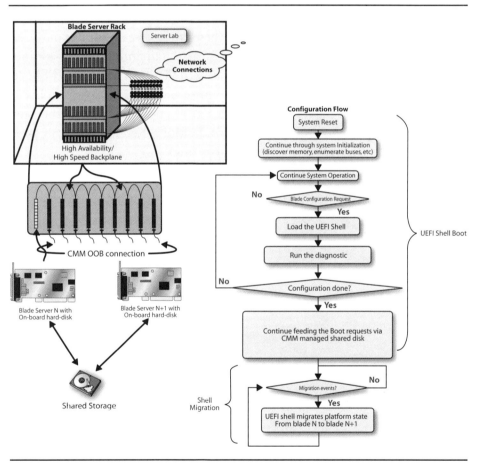

Figure 4.12 Migration of UEFI settings from one blade to another

Even though this example shows a migration across a series of blades in a rack, it would have been equally applicable across a class of enterprise client machines, handheld devices, or other appliances. The key common elements across these platforms are the UEFI-based firmware, the UEFI Shell, the ability to reach the common repository of settings, and the cloning application.

Going Forward

Subsequent chapters provide guidance on how UEFI-based technology such as the UEFI Shell can assist in these latter state evolutions of the platform. For example, configuration in state4 can entail enrollment of additional devices, such as "taking ownership" of Trusted Platform Modules (TPMs), the cloning of machines such that an enterprise owner of a large number of units can personalize them for their particular business needs, or further storage options can be applied, such as configuration of a Redundant Array of Independent Disks (RAID) with additional options.

Chapter **5**

Manufacturing Using the UEFI Shell

Don't sweat it—it's not real life. It's only ones and zeroes.

—Eugene Spafford

We are told we live in the information age. Before that we lived in the space age and, before that, the atomic age. Our forefathers lived in the industrial age, through the industrial revolution, the age of reason, several other ages back to the middle ages, then back more ages to the Hellenistic age, and the iron, bronze, and stone ages.

With the way ages are described, we'd be forgiven if we thought one technological age replaced all the previous ones. That's not what happens. Ages clearly overlap. Furthermore, each age is built on the previous ages and uses the knowledge accumulated in those ages. The practitioners of those older arts continue to refine their skills and technologies: modern container ships aren't made of space, they're made of good old industrial age steel. Modern buildings aren't made of information, they're made of stone and wood and glass, products of several ages, successively refined.

Artists have tried to show the information age with only limited success. They typically show little pellets of information zooming through tubes or shimmering webs of connections between nodes encircling the earth. Movies show users swimming through matrices of information, occasionally bumping into firewalls. The reality of the information age is quite different. All of the bits and pieces that store and manipulate information are real tangible physical objects: keyboards, routers, cables, power supplies, flash drives, laptops, and so on.

The way those objects are created owes more to the processes of the industrial age than any newer age. Like the steam locomotives and Model Ts of a previous age, the objects of the information age must be conceived of and then designed. With the consistency required by this age they must then be manufactured to very high tolerances. Manufacturing of computers and computer products straddles the ages.

Computer manufacturing itself is not uniform. Motherboards must be built, as must add-in devices of every sort. The various components must then be integrated together to form systems. The systems must then be provided with software and configured. The UEFI Shell is useful at all of the stages.

One of the earliest applications of the UEFI Shell was in manufacturing testing and automation. This is not surprising since the requirements of manufacturing align quite closely with what the UEFI Shell delivers.

Disclaimer

Manufacturing is a complex and changing area of expertise. In the short space allocated here, we can only provide a brief description of how manufacturing works and why. As with any discipline, it has a language all of its own, with less than complete consistency from company to company. As such, the terminology used here may not be the terminology you're used to.

The descriptions here are intended as a brief overview in order to motivate the following discussion so an important area of the manufacturing process might be given shorter coverage than you might expect.

This chapter is intended to serve several audiences. It is an overview of manufacturing, its challenges, and the UEFI Shell's utility for those who aren't familiar with the field. It is intended to describe the value of using the UEFI Shell to those who might want to bring it to a manufacturing environment. It is also an overview of some of the UEFI Shell's useful features for those who work in computer manufacturing environments.

Manufacturing 101

Manufacturing decisions are driven by a number of factors. This section summarizes some of the most common and most critical.

Manufacturing Economics

Manufacturing is about time and money. In many ways the two are treated as interchangeable: the more time the more money. Most decisions made during manufacturing try to minimize expenditure of one or the other. The refinement of over 150 years of manufacturing experience has led to deep understanding of the parameters available and how to adjust them.

Manufacturing costs can be broken into two categories: recurring expenses and nonrecurring expenses. Recurring costs are costs incurred each time an item is produced: the labor that goes into creating the item and the items in the bill of materials (BOM—the parts that the item is made out of) are usually key examples. Nonrecurring costs include the design and engineering costs and the jigs and machines used to manufacture the item. For example, a milling machine is typically not purchased for creating a single item. In manufacturing computer components, manufacturing generally argues to make the new generation's products similar to the old ones not just because manufacturing is by its nature adverse to risk but also because many of the costs are reduced.

Manufacturing is about scale: what number of a given item is to be produced and how quickly. If the goal is to produce thousands of an item, it will be manufactured differently than if the goal is to produce millions of that item. If you wanted to create three chairs for an entire production run, you would use very different tools and techniques than if you planned a production run of 100,000. The decision-making process concerning the level of investment in nonrecurring tools is complex and there are times when the tradeoffs balance each other out. In such cases, other factors enter into the equation: What is the workforce used to? How much training on some piece of new equipment is required? How reliable is the equipment? Will it arrive on time? Manufacturing tends to be conservative to minimize risk. It is better to be certain of having something in 90 days than to take the chance of having something in 60 days that may take 365 days.

Manufacturing is about ensuring quality. In the 1970s and 1980s we learned that "You can't test in quality." That may be true or not but much of manufacturing is about testing. You build a little, you test a little, you build some more, you test some more.

Quality itself is, outside the manufacturing world, somewhat hard to define. When it comes to manufacturing, however, quality is almost synonymous with consistency: Is the latest item the same as the previous one? Good and bad are, in this area at least, subjective terms. Different is more objective so change forms the basis of quality if for no other reason than because differences are measurable. The theory goes as well that, if you start with something that works and you make copies of that item, they'll work too. The fly in the ointment is that some differences are relevant and some are not. The data gathered does allow for a better decision as to what's important.

Lines

If you walk onto a higher volume manufacturing floor, you'll see machines connected one to the next, usually tended to by people. At some points along the way, people work with equipment to do tasks that can't be or haven't been automated. Other points are entirely automated with workers simply monitoring the equipment.

At a more formal level, a manufacturing floor contains one or more lines. Each line is divided up into stations. The initial components go in at one end of the line and are processed and tested at each station along the line, ending up with finished goods coming out the end of the line, as shown in Figure 5.1.

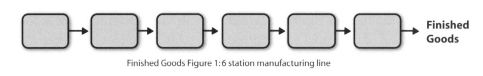

Finished Goods Figure 1:6 station manufacturing line

Figure 5.1 Six Station Manufacturing Line

Throughput, or *beat rate* (from the consistent tapping of a drum during a march of soldiers) is the standard measure of manufacturing performance: how many functional items does the line produce for a given rate of time?

With this piece of data, planners can determine how many lines are required to meet a certain demand.

Consider the simple case of a line producing widgets, shown in Figure 5.2. The line produces 100 widgets per hour. If the demand is 800 widgets per day, one 8 hour shift will produce the required quantity (8 × 100 = 800).

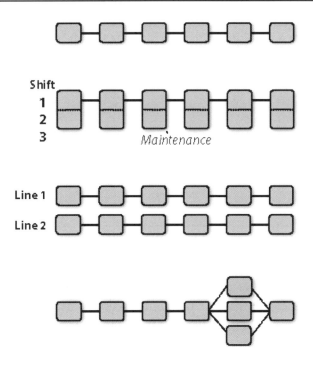

Figure 5.2   Line Capable of 800 Widgets

If the demand increases to 1600, you either add another shift (2 × 8 × 100 = 1600), as shown in Figure 5.3, or add another line (8 × 2 × 100 = 1600), as shown in Figure 5.4. The costs of workers versus the cost of the machinery associated with the line indicate which path makes more sense. As usual, real life isn't quite as simple as the calculations shown here. Shift workers don't appear and disappear instantaneously, for example. New machinery takes time to install and may require a new facility. The tradeoffs between investment and flexibility are not trivial.

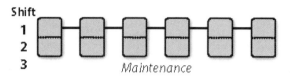

Figure 5.3 Use Two Shifts to Make 1600 Widgets

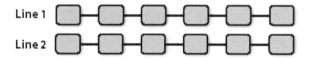

Figure 5.4 Use Two Lines to Make 1600 Widgets

The other alternative to going from 800 to 1600 is to make the line produce 200 widgets per hour. To do so, analysis of the line is undertaken to determine the slow parts of the line. If one station is slow, can it be split into two or three parts, each taking its share of the production, as illustrated in Figure 5.5? Can a slow manual process be automated?

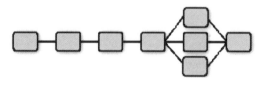

Figure 5.5 Modified Line to Make 1600 Widgets

Phases

For convenience, lines can be conceptually broken up into larger pieces we'll call *phases*. Each phase then consists of one or more stations. The phases are more consistent across types of manufacturing than individual phases.

The phases we see in most manufacturing fall into three areas, which are more commonly referred to by the type of testing that occurs during each phase.

The first phase tests the components and sub-assemblies of the article. The next phase tests the final article. The third phase subjects random finished articles to more testing. This last phase allows for improved consistency of all finished articles at a fraction of the cost.

The names for each phase vary from industry to industry, company to company, and organization to organization.

Motherboards

The motherboard is the base card in a system. In mobile computing, it may actually be a few cards due to chassis constraints. In contrast to desktop and mobile platforms, server motherboards may not have sites for the processors. Server motherboards are also larger and have more parts whereas mobile (and sub-mobile) motherboards tend to be more densely packed. As far as the UEFI Shell is concerned, these physical differences are outweighed by the systems' similarities.

There are usually three series of tests for high volume motherboard construction: circuit testing, functional testing, and quality monitoring.

Circuit Testing

In the first series, motherboards are subjected to a series of electrical tests before any code is executed. Is there continuity on the board? Are important circuits such as power delivery providing the right levels of power? Since no code is executed during this phase, the shell is not of much use on the system under test. Instead, monitoring computers use sophisticated hardware interfaces to probe components. Some of the machines doing the testing might be able to use the shell but that is for a different chapter.

Functional Testing

Functional testing is literally that: testing to see if the newly manufactured motherboard is functional. In plainer terms, does the thing work? Unlike circuit testing, functional tests are run on the unit under test (UUT). In years past, tests were generally moved around on floppies or CDs. Now UUTs get their tests downloaded to them over a network from a test server. The UUT then either fails or reports its data back up the network to systems that process the results.

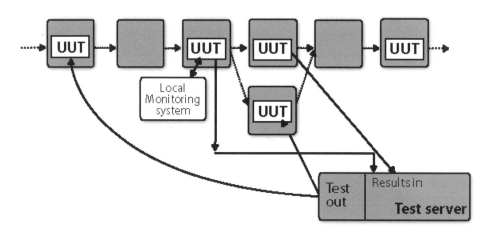

Figure 5.6 Network connections during functional testing

The test server typically remains connected through all or most all of the board's journey through functional testing so that the time consuming task of reestablishing a network connection does not have to be repeated. As such, the test server must track how far a system is along the flow and what tests it requires next.

Due to limitations in the firmware LAN connections (which UEFI and the UEFI Shell can resolve), the test server is also almost always the system that accumulates results. The results are used for both analysis of the UUT and trend data as well.

In many cases the system may be hooked up to local monitoring computers although this is becoming rarer as more automation is available.

Quality Monitoring

Quality monitoring is a manifestation of the concept of statistical quality control. In functional testing, all boards were subjected to a battery of tests. In quality monitoring a statistically significant sample are then subjected to even more tests. Initially that sample is 100 percent of the items from functional test. As confidence is achieved that small numbers of systems are failing the quality monitoring tests, the sample size is reduced. Typically, during volume production of a solid product, 20 to 25 percent of all boards might go through quality monitoring.

The tests selected for quality monitoring are typically of longer duration or:

- Have higher test facility costs than in functional testing
- Are less likely to demonstrate issues
- Are likely to be consistent problems rather than item-specific.

For example, four corner testing (high humidity + high temperature, high humidity + low temperature, low humidity + low temperature, low humidity + high temperature) might take along longer than the total time it takes to do all of functional testing (many hours for client product, many days for servers). Four corner test facilities are expensive, particularly when multiplied by the number of chambers required to keep up with (even 20 percent of) the beat rate.

The output of manufacturing is *finished goods* and shipping. One of many nightmares that manufacturing personnel seek to avoid is to have to reopen finished goods to fix product or to simply have to scrap finished goods.

Using the UEFI Shell to Manufacture Motherboards

With this background, we can now look at how operating systems, particularly the Shell, can affect manufacturing flow.

Using DOS to Manufacture Motherboards

Even today much manufacturing uses DOS for tests run at functional test and quality monitoring stations. Those looking from the outside might put this apparent conservatism up to institutional inertial and a high comfort level on the part of the developers. The argument goes that all of the DOS tools already exist, they've worked for many years, and we know how to tweak them from product to product.

Although there is a lot of rationale in not changing what works, the underlying reasons for using DOS are somewhat different.

While the system is booting, no real useful testing is going on. The quicker a system boots the more testing that can be done per unit time. DOS boots in 5–10 seconds whereas it might take 90 seconds to boot a large OS.

Computer manufacturing is the largest user of network boot since it allows for boot without add-in devices (like disks) that might not have been installed yet. The disks probably contain the end user operating system as well rather than the test OS. Booting from the network has the added benefit of centralizing boot so that changes to the process can be integrated in a controlled fashion and nearly instantaneously. The standard boot framework is known as PXE, which uses a DOS intermediary. With DOS, you can just stop there.

DOS also has no protections against direct access to hardware. It may seem kind of obvious but the implications are hard to overestimate: if you are testing hardware, you need full access to that hardware. Larger operating systems are successful in part because one application can't disrupt another by writing into its memory or modifying underlying hardware configuration. These benefits must all be worked around when testing hardware.

DOS uses FAT, the most common format for file interchange in the world. While not a direct requirement, an agreed upon format for use by both the unit-under-test and the system monitoring the tests is necessary.

The UEFI Shell and DOS

The good news is the UEFI Shell retains DOS' quick boot performance, quick network boot time, lack of protections, and FAT. There are also available libraries for the standard C I/O libraries.

So, if the two are so similar, why use UEFI Shell rather than DOS? In many ways, the UEFI Shell was designed as a DOS that is extended to include the modern features that around 35 years of experience has demonstrated DOS lacking.

Finding and Using Basic Resources

The UEFI APIs visible natively via the Shell allow test applications to know what peripherals the firmware (BIOS) found, where they are, and what resources the firmware is using.

For example, a memory test that writes over itself or the network stack will not be able to return results. The UEFI GCD services describe the various types of memory in the system and what they are used for. Memory services already required and used by the BIOS and operating system allow for allocation of memory with different cache attributes and, if required, at particular addresses.

One worry is that this will slow tests down. Not true. The performance is not noticeable for all but the most extreme tests and there other variables (differences in cache size, processor technology, and so on) outweigh any variation caused by 64-bit accesses.

DOS was designed in a time when the personal computer could only address 1 megabyte of memory, so it is limited to 640 KB in its basic form. With arduous extensions, it can go to 4 GB. Only with extremely unnatural acts can one address above 4 GB in DOS. Workarounds become difficult and the creation of new tools becomes more error-prone.

The problem is that access to higher and higher areas of the memory map is becoming more and more commonplace. Graphics controllers routinely map 256 MB of RAM into the PCIe spaces. The trend is also for processor and chipset I/O locations to be memory mapped, usually at very high sub-4GB addresses (or in servers, above 4 GB), the limitations of DOS are becoming painful.

And it gets worse than that. Trends are also for memory addressability in even client (desktop and mobile) systems to exceed 4 GB. Since some of the memory below 4GB is used by the firmware, APICs, PCI/PCIe memory, and the like, this means some of the RAM in full-up configuration testing is likely to be above 4 GB.

On the other hand, the Shell's native environment (on x64 systems) is 64-bit. It finds accessing above 1 MB, and even above 4 GB trivial. You simply load the value in a pointer and access the memory.

Useful Interfaces

In DOS, The interfaces for all buses and devices to be tested must be carried by the tests themselves since the stacks underlying DOS (the BIOS) are not visible. With the UEFI Shell, tests can hook in at any of several levels to access devices. A hard disk interface can be tested at any level from the file level, block level, or device level, and without disrupting the UEFI Shell. In DOS, you have to worry about the side effects of your tests on the viability of DOS if you touch the hardware. If you use intermediate level APIs provided in the PI specification, you are playing inside the system rather than against it.

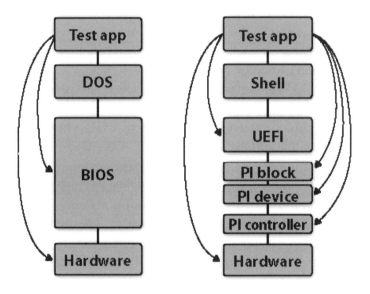

Figure 5.7   Accessible intermediate interfaces allow improved test module portability, increased system stability.

Of course, if you feel you must directly manipulate the hardware, the UEFI Shell, like DOS, puts up no defenses.

This would allow, for example, a general purpose low level disk interface test to be deployed on various versions of SCSI and SATA interfaces since the tests would use the block or controller level interfaces. Even if the rules were to require tests to touch hardware rather than rely on firmware, this methodology, enables testing for the interfaces to go on while the "real" tests are being developed. Those tests might then only be deployed in the quality monitoring phase.

One reason to attempt to use intermediate interfaces is that you are less likely to leave the system in an unstable state, a state that means you can't return back to the firmware to reload the next OS in the boot sequence. Using DOS and the old BIOS, once the system is booted, the only recourse when you're done with your tests and wish to go to a large scale OS is to reboot. Using UEFI, the Shell is an application of the firmware and so can return back to the firmware. This avoids most of the expense of a reboot.

A reboot is not always avoidable but using Shell APIs is still useful. Consider testing a discrete TPM for example. Testing requires three stages: initialization of the TPM, test, and clearing the TPM. By the TPM specification, each stage is separated by a reset. If you do all three stages in a major OS, you'll need three stages at about 90 seconds a stage or 270 seconds or 4.5 minutes. If you do all three stages in DOS or Shell, you'll need around 60 seconds or 1 minute. UEFI and the Shell have richer TPM APIs than BIOS, which makes the job that much easier and more portable.

Interoperability at various levels, along with the availability of specified defined interfaces and their accompanying include files, allows different companies to share components created with different tools. This enables a world in the near future where we can expect to see UEFI Shell-based component level tests provided by components developers. These tests can be integrated into the flow on the manufacturing line, thus reducing cost to create tests and increasing quality.

For example, what if marketing starts to require a new peripheral controller for the next version of USB or 1394 to be added to the board? In the DOS/ BIOS world, the test team would have to learn the specifications, and write a test for the new devices. In the UEFI Shell world, part of the requirements for accepting a chip would be for test UEFI Shell applications to be provided by the vendor. The process is now one of being convinced that the tests are rigorous enough and fast enough and integrating them in.

Scripting Improvements

DOS has a familiar set of scripting features. The Shell's scripting features which are similar to but much richer than DOS' scripting features. It's "IF" and looping constructs are much richer and less error prone. The relevant Shell commands have a specified set of well defined output formats (the –sof output formats) that are easy to parse by the automated tools that process test results. Reformatting test output into this style is not required but evolving to the style over time can make results processing easier.

Access to Present and Future Technology

DOS applications boot off of the network using a series of interfaces known as PXE. So does the UEFI Shell. When PXE is made obsolete by IPv6, the UEFI Shell (adopting the features from UEFI) has an answer that is transparent to all but the networking stack itself.

UEFI has a richer networking stack once loaded as well. This means, for example, that richer and possibly faster protocols can be used including internet protocols. This doesn't mean that a manufacturing floor need become visible to the entire world via the Internet but it does mean that more advanced network management tools become available. The richer networking environment also means that it is possible for a UUT to connect to more than one test server. This does cost some time so the tradeoffs must be weighed but also means that it is easier to create a test server and a results server, for example.

DOS tools are becoming old and are not well supported. The UEFI Shell, UEFI, and PI are intentionally defined using the same industry-wide tools and standards as the OS-based rest of the system programming world. Implementations exist or are arriving soon for all major development environments including Microsoft Windows, Linux with gcc, and the Intel C Compiler.

The UEFI specification describes "bindings" that define the calling sequences between modules. These calling sequences are of necessity C-friendly since the compilers are a lot less easy to change than assembly interfaces. On the other hand, for the times you needs assembly, newer versions of the same assemblers you've used for DOS are available. It is impressive to note, however, that the vast majority of tests run today are all or almost all in high-level languages.

Conversion from DOS to UEFI Shell

For all of its extensions to DOS and its advantages, the UEFI Shell is not DOS. There is effort required to move from one to the other.

The real-life experiences in moving tests from DOS to the UEFI Shell and depend on several factors, among them:

- Experience with UEFI and its concepts. Starting the conversion without learning the basics is, as with most things, a sure way to fail or at least find the going tough.

- The state of the tests themselves. Are the tests well written programs? Are they easy to maintain (given the complexity of the task)? If so, conversion is generally easier.

- Are developers knowledgeable in the tests still available for the job? Having to resurrect design documents is both a burden and an opportunity to create better documentation and to better understand test coverage.

- Is conversion alone the task? Major variability in project duration and cost seeps in when well-meaning developers start to see opportunities to improve and rewrite the tests during the migration from DOS to the UEFI Shell. Although not a cost of conversion per se, this issue can double the time to useful tests.

- There is some clean-up that will inevitably happen and some that will be required during conversion. In particular, the libraries and functions that hide all of the magic mode conversions from 16 to 32 to 64 bits will probably be slated for improvement. Once this effort gets underway it goes fairly quickly. Removing code is easier than adding it.

- Acceptance of the new interfaces and design. The UEFI Shell is not Linux and not DOS. Attempting to make it into the environment one is familiar with leads to extra effort for little results. The most successful transitions have been where the developers understood the tests and understood the new environment and the reasons for it and got about the business.

Add-In Devices

Add-in devices cover a range of items from cards to chips to subassemblies to USB devices.

In many ways, add-in devices are under the same constraints and follow many of the same processes as motherboards. There are a few areas where they differ.

The one major area where there is a difference is that much of the system being tested is functional. The media that is loading the tests is not suspect nor is the basic functionality of the system. The test systems are typically designed to isolate the one 'non-trusted' new appendage.

The UEFI Shell for Add-In Devices

So, why use the UEFI Shell instead of a large OS? In some sense, the usefulness of the UEFI Shell in this environment is a function of the type of device being tested. For example, testing an add-in card will require a reboot to add the new card whereas a USB device, for example, can be plugged in without reset (although experience may have taught the test team to treat new USB devices as if they needed reboots).

There are reasons to use the UEFI Shell, and UEFI, for testing even USB devices. One the one hand, the test author avoids all of the complexity required to wrestle early control of the USB stack away from a large OS's drivers. On the other hand, using DOS, the test author must deal with the idiosyncrasies of the host controllers directly. The test author also avoids all of the complexity required to create and maintain the host controller drivers (since they are validated by other teams). The drivers are much simpler than those for a big operating system making testing simpler. Some of the same benefits for manufacturing systems also appear here including the more rapid boot times and the less intrusive operating environment.

The UEFI Shell carves a useful middle ground. It offers several levels of access to the USB stack without all of the protection a big OS requires. As such it immunizes the test author from changes in the host controller, as has happened with first the addition of EHCI to UHCI or OHCI and now EHCI's take over of the USB 1.1 controllers' functions at about the time a new controller is being designed for (for example a theoretical) USB3.

Systems

System level manufacturing is sometimes called integration because it is mostly a process of a taking a number of subassemblies from different manufacturers and integrating them together in a chassis to form a complete system.

There is more variability in the scale of system manufacturing than in the other types discussed here. It is quite common to see system integrators that which create less than 100 systems per year. On the other hand, the larger system houses create millions or tens of millions of systems per year. This variation leads to different choices in the level of automation, style of testing, and complexity of process.

Not all integrators even do the same thing. For example, a large system manufacturing house might build a system that is then purchased by a shop that specializes in supporting certain industries. That shop then adds new hardware and new software to the system, reconfigures it, and ships it down the line to a dealer who may in turn localized it and add a peripheral requested by a customer before delivering and installing the system.

Each of the three do some sort of integration and yet they do different things that are of value to the end customer. Early on, it might look quite similar to motherboard manufacturing while the latter stages look quite similar to a staged deployment of new systems by the IT group of a large company. Some of the features of the UEFI Shell and UEFI that are IT friendly might be quite unnecessary to a motherboard manufacturer but would be quite useful to an integrator closer to the end user.

An example of this would be the support for system and add-in card configuration provided through UEFI's Human Interface Infrastructure (HII) as mentioned previously. Through this set of APIs, a system's options can be queried and configurations created. A common way to do this is to create a "golden system," extract its configuration, and download that via the HII APIs to the remainder of the systems.

At many of the stages, low level tests are run, followed by firmware updates, followed, without reboot, by the first stages of operating system installation. DOS would require a reboot between the low level tests and first stage OS boot. As described in the motherboard section, if the tests are written within the bounds of UEFI, there is no requirement for a reboot. Simply tell the shell to return to the firmware loader and the loader will proceed to the next boot device.

UEFI and the UEFI Shell also provide a richer set of methods to verify that the system is built correctly. For example, using UEFI protocols a program can determine which card is in which slot. In some cases, this level of detail is required contractually. A UEFI Shell application can both use UEFI to query the data and provide a report for audit purposes.

Summary

As we've seen, the value of the UEFI Shell in manufacturing computer devices is considerable.

- A quick boot compared with large operating systems like Microsoft Windows and Linux improves beat rate.

- DOS-like lack of protection allows for rich test programs.

- DOS-like network boot allows for backward compatibility with network while using faster boot over time due to the promise of improved LAN driver speed with UEFI drivers.

- Support for modern computer architectures and modern buses allow for easier testing of things such as more than 4 gigabytes of memory, PCIe peripherals, and the like.

- Rich scripting supports creation of reusable test modules that can be glued together in different ways to support different products.

- Script-friendly output from UEFI Shell commands makes writing tools and processing results easier.

- Rich interfaces allow script-driven cross-vendor, cross-product reconfiguration tools.

- By following a few rules for UEFI Shell programs, the number of reboots during a manufacturing process can be reduced. This is because the reboot is not required when leaving the UEFI Shell to boot a larger operating system.

The UEFI Shell is the obvious DOS replacement. Now that the UEFI Shell specification itself, along with underlying UEFI and PI-defined interface specifications, are owned by an industry forum, the interfaces are likely to be stable for generations of products.

Chapter 6

Bare Metal Provisioning

Winning starts with beginning.

—Robert H. Schuller

One of the most apt uses for the UEFI Shell is in the base metal provision-ing of a system. Recall from the earlier chapters on the states of the machine that there is a point where the system board has been manufactured, peripherals have been attached and tested, but there is not necessarily an op-erating system.

The act of configuring the operating system or providing a new operating system is called *bare metal provisioning*. We refer to this action as *bare metal* because the only services exposed by the platform at this point are carried with the system board, namely its UEFI firmware. This differs from OS-hosted provisioning wherein a fully extant operating system with all of its capabilities is used to host the provisioning session. In the bare-metal case, the system firmware provides the I/O and console interfaces to the provisioning agent.

To illustrate the usage of the UEFI Shell for provisioning, a network-based deployment scenario will be reviewed. During this scenario, the various facets of the UEFI Shell and its utility will be demonstrated.

Provisioning with the UEFI Shell

In this scenario, we'll return to our system platform, which we will refer to as the "UEFI Client," shown in Figure 6.1. It is only a client inasmuch as it will interact with a provisioning server. The "client" could itself be a mobile device, Mobile Internet Device (MID), desktop PC, or server. The client moniker only designates its role in the networking scenario.

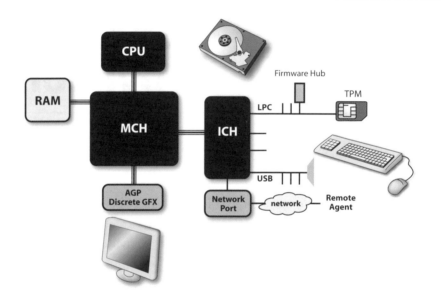

Figure 6.1   Client Platform

This client platform, depending upon its market segment, may or may not have a local disk, video, keyboard or mouse. But what any platform will have for this scenario includes a central processing unit, chipset, memory, flash part with the UEFI firmware, and most importantly, a network connection with a appropriate network interface controller (NIC) and networking UEFI drivers.

UEFI Networking Stack

The UEFI drivers in this scenario include the UEFI2.2 networking stack. This networking stack supports ARP, UDP, TCP, the PXE network-boot application, optional ISCSI, and a variant for both IPV4 and IPV6, as shown in Figure 6.2.

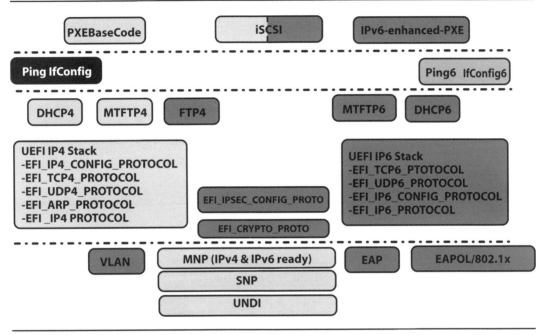

Figure 6.2   Networking Stack

The diagram in Figure 6.2, from the bottom up, shows the hardware elements of the stack, such as the Universal Network Device Interface (UNDI), which abstracts the NIC send and receive datagram capability. This raw UNDI interface is abstracted via the Simple Network Protocol (SNP). The SNP, in turn, is abstracted by the Managed Network Protocol (MNP). As opposed to the earlier EFI network technology wherein only one application could open the SNP exclusively, the MNP allows for many concurrent listeners, thus allowing for several services to concurrently operate. What this means is that an Extensible Authentication Protocol (EAP) handler looking for layer 2 messages can coexist with both the UEFI IP4 and UEFI IP6 stack applications such as PXE boot and ISCSI.

The multiple-consumer nature of the MNP and the UEFI2 nature stack is important because many of the network-based provisioning scenarios are "blended." The blending is borne of the fact that the scenario may entail some network authentication action as a preamble in order to allow the client onto the provisioning network, then an ISCSI mount in order to have a file system, and finally, a PXE boot such that an installer or test application can be downloaded. The latter UEFI application, in turn, will access to the file system on ISCSI while performing its own network-specific file operations.

Securing the Network

Because of the expanded natures of local area networks (LANs), wide-area networks (WANs), and networks of networks, such as the Internet, providing secure interaction among agents on the wire is imperative. One of these scenarios is shown in Figure 6.3, which elucidates a network download and the salient trust elements.

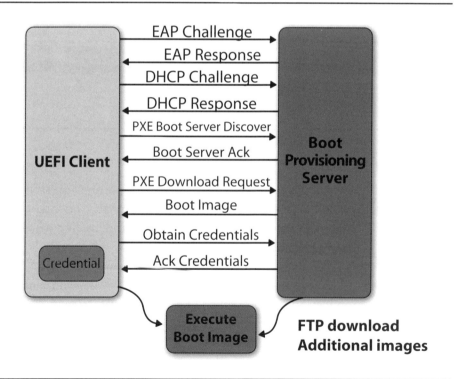

Figure 6.3   PXE Boot

The notable aspect of this download is the initial EAP transaction. Historically, PXE began with a DHCP discovery message in order to ascertain the location of the boot server. But corporate IT departments have some concerns with this former model. IT typically hosts the boot provisioning server, and the concept of a "bare-metal" machine joining their corporate network is a concern. With the advent of 802.1x controlled ports and EAP, though, the client machine can be configured such that it must satisfy a challenge-response prior to joining the network, as shown in Figure 6.4. This entails the client responding to a set of EAP layer 2 messages from the switch; the messages are in turn transmitted to the authentication server via the well-known Radius protocol.

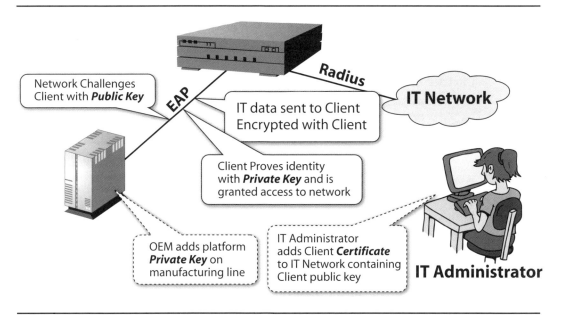

Figure 6.4   802.1x/EAP Challenge-Response

Once the client machine has been authenticated via the EAP challenge/response, it is allowed onto the network. UEFI 2.2 supports both the 802.1x state machine in the firmware and the ability to register a plurality of different EAP handlers. These handlers can include pre-shared key (PSK) methods, such as CHAP, and can be extended to more sophisticated single or mutual authentication methods based upon asymmetric cryptography like RSA, including but not limited to a Transport Layer Security (TLS) handshake.

As the needs arise, other network perimeter EAP methods can be included in the UEFI clients, such as EAP Kerberos or the Trusted Computer Group's EAP Trusted Network Connect (TNC). The former is interesting as it will allow the UEFI Client to participate into an extant enterprise network topology, and the latter is useful since the pre-OS posture of the UEFI client, such as its code identity as described in the Trusted Platform Module's (TPM) Platform Configuration Registers (PCR) can be used to assess the posture of the UEFI client prior to letting it on the network.

EAP is at layer 2, so it works on IPV4 or IPV6 networks. After gaining access to the network, the UEFI client can attempt a DHCPv4 or DHCPv6-based network discover request. The ability to do either or both is enabled via UEFI and its dual stack. With the imminent exhaustion of the 32-bit Internet Protocol version 4 addresses, deploying UEFI 2.2 firmware with Internet Protocol version 6 support is key. IPV6 opens up the address space to 128-bits. And as UEFI firmware proliferates to compute platforms beyond towards PC's and servers (UEFI for appliances, non-standard platforms, and so on), the ability to support IPV6 networking in the pre-OS is imperative.

After the UEFI PXE application has negotiated with the boot server for a server name and IP address, it can commence the download of the boot image. In UEFI, the boot image isn't the small 16-bit file of some tens of kilobytes as in conventional BIOS but is instead a fully-qualified Portable Executable Common Object File Format (PE/COFF) image. The UEFI executable is downloaded to the client machine for execution.

Now recall how earlier we mentioned that IT may set up EAP for authenticating the client such that a rogue UEFI machine may not wander onto IT networks. A similar concern emerges with respect to the downloaded executable. The UEFI client wants to defend itself from any random bits on the network, especially given the distributed nature of today's topologies, rogue wireless access points, and other venues for Man-in-the-Middle (MITM) attacks on the wire to occur.

The credential listed in Figure 6.4 would be something like an x509v2 certificate with a public verification key. The UEFI firmware uses the public key to verify the digital signature of the boot image in order to ensure that it hasn't been modified by an unauthorized party during transit. UEFI2.2

introduced the use of Authenticode image signing such that the trust hierarchy can be flat or nested, allowing for various deployment options. In addition, the rich UEFI network stack allows for the firmware to check for certificate expiry for possible future revocation models (such as if the private key associated with the public key in the certificate has been divulged).

A sample certificate is shown in Figure 6.5

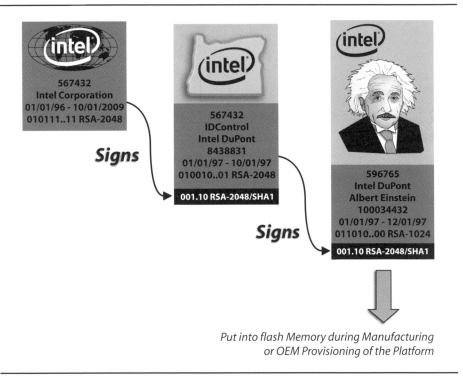

Figure 6.5   Example of an x509v2 Digital Certificate

Important fields include name information, the expiry date, and the signature. The signature in this example includes an SHA-1 digest of the data signed by a 2048-bit RSA asymmetric key. This example also includes a 2-level deep hierarchy where the authority in this case is Intel.

To bring all of these elements together, Figure 6.6 shows a flowchart of the end-to-end process of booting. It includes the actions of both the boot server and client machine.

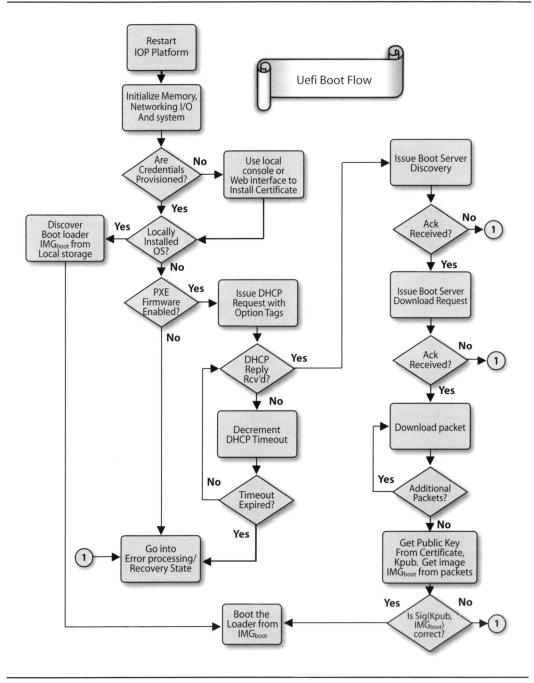

Figure 6.6   Overall Boot Flow

Figure 6.6 shows the overall network boot process. The first portion is the use of the Dynamic Host Configuration Protocol (DHCP) by the UEFI client in order to query the network for both an IP address and the availability of a boot server. The DHCP offer from the client and response from server are important in that the client tells the boot server the "type" of client, such as x64 UEFI. The server, in turn, responds if it can support providing images to the machine.

One important image that can be downloaded to the platform is the UEFI Shell. Given that there are a plurality of activities that need to occur during provisioning, such as downloading additional files to image on the disk, activating certain devices like TPMs, the shell can be used to orchestrate their invocation and pass results.

Speeding Up the Network

One of the advantages of performing network downloads is the introduction of the File Transfer Protocol (FTP) into UEFI. One of the historical complaints about the network boot experience is the use of PXE and UDP. The user datagram protocol (UDP), upon which the trivial file transfer protocol (TFTP) is built, was originally chosen because of its simplicity, thus leading to smaller code implementations in the pre-OS. But TFTPs disadvantages include the fact that it is connectionless (because of UDP), has small blocks, and requires several ACKs. This makes TFTP a very non-scalable protocol. FTP, on the other hand, is build upon the Transmission Control Protocol (TCP). TCP is a connection-oriented protocol that features much more robust download capabilities.

Going forward with PXE, the DHCP handshake will be extended to allow for today's TFTP downloads, FTP, or even HTTP. The latter two can include the secure variants of FTP-S and HTTP-S, if necessary. The Hyper Text Transfer Protocol (HTTP) will offer the most flexible download going forward since it is routable across firewalls and HTTP is already supported in web servers. Of course, the Internet today runs on HTTP, so aligning the network boot paradigm with this technology ensures that the platform investment will carry forward.

Example of Putting It Together

To tie the notion of a connection-oriented protocol like FTP back to the shell, though, below is an extract of a File Transfer Protocol (FTP) utility that is built upon the UEFI TCP support.

This program leverages the UEFI, which uses the UEFI Transmission Control Protocol (TCP) to download a file. TCP is a connection-oriented protocol with guaranteed delivery with handshakes. This is in contrast to the Trivial File Transport Protocol (TFTP), which is based upon Universal Datagram Protocol (UDP). UDP does not have any delivery guarantees.

```
256 #include "miniftp.h"
257 #include "utility.h"
258 #include "script.h"
259 #include "Log.h"
260 #include "Cli.h"
261
262
```

Lines 256–260

The header files contain basic support routines for the FTP utility.

```
263
264
265
266 MINIFTP_UI        Ui;
267 BOOLEAN           ToExit        = FALSE;
268 BOOLEAN           IsConnected   = FALSE;
269 BOOLEAN           UseScript     = FALSE;
270 BOOLEAN           HasLogin      = FALSE;
271 BOOLEAN           NeedLog       = FALSE;
272 BOOLEAN           AppendLogFile = FALSE;   // append log
273                                   file if log file is exit
274 EFI_HANDLE        BackupImageHandle;
275 EFI_IP_ADDRESS    FtpServerIp;
276
277 CHAR16            ScriptFileName[256];
278 CHAR16            LogFileName[256];
279
```

Lines 261–273

These lines declare global variables used by the FTP utility.

```
280
281
282 VOID
283 PrintUsage (
284   VOID
285   );
286
287
288 EFI_STATUS
289 ParseArgs (
290   VOID
291   );
292
293
```

Lines 275–285

These lines provide forward declaration of service routines.

```
294
295
296
297 EFI_STATUS
298 EFIAPI
299 InitializeMiniFtp (
300   IN EFI_HANDLE          ImageHandle,
301   IN EFI_SYSTEM_TABLE     *SystemTable
302   );
303
304  EFI_GUID        MiniFtpGuid = EFI_MINIFTP_GUID;
305
306 //
307 // Name:
308 //    InitializeMiniFtp -- Entry point
309 // In:
310 //    ImageHandle
311 //    SystemTable
312 // Out:
313 //    EFI_SUCCESS
314 //
315 EFI_BOOTSHELL_CODE(EFI_APPLICATION_ENTRY_POINT(Initialize
316 MiniFtp))
317 EFI_STATUS
318 EFIAPI
319 InitializeMiniFtp (
```

```
320    IN EFI_HANDLE              ImageHandle,
321    IN EFI_SYSTEM_TABLE        *SystemTable
322    )
323 /*++
324  Routine Description:
325    Initial FTP shell application
326
327  Arguments:
328    ImageHandle -
329    SystemTable -
330 Returns:
331 --*/
332 {
333    EFI_STATUS          Status;
334    CLI_COMMAND_CONTEXT Context;
335    //
336    // We are now being installed as an internal command
337 driver, initialize
338    // as an nshell app and run
339    //
340    EFI_SHELL_APP_INIT (ImageHandle, SystemTable);
341
342    BackupImageHandle = ImageHandle;
343
344    Status          = ParseArgs ();
345    if (EFI_ERROR (Status)) {
346      PrintUsage ();
347      return Status;
348    }
349    Status = EfiMiniFtpLogInit (LogFileName);
350    if (EFI_ERROR (Status)) {
351      Print (L"Failed to initialize log file.\n\r");
352      goto done;
353    }
354    if (UseScript) {
355      Status = RunScript (ScriptFileName);
356      goto done;
357    }
358    //
359    // EnablePageBreak(1, TRUE);
360    //
361    // Main loop
362    //
```

```
363    StrCpy (Context.Prompt, DEFAULT_PROMPT);
364    do {
365      GetCommandLine (&Context);
366      ToExit = ProcessCommandLine (&Context);
367      ResetCliContext (&Context);
368    } while (!ToExit);
369  done:
370    EfiMiniFtpLogFinal ();
371
372    if (!UseScript) {
373      //
374      //     Out->ClearScreen(Out);
375      //
376      Out->EnableCursor (Out, TRUE);
377    }
378
379    return Status;
380  }
381
```

Lines 286–369

These lines contain the code for the main body of the FTP application.

```
382
383
384
385 EFI_STATUS
386 ParseArgs (
387    VOID
388    )
389 /*++
390 Routine Description: Parse the input parameter. Miniftp
391 support parameter as
392 follows:
393    Usage           : Miniftp [-f <Script> ] [-l
394 <LogFilename>] [-a]
395    <Script>        : The name of script to run.
396    <LogFilename>  : The name of log file. ('-a' will
397                    be in effect if choose to write log file )
398                    [-a]: append information in log file, if
399                          the log file exists
400
401 Arguments:
402 Returns:
```

```
403      EFI_SUCCESS           -   success
404      EFI_INVALID_PARAMETER -   parameter is error or not
405 supported in MiniFTP
406 --*/
407 {
408   EFI_STATUS   Status;
409   UINTN        Index;
410   CHAR16       *Char;
411   BOOLEAN      ServerIpConfigured;
412   BOOLEAN      IsIPv4;
413
414   ServerIpConfigured  = FALSE;
415   Status              = EFI_SUCCESS;
416
417   for (Index = 1; Index < SI->Argc; Index++) {
418     if (SI->Argv[Index][0] == '-') {
419       Char = SI->Argv[Index] + 1;
420       switch (*Char) {
421          case 'S':
422          case 's':
423          if ((Index == SI->Argc - 1) || (SI->Argv[Index +
424             1][0] == '-')) {
425          //
426          // No value after "-s", Error!
427          //
428             return EFI_INVALID_PARAMETER;
429          }
430
431          IsIPv4 = FALSE;
432          Status = StrToInetAddr (SI->Argv[Index + 1],
433                     &FtpServerIp, &IsIPv4);
434          if (EFI_ERROR (Status)) {
435             goto Done;
436          }
437
438     ServerIpConfigured = TRUE;
439     break;
440
441     case 'f':
442     case 'F':
443       if (Index == SI->Argc - 1) {
444         return EFI_INVALID_PARAMETER;
445       }
```

```
446
447     UseScript = TRUE;
448     StrCpy (ScriptFileName, SI->Argv[Index + 1]);
449     break;
450
451   case 'l':
452   case 'L':
453     if (Index == SI->Argc - 1) {
454       return EFI_INVALID_PARAMETER;
455     }
456
457     NeedLog = TRUE;
458     StrCpy (LogFileName, SI->Argv[Index + 1]);
459     break;
460
461   case 'a':
462   case 'A':
463       if (NeedLog == TRUE) {
464         AppendLogFile = TRUE;
465       }
466       break;
467   default:
468       Status = EFI_INVALID_PARAMETER;
469       goto Done;
470     }
471   }
472   Done:
473     return Status;
474   }
475 }
476
477
```

Lines 371–461

These lines contain the argument parsing code.

```
478
479
480
481 VOID
482 PrintUsage (
483   VOID
484   )
485 /*++
```

```
486
487  Routine Description:
488  --*/
489  {
490    Print (
491      L"MiniFtp Client 0.01\n\r"L"Copyright (C) Intel Corp
492  2009. All rights reserved.\n\r"L"\n\r"    L"Usage :
493  Miniftp [-f <Script> ] [-l <LogFilename>] [-a]\n\r"L"\n"
494  L"  <Script>       : The name of script to run.\n\r"L"
495  <LogFilename> : The name of log file to create.\n\r"
496      L"   [-a]          : Append Log file if log file is
497  exist.\n\r"
498      );
499  }
```

Lines 463–482

These lines contain the help print routine.

The ability to create a FTP utility in UEFI is something that could not be done in BIOS. For one thing, the BIOS networking stack only exposed UDP in the base code, not a TCP interface. Also, BIOS does not have a consistent shell/command-line interface built into the ROM in the same fashion as the ability to integrate the UEFI Shell.

In addition to the use of FTP, the UEFI Shell can integrate the FTP utility as a built-in command, and the integrated FTP+UEFI Shell could be integrated into the ROM, could be put on the UEFI System partition, or could be PXE-booted itself, in order to allow for a rich set of scenarios.

Summary

This chapter has shown how emergent UEFI platform networking capabilities, combined with the UEFI shell, allow for rich provisioning scenarios. These scenarios allow for flexibility without compromising scale or security of the solution.

Chapter 7

Configuration of Provisioned Material

Innovation distinguishes between a leader and a follower.

—Steve Jobs

Once material gets placed on a target system, one of the inevitable next steps would be the configuration of this material. Since much of the inherent configuration mechanisms that are available in the UEFI firmware environment are also supported in the UEFI Shell environment, this chapter's material will touch on configuration capabilities available in both environments.

The BIOS has never been known for having a great user interface. The ROM sizes were too limited and the video interfaces too unpredictable to support high-end graphical interfaces.

Much of the design that the UEFI configuration infrastructure covers has been heavily studied and analyzed by modern operating systems. The results of these efforts are what have turned into the configuration infrastructure that first was documented in the UEFI 2.1 specification.

Initialization Timeline

During platform initialization, several distinct steps occur. To simplify the timeline, the illustration in Figure 7.1 simply covers four general phases of operation for the system. These phases are intended to illustrate when configuration of the platform is possible. Note that configuration services are available very early in platform initialization.

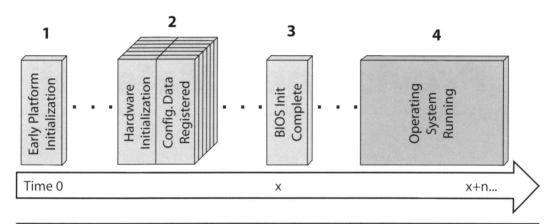

Figure 7.1   The Platform Initialization Timeline

Figure 7.1 gives a simplified view of the phase of operations for a platform:

■ *Phase 1.* During early initialization, the UEFI-compatible BIOS initializes some of the underlying components of the platform (such as CPU, chipset, and memory). This also includes establishing the UEFI infrastructure such that the common UEFI components (such as the UEFI configuration infrastructure) are available to be used by later phases of operation.

■ *Phase 2.* In the later phase the BIOS starts to launch drivers (often located in add-in device option ROMs) that have configuration-related material associated with certain configurable devices. This configuration data is registered with the BIOS through something known as the Human Interface Infrastructure (HII) services. Also between Phase 2 and 3 is usually when a local user would interact with the platform to configure it (picture a user at a BIOS setup menu.)

- *Phase 3.* The BIOS initialization is complete and the BIOS proceeds to launch the boot target (which is usually an operating system for most platforms).

- *Phase 4.* The boot target is launched and running. For most platforms, this is the phase that the machine remains in for most of the time.

It should also be noted that a very common scenario for platform configuration is when a remote administrator interacts with a platform. This can be done with either the assistance of an operating system, as illustrated in Figure 7.2, or with a platform that contains an out-of-band management controller. Since the BIOS is often not interactive while the operating system is running, this poses some issues for updating BIOS-based configuration settings during the later phases of platform operation. Figure 7.2 shows a slightly modified example of the previous timeline, which now enables late configuration setting updates through a mechanism that applies the changes across a system reset, leveraging the underlying UEFI configuration infrastructure.

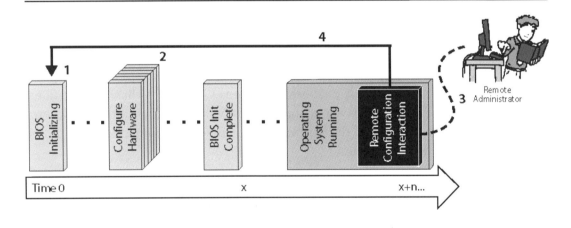

Figure 7.2 Timeline Illustrating How Late Requests for BIOS Setting Changes Can Be Accommodated

- *Step 1.* The UEFI-compliant BIOS initializes like it normally does.

- *Step 2.* The configuration step is usually based on some previously chosen settings that the user/administrator had previously applied to that device. These settings are stored in some nonvolatile location.

During this step, the settings are typically read from the nonvolatile storage and the device is configured accordingly.

■ *Step 3.* The platform is running the operating system in this illustration and has some interaction with a remote administrator. The remote administrator requests some BIOS setting changes to occur on the platform and some agent proxies this request by a couple of methods:

  – *Capsules.* The UEFI infrastructure supports an UpdateCapsule() service, which allows for an OS-present agent to call into the BIOS and communicate some configuration request, which will typically be acted upon across a platform reset. This is a very flexible method of enabling across-reset update since it can potentially allow for updates of both on-motherboard devices as well as third-party devices (which often use their own proprietary local nonvolatile storage). Platform behavior changes typically do not occur until the platform has reset and the hardware has then been reconfigured based on the desired settings.

  – *EFI Variable.* The UEFI infrastructure provides abstractions to a platform nonvolatile storage service (that is, an EFI variable). This is primarily used by the motherboard devices and the setting requests can be directly established from the OS-present phase of operations. Platform behavior changes typically do not occur until the platform has reset and the hardware has then been reconfigured based on the desired settings.

■ *Step 4.* Once the remote configuration update request has been received and acted upon, the platform typically resets so that the boot timeline is restarted. It should be noted, though, that during this subsequent boot the items that normally occur in Step 2 would still occur, but typically based on the aforementioned configuration updates in the current configuration settings.

Configuration Infrastructure Overview

The modern UEFI configuration infrastructure that was first described in the UEFI 2.1 specification is known as the Human Interface Infrastructure (HII). HII includes the following set of services:

■ *Database Services.* A series of UEFI protocols that are intended to be an in-memory repository of specialized databases. These database services are focused on differing types of information:

– Database Repository – This is the interface that drivers interact with to manipulate configuration related contents. It is most often used to register data and update keyboard layout related information.

– String Repository – This is the interface that drivers interact with to manipulate string-based data. It is most often used to extract strings associated with a given token value.

– Font Repository – The interface to which drivers may contribute font-related information for the system to use. Otherwise, it is primarily used by the underlying firmware to extract the built-in fonts to render text to the local monitor. Note that since not all platforms have inherent support for rendering fonts locally (think headless platforms), general purpose UI designs should not presume this capability.

– Image Repository – The interface to which drivers may contribute image-related information for the system to use. This is for purposes of referencing graphical items as a component of a user interface. Note that since not all platforms have inherent support for rendering images locally (think headless platforms), general purpose UI designs should not presume this capability.

■ *Browser Services.* The interface that is provided by the platform's BIOS to interact with the built-in browser. This service's look-and-feel is implementation-specific, which allows for platform differentiation.

■ *Configuration Routing Services.* The interface that manages the movement of configuration data from drivers to target configuration applications. It then serves as the single point to receive configuration information from configuration applications, routing the results to the appropriate drivers.

■ *Configuration Access Services.* The interface that is exposed by a driver's configuration handler and is called by the configuration routing services. This service abstracts a driver's configuration settings and also provides a means by which the platform can call the driver to initiate driver-specific operations.

Using the Configuration Infrastructure

The overview introduced the components of the UEFI configuration infrastructure. This section discusses with a bit more detail how one goes about using aspects of this infrastructure. The following steps are initiated by a driver that is concerned with using the configuration infrastructure:

■ *Initialize hardware.* The primary job of a device driver is typically to initialize the hardware that it owns. During this process of physically initializing the device, the driver is also responsible for establishing the proper configuration state information for that device. These typically include doing the following:

— *Installing required protocols.* Protocols are interfaces that will be used to communicate with the driver. One of the more pertinent protocols associated with configuration would be the Configuration Access protocol. This is used by the system BIOS and agents in the BIOS to interact with the driver. This is also the mechanism by which a driver can provide an abstraction to a proprietary nonvolatile storage that under normal circumstances would not be usable by anyone other than the driver itself. This is how configuration data can be exposed for add-in devices and others can send configuration update requests without needing direct knowledge of that device.

— *Creating an EFI device path on an EFI handle.* A device path is a binary description of the device and typically how it is attached to the system. This provides a unique name for the managed device and will be used by the system to refer to the device later.

■ *Register Configuration Content.* One of the latter parts of the driver initialization (once a device path has been established) is the registration of the configuration data with the underlying UEFI-compatible BIOS. The configuration data typically consists of sets of forms and strings that contain sufficient information for the platform to render pages for a user to interact with. It should also be noted that now that the configuration data is encapsulated in a binary format, what was previously an opaque meaningless set of data is now a well-known and exportable set of data that greatly expands the configurability of the device by both local and remote agents as well as BIOS and OS-present components.

■ *Respond to Configuration Event.* Once the initialization and registration functions have completed, the driver could potentially remain dormant until called upon. A driver would most often be called upon to act on a configuration event. A configuration event is an event that occurs when a BIOS component calls upon one of the interfaces that the driver exposed (such as the Configuration Access protocol) and sends the driver a directive. These directives typically would be something akin to "give me your current settings" or "adjust setting X's value to a 5".

Driver Model Interactions

The drivers that interact with the UEFI configuration infrastructure are often compliant with the UEFI driver model, as the examples shown in Figure 7.3 and Figure 7.4. Since driver model compliance is very common (and highly recommended) for device drivers, several examples are shown below that describe in detail how such a driver would most effectively leverage the configuration infrastructure.

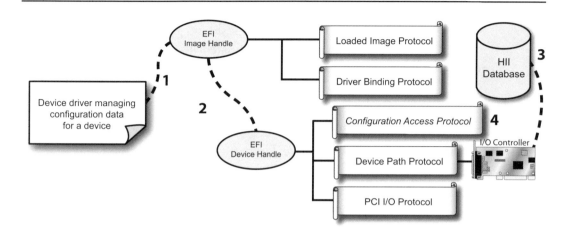

Single driver managing a device

Figure 7.3   A Single Driver that Is Registering Its Configuration Data and Establishing Its Environment in a Recommended Fashion

■ *Step 1.* During driver initialization, install services on the controller handle.

■ *Step 2.* During driver initialization, discover the managed device. Create a device handle and then install various services on it.

■ *Step 3.* During driver initialization, configuration data for the device is registered with the HII database (through the NewPackageList() API) using the device's device handle. A unique HII handle is created during the registration event.

■ *Step 4.* During system operation, when a configuration event occurs, the system addresses (through the Configuration Access protocol) the configuration services associated with the device.

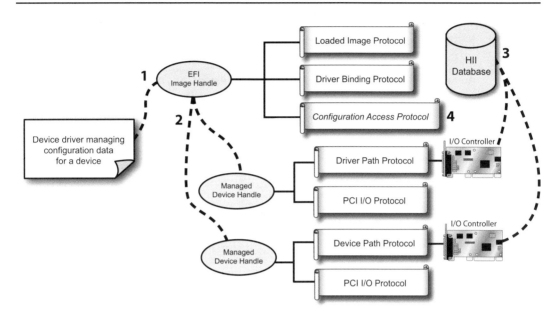

Single driver managing more that one devices

Figure 7.4 A Single Driver that Is Managing Multiple Devices, Registering Its Configuration Data, and Establishing Its Environment in a Recommended Fashion

- *Step 1.* During driver initialization, install services on the controller handle.

- *Step 2.* During driver initialization, discover the managed device(s). Create device handle(s) and then install various services on them.

- *Step 3.* During driver initialization, configuration data for each device is registered with the HII database (through the NewPackageList() API) using each device's device handle. A unique HII handle is created during the registration event.

- *Step 4.* During system operation, when a configuration event occurs, the system addresses (through the Configuration Access protocol) the configuration services associated with the driver. In this example, the configuration services will be required to disambiguate references to each of its managed devices by the passed in HII handle.

Provisioning the Platform

Figure 7.5 is an illustration that builds on the previously introduced concepts and shows how the remote interaction would introduce the concept of bare-metal provisioning (putting content on a platform without the aid of a formal operating system). This kind of interaction could be used in the manufacturing environment to achieve the provisioning of the platform or in the after-market environment where one is remotely managing the platform and updating it.

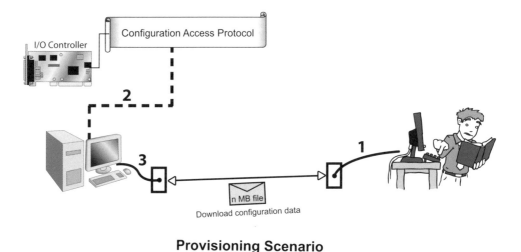

Provisioning Scenario

Figure 7.5   Remote Interaction Occurs with a Target System; the System in Turn Accesses the Configuration Abstractions Associated with a Device orSet of Devices

■ *Step 1.* Remote administrator sends a query to a target workstation. This query could actually be a component of a broadcast by the administrator to all members of the network.

■ *Step 2.* Request received and an agent (possibly a shell-based one) proxies the request to the appropriate device.

■ *Step 3.* The agent responds based on interaction with the platform's underlying configuration infrastructure.

Configuring through the UEFI Shell

One of the usage models associated with the UEFI Shell is for the running of programs or scripts within it so that it can automatically execute a variety of tasks and leverage the power of the overall BIOS environment. Some of the built-in commands associated with certain support levels of the UEFI Shell provide both basic and advanced features. These features expose the ability to configure the system as well as query the system for some rather complicated sets of data through scripts. Having this capability in scripting certainly does not preclude the ability for anyone to leverage the full extent of the UEFI BIOS's capabilities through a binary program.

Basic Configuration

Some of the common commands that provide basic interaction with the configuration infrastructure include:

- *drvcfg.* This command invokes the platform's configuration infrastructure. This command is used primarily for the following purposes:

  - To invoke the system's browser through a script so that it displays a given device's setup pages.

  - To provide the ability to set a specific set of default behaviors for a given device.

  - To set a device's configuration from a user-defined group of settings contained in a file.

- *drvdiag.* This command invokes the Driver Diagnostics Protocol. This provides a script the ability to interact with the diagnostics services that a driver may expose in its list of services.

Command-line Usage for drvcfg

This section provides a set of examples of common usages for the drvcfg command, followed by the appropriate command-line syntax. The full command-line syntax is as follows:

```
drvcfg [-l XXX] [-c] [-f <Type>|-v|-s] [DriverHandle
[DeviceHandle [ChildHandle]]] [-i filename] [-o filename]
```

To display the list of devices that are available for configuration:

```
Shell> drvcfg
```

To display the list of devices and child devices that are available for configuration:

```
Shell> drvcfg —c
```

To force defaults on all devices:

```
Shell> drvcfg —f 0
```

To force defaults on all devices that are managed by driver 0x17:

```
Shell> drvcfg —f 0 17
```

To force defaults on device 0x28 that is managed by driver 0x17:

```
Shell> drvcfg —f 0 17 28
```

To force defaults on all child devices of device 0x28 that is managed by driver 0x17:

```
Shell> drvcfg —f 0 17 28 —c
```

To force defaults on child device 0x30 of device 0x28 that is managed by driver 0x17:

```
Shell> drvcfg —f 0 17 28 30
```

To validate options on all devices:

```
Shell> drvcfg —v
```

To validate options on all devices that are managed by driver 0x17:

```
Shell> drvcfg —v 17
```

To validate options on device 0x28 that is managed by driver 0x17:

```
Shell> drvcfg —v 17 28
```

To validate options on all child devices of device 0x28 that is managed by driver 0x17:

```
Shell> drvcfg —v 17 28 —c
```

To validate options on child device 0x30 of device 0x28 that is managed by driver 0x17:

```
Shell> drvcfg —v 17 28 30
```

To set options on device 0x28 that is managed by driver 0x17:

```
Shell> drvcfg —s 17 28
```

To set options on child device 0x30 of device 0x28 that is managed by driver 0x17:

```
Shell> drvcfg —s 17 28 30
```

To set options on device 0x28 that is managed by driver 0x17 in English:

```
Shell> drvcfg —s 17 28 —l eng
```

To set options on device 0x28 that is managed by driver 0x17 in Spanish:

```
Shell> drvcfg —s 17 28 —l spa
```

Command-line Usage for drvdiag

This section provides a set of examples of common usages for the drvdiag command, followed by the appropriate command-line syntax. The full command-line syntax is as follows:

```
drvdiag [-c] [-l XXX] [-s|-e|-m] [DriverHandle
[DeviceHandle [ChildHandle]]]
```

To display the list of devices that are available for diagnostics:

```
Shell> drvdiag
```

To display the list of devices and child devices that are available for diagnostics:

```
Shell> drvdiag —c
```

To run diagnostics in standard mode on all devices:

```
Shell> drvdiag —s
```

To run diagnostics in standard mode on all devices in English:

```
Shell> drvdiag —s —l eng
```

To run diagnostics in standard mode on all devices in Spanish:

```
Shell> drvdiag —s —l spa
```

To run diagnostics in standard mode on all devices and child devices:

```
Shell> drvdiag —s —c
```

To run diagnostics in extended mode on all devices:

```
Shell> drvdiag —e
```

To run diagnostics in manufacturing mode on all devices:

```
Shell> drvdiag —m
```

To run diagnostics in standard mode on all devices managed by driver 0x17:

```
Shell> drvdiag —s 17
```

To run diagnostics in standard mode on device 0x28 managed by driver 0x17:

```
Shell> drvdiag —s 17 28
```

To run diagnostics in standard mode on all child devices of device 0x28 managed by driver 0x17:

```
Shell> drvdiag —s 17 28 —c
```

To run diagnostics in standard mode on child device 0x30 of device 0x28 managed by driver 0x17:

```
Shell> drvdiag —s 17 28 30
```

Advanced Configuration Abilities

Some of the common commands that provide basic interaction with the configuration infrastructure include:

- *memmap.* This command displays the memory map associated with the UEFI environment.

- *dblk.* This command allows a script to interact with the underlying block (storage) device so that it can display the contents of one or more of its blocks/sectors.

- *dmem.* This command displays the contents of system memory or device memory. If an address is not specified, then the contents of the EFI system table are displayed. Otherwise, memory starting at a particular address is displayed. This is especially useful for displaying the contents of certain memory ranges like a device's PCI configuration space.

- *mm.* This command allows the user to display or modify the I/O register, memory contents, or PCI configuration space.

Command-line Usage for memmap

This section provides an example of the memmap command. The full command-line syntax is as follows:

```
memmap [-b] [-sfo]
```

```
fs0:\> memmap

Type       Start           End            # Pages      Attributes
available  0000000000750000-0000000001841FFF  00000000000010F2  0000000000000009
LoaderCode 0000000001842000-00000000018A3FFF  0000000000000062  0000000000000009
available  00000000018A4000-00000000018C1FFF  000000000000001E  0000000000000009
LoaderData 00000000018C2000-00000000018CAFFF  0000000000000009  0000000000000009
BS_code    00000000018CB000-0000000001905FFF  000000000000003B  0000000000000009
BS_data    0000000001906000-00000000019C9FFF  00000000000000C4  0000000000000009
...
RT_data    0000000001B2B000-0000000001B2BFFF  0000000000000001  8000000000000009
BS_data    0000000001B2C000-0000000001B4FFFF  0000000000000024  0000000000000009
reserved   0000000001B50000-0000000001D4FFFF  0000000000000200  0000000000000009

   reserved  :    512 Pages (2,097,152)
   LoaderCode:     98 Pages (401,408)
   LoaderData:     32 Pages (131,072)
   BS_code   :    335 Pages (1,372,160)
   BS_data   :    267 Pages (1,093,632)
   RT_data   :     19 Pages (77,824)
   available :  4,369 Pages (17,895,424)
Total Memory: 20 MB (20,971,520) Bytes
```

Command-line Usage for dblk

This section provides a set of examples of common usages for the dblk command, followed by the appropriate command-line syntax. The full command-line syntax is as follows:

```
dblk device [lba] [blocks] [-b]
```

To display one block of blk0, beginning from block 0:

```
Shell>dblk blk0
```

To display one block of fs0, beginning from block 0x2:

```
Shell>dblk fs0 2
```

To display 0x5 blocks of fs0, beginning from block 0x12:

```
Shell>dblk fs0 12 5
```

To display 0x10 blocks of fs0, beginning from block 0x12:

```
Shell>dblk fs0 12 10
```

The attempt to display more than 0x10 blocks will display only 0x10 blocks:

```
Shell>dblk fs0 12 20
```

To display one block of blk2, beginning from the first block (blk0):

```
fs1:\tmps1> dblk blk2 0 1
```

```
LBA 0000000000000000 Size 00000200 bytes BlkIo 3F0CEE78
00000000: EB 3C 90 4D 53 44 4F 53-35 2E 30 00 02 04 08 00  *.<.MSDOS5.0.....*
00000010: 02 00 02 00 00 F8 CC 00-3F 00 FF 00 3F 00 00 00  *........?...?...*
00000020: 8E 2F 03 00 80 01 29 2C-09 1B D0 4E 4F 20 4E 41  *./....),...NO NA*
00000030: 4D 45 20 20 20 20 46 41-54 31 36 20 20 20 33 C9  *ME    FAT16   3.*
00000040: 8E D1 BC F0 7B 8E D9 B8-00 20 8E C0 FC BD 00 7C  *........ ......*
00000050: 38 4E 24 7D 24 8B C1 99-E8 3C 01 72 1C 83 EB 3A  *8N$.$....<.r..:*
00000060: 66 A1 1C 7C 26 66 3B 07-26 8A 57 FC 75 06 80 CA  *f...&f;.&.W.u...*
00000070: 02 88 56 02 80 C3 10 73-EB 33 C9 8A 46 10 98 F7  *..V....s.3..F...*
00000080: 66 16 03 46 1C 13 56 1E-03 46 0E 13 D1 8B 76 11  *f..F..V..F....v.*
00000090: 60 89 46 FC 89 56 FE B8-20 00 F7 E6 8B 5E 0B 03  *`.F..V.. ....^..*
000000A0: C3 48 F7 F3 01 46 FC 11-4E FE 61 BF 00 00 E8 E6  *.H...F..N.a.....*
000000B0: 00 72 39 26 38 2D 74 17-60 B1 0B BE A1 7D F3 A6  *.r9&8-t.`.......*
000000C0: 61 74 32 4E 74 09 83 C7-20 3B FB 72 E6 EB DC A0  *at2Nt... ;.r....*
000000D0: FB 7D B4 7D 8B F0 AC 98-40 74 0C 48 74 13 B4 0E  *........@t.Ht...*
000000E0: BB 07 00 CD 10 EB EF A0-FD 7D EB E6 A0 FC 7D EB  *..............*
000000F0: E1 CD 16 CD 19 26 8B 55-1A 52 B0 01 BB 00 00 E8  *.....&.U.R......*
00000100: 3B 00 72 E8 5B 8A 56 24-BE 0B 7C 8B FC C7 46 F0  *;.r.[.V$......F.*
00000110: 3D 7D C7 46 F4 29 7D 8C-D9 89 4E F2 89 4E F6 C6  *=..F.)....N..N..*
00000120: 06 96 7D CB EA 03 00 00-20 0F B6 C8 66 8B 46 F8  *........ f.F.*
00000130: 66 03 46 1C 66 8B D0 66-C1 EA 10 EB 5E 0F B6 C8  *f.F.f..f....^...*
00000140: 4A 4A 8A 46 0D 32 E4 F7-E2 03 46 FC 13 56 FE EB  *JJ.F.2....F..V..*
00000150: 4A 52 50 06 53 6A 01 6A-10 91 8B 46 18 96 92 33  *JRP.Sj.j...F...3*
00000160: D2 F7 F6 91 F7 F6 42 87-CA F7 76 1A 8A F2 8A E8  *......B...v.....*
00000170: C0 CC 02 0A CC B8 01 02-80 7E 02 0E 75 04 B4 42  *...........u..B*
00000180: 8B F4 8A 56 24 CD 13 61-61 72 0B 40 75 01 42 03  *...V$..aar.@u.B.*
00000190: 5E 0B 49 75 06 F8 C3 41-BB 00 00 60 66 6A 00 EB  *^.Iu...A...`fj..*
000001A0: B0 4E 54 4C 44 52 20 20-20 20 20 20 0D 0A 52 65  *.NTLDR      ..Re*
000001B0: 6D 6F 76 65 20 64 69 73-6B 73 20 6F 72 20 6F 74  *move disks or ot*
000001C0: 68 65 72 20 6D 65 64 69-61 2E FF 0D 0A 44 69 73  *her media....Dis*
000001D0: 6B 20 65 72 72 6F 72 FF-0D 0A 50 72 65 73 73 20  *k error...Press *
000001E0: 61 6E 79 20 6B 65 79 20-74 6F 20 72 65 73 74 61  *any key to resta*
000001F0: 72 74 0D 0A 00 00 00 00-00 00 00 AC CB D8 55 AA  *rt...........U.*
```

```
Fat 16 BPB  FatLabel: 'NO NAME   '  SystemId: 'FAT16  '  OemId: 'MSDOS5.0'
SectorSize 200  SectorsPerCluster 4 ReservedSectors 8  # Fats 2
Root Entries 200  Media F8  Sectors 32F8E  SectorsPerFat CC
SectorsPerTrack 3F Heads 255
```

Command-line Usage for dmem

This section provides example usages of the dmem command. The full command-line syntax is as follows:

```
dmem [-b] [address] [size] [-MMIO]
```

To display the EFI system table pointer entries:

```
fs0:\> dmem

Memory Address 000000003FF7D808 200 Bytes
3FF7D808: 49 42 49 20 53 59 53 54-02 00 01 00 78 00 00 00  *IBI SYST....x...*
3FF7D818: 5C 3E 6A FE 00 00 00 00-88 2E 1B 3F 00 00 00 00  *\>j........?....*
3FF7D828: 26 00 0C 00 00 00 00 00-88 D3 1A 3F 00 00 00 00  *&.........?....*
3FF7D838: A8 CE 1A 3F 00 00 00 00-88 F2 1A 3F 00 00 00 00  *...?......?....*
3FF7D848: 28 EE 1A 3F 00 00 00 00-08 DD 1A 3F 00 00 00 00  *(..?......?....*
3FF7D858: A8 EB 1A 3F 00 00 00 00-18 C3 3F 3F 00 00 00 00  *...?..........*
3FF7D868: 00 4B 3F 3F 00 00 00 00-06 00 00 00 00 00 00 00  *.K............*
3FF7D878: 08 DA F7 3F 00 00 00 00-70 74 61 6C 88 00 00 00  *...?....ptal...*
3FF7D888: 00 00 00 00 00 00 00 00-00 00 00 00 00 00 00 00  *...............*
3FF7D898: 00 00 00 00 00 00 00 00-00 00 00 00 00 00 00 00  *...............*
3FF7D8A8: 00 00 00 00 00 00 00 00-00 00 00 00 00 00 00 00  *...............*
3FF7D8B8: 00 00 00 00 00 00 00 00-00 00 00 00 00 00 00 00  *...............*
3FF7D8C8: 00 00 00 00 00 00 00 00-00 00 00 00 00 00 00 00  *...............*
3FF7D8D8: 00 00 00 00 00 00 00 00-00 00 00 00 00 00 00 00  *...............*
3FF7D8E8: 00 00 00 00 00 00 00 00-00 00 00 00 00 00 00 00  *...............*
3FF7D8F8: 00 00 00 00 00 00 00 00-70 68 06 30 88 00 00 00  *........ph.0...*
3FF7D908: 65 76 6E 74 00 00 00 00-02 02 00 60 00 00 00 00  *evnt.......`...*
3FF7D918: 18 6F 1A 3F 00 00 00 00-10 E0 3F 3F 00 00 00 00  *.o.?..........*
3FF7D928: 10 00 00 00 00 00 00 00-40 C0 12 3F 00 00 00 00  *........@..?...*
3FF7D938: 10 80 13 3F 00 00 00 00-00 00 00 00 00 00 00 00  *...?..........*
3FF7D948: 00 00 00 00 00 00 00 00-40 7D 3F 3F 00 00 00 00  *........@.....*
3FF7D958: 50 6F 1A 3F 00 00 00 00-00 00 00 00 00 00 00 00  *Po.?..........*
3FF7D968: 00 00 00 00 00 00 00 00-00 00 00 00 00 00 00 00  *...............*
3FF7D978: 00 00 00 00 00 00 00 00-70 74 61 6C 88 00 00 00  *........ptal...*
3FF7D988: 00 00 00 00 00 00 00 00-00 00 00 00 00 00 00 00  *...............*
3FF7D998: 00 00 00 00 00 00 00 00-00 00 00 00 00 00 00 00  *...............*
3FF7D9A8: 00 00 00 00 00 00 00 00-00 00 00 00 00 00 00 00  *...............*
3FF7D9B8: 00 00 00 00 00 00 00 00-00 00 00 00 00 00 00 00  *...............*
3FF7D9C8: 00 00 00 00 00 00 00 00-00 00 00 00 00 00 00 00  *...............*
3FF7D9D0: 00 00 00 00 00 00 00 00-00 00 00 00 00 00 00 00  *...............*
3FF7D9E8: 00 00 00 00 00 00 00 00-00 00 00 00 00 00 00 00  *...............*
3FF7D9F8: 00 00 00 00 00 00 00 00-70 68 06 30 A0 00 00 00  *........ph.0...*

Valid EFI Header at Address 000000003FF7D808
-------------------------------------------
System: Table Structure size 00000078 revision 00010002
ConIn (3F1AD388) ConOut (3F1AF288) StdErr (3F1ADD08)
Runtime Services 000000003F3FC318
```

```
Boot Services      000000003F3F4B00
SAL System Table 000000003FF22760
ACPI Table         000000003FFD9FC0
ACPI 2.0 Table     00000000000E2000
MPS Table          000000003FFD0000
SMBIOS Table       00000000000F0020
```

To display memory contents from 1af3088 with size of 16 bytes:

```
Shell> dmem 1af3088 16
Memory Address 0000000001AF3088 16 Bytes
01AF3088: 49 42 49 20 53 59 53 54-00 00 02 00 18 00 00 00 *IBI SYST........*
01AF3098: FF 9E D7 9B 00 00                               *......*
```

To display memory mapped I/O contents from 1af3088 with size of 16 bytes:

```
Shell> dmem 1af3088 16 -MMIO
```

Command-line Usage for drvdiag

This section provides example usages of the drvdiag command. The full command-line syntax is as follows:

```
mm address [value] [-w 1|2|4|8] [-MEM | -MMIO | -IO | -PCI | -PCIE]
```

To display or modify memory:

```
Address 0x1b07288, default width=1 byte:
fs0:\> mm 1b07288
MEM   0x0000000001B07288 : 0x6D >
MEM   0x0000000001B07289 : 0x6D >
MEM   0x0000000001B0728A : 0x61 > 80
MEM   0x0000000001B0728B : 0x70 > q

fs0:\> mm 1b07288
MEM   0x0000000001B07288 : 0x6D >
MEM   0x0000000001B07289 : 0x6D >
MEM   0x0000000001B0728A : 0x80 >          *Modified
MEM   0x0000000001B0728B : 0x70 > q
```

To modify memory: Address 0x1b07288, width = 2 bytes:

```
Shell> mm 1b07288 -w 2
MEM   0x0000000001B07288 : 0x6D6D >
MEM   0x0000000001B0728A : 0x7061 > 55aa
MEM   0x0000000001B0728C : 0x358C > q

Shell> mm 1b07288 -w 2
MEM   0x0000000001B07288 : 0x6D6D >
MEM   0x0000000001B0728A : 0x55AA >          *Modified
MEM   0x0000000001B0728C : 0x358C > q
```

To display I/O space: Address 80h, width = 4 bytes:

```
Shell> mm 80 -w 4 —IO
IO   0x0000000000000080 : 0x000000FE >
IO   0x0000000000000084 : 0x00FF5E6D > q
```

To modify I/O space using non-interactive mode:

```
Shell> mm 80 52 -w 1 -IO
Shell> mm 80 -w 1 -IO
IO   0x0000000000000080 : 0x52 > FE     *Modified
IO   0x0000000000000081 : 0xFF >
IO   0x0000000000000082 : 0x00 >
IO   0x0000000000000083 : 0x00 >
IO   0x0000000000000084 : 0x6D >
IO   0x0000000000000085 : 0x5E >
IO   0x0000000000000086 : 0xFF >
IO   0x0000000000000087 : 0x00 > q
```

To display PCI configuration space, ss=00, bb=00, dd=00, ff=00, rr=00:

```
Shell> mm 0000000000 -PCI
PCI   0x0000000000000000 : 0x86 >
PCI   0x0000000000000001 : 0x80 >
PCI   0x0000000000000002 : 0x30 >
PCI   0x0000000000000003 : 0x11 >
PCI   0x0000000000000004 : 0x06 >
PCI   0x0000000000000005 : 0x00 > q
```

To display PCIE configuration space, ss=00, bb=06, dd=00, ff=00, rrr=000:

```
Shell> mm 00060000000 -PCIE
PCIE   0x0000000060000000 : 0xAB >
PCIE   0x0000000060000001 : 0x11 >
PCIE   0x0000000060000002 : 0x61 >
PCIE   0x0000000060000003 : 0x43 >
PCIE   0x0000000060000004 : 0x00 > q
```

Chapter 8

The Use of UEFI for Diagnostics

To err is human - and to blame it on a computer is even more so.

—Robert Orben

This chapter describes some usages of the UEFI Shell for diagnostics. Although the PC ecosystem has rich examples of robust platform software and hardware components, occasionally things go awry. In those cases, the machine state needs to be diagnosed or assessed. To that end, the act of performing diagnostics is a key action for platform deployment and lifecycle maintenance.

Today, disk operating systems such as MS-DOS or PC DOS are still used by many platform manufacturers as a diagnostics environment because of the single-tasking nature of DOS, the large library of extant DOS utilities, the fact that DOS layers directly on PC/AT BIOS as its I/O stack, and the lack of memory protection in DOS. For the purposes of a modern OS, these features of DOS are abhorrent, but for diagnosing a machine or determining root-cause of a failure, this close mapping to the hardware and controlled environment is appreciated. But DOS has various downsides for diagnostics on contemporary platform hardware, including a limited memory map, 16-bit operating mode, and difficulties in getting modern software ported to this environment.

This description of DOS is not intended to be pejorative. In fact, the existence of DOS coupled with PC/AT BIOS has been a contributing factor to the PC ecosystem success and customer-visible value of Moore's Law and the associated platform.

The *beyond DOS* aspect of the book title, though, describes how scenarios like DOS diagnostics now have an opportunity to move to UEFI. Int21h in DOS maps the appropriate UEFI service, for example. In addition, the full machine addressability of UEFI, richness of the UEFI and shell specifications, the ability to in fact access UEFI Platform Initialization (PI) interfaces if they're available, and open software infrastructure like the EFI Development Kits at www.tianocore.org, are key enabling elements of this migration.

Types of Diagnostics

In the context of a UEFI system, many actors can contribute to the diagnostics role. We mentioned above the available, generic infrastructure that the UEFI Shell and main specifications at www.uefi.org provide, but within those specifications are some purpose-designed abstractions for diagnostics. One example would be the EFI_DRIVER_DIAGNOSTICS_PROTOCOL. The intent of a protocol such as this, like other UEFI interfaces, is to bind the API to the entity that can produce the domain-specific behavior. What we mean by that is the UEFI driver that provides a capability, such as block abstraction from a disk driver, can also provide a diagnostics interface in cases of a failure of the underlying media or hardware.

So why is a device-specific abstraction valuable? This gives a platform manufacturer the opportunity to write a generic "disk diagnostics" capability into a shell application that can access the plurality of disk block instances via each driver's EFI_DRIVER_DIAGNOSTICS_PROTOCOL. Without this per-driver API publication, such a "disk diagnostics" utility would have to contain vendor-specific information and code flows from the sundry disk controller vendors in the industry.

Regarding the usage of EFI_DRIVER_DIAGNOSTICS protocol mentioned above, the UEFI Shell specification codifies a usage via the `drvdiag` command.

Another type of diagnostic can be one that accesses the platform resources, such as the PCI bus. To that end, the UEFI Shell has the mm and pci commands to allow peeking (reading) and poking (writing) memory-mapped I/O, direct I/O, PCI configuration access, and PCI memory-mapped device access, respectively. And like other UEFI Shell commands, these hardware accesses can be done in an interactive mode or via scripting, with console and/or log file recording being possible, too.

The final discussion of a class of diagnostic entails the use of the UEFI Shell to ascertain information from the System Management BIOS tables. This example provides working reference code and is intended to tie together some of the earlier discussions around available software frameworks, infrastructure in both the UEFI main specification and UEFI Shell specifications, and a use-case that provides customer-visible value from using this technology.

The System Management BIOS (SMBIOS) tables are a set of data structures in memory that are referenced by the GUID in the UEFI system table, namely

```
#define SMBIOS_TABLE_GUID \
{0xeb9d2d31,0x2d88,0x11d3,0x9a,0x16,0x0,0x90,0x27,0x3f,0xc1,0x4
d}
```

The location of the SMBIOS table relative to other UEFI objects is shown in Figure 8.1. The important point to note is the location of the industry standard hand-off tables in the lower left-hand side of the diagram.

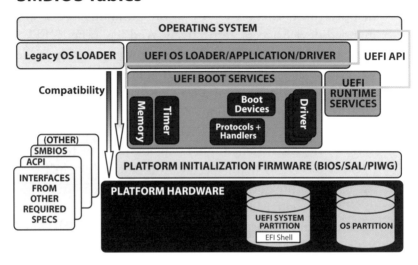

Figure 8.1 System Diagram with UEFI

This chapter describes a scenario wherein the system is not operational and different asset information is discovered using capabilities of the UEFI Shell. Before we describe the tool to ascertain the SMBIOS data, a little background information will be provided.

SMBIOS Table Organization

The purpose of utility (named SMBIOSVIEW) is to get data from SMBIOS tables and translate the packed information into a human-readable form. As such, the SMBIOS structure table organization is the first issue to design with respect to this diagnostic UEFI Shell-based utility.

According to SMBIOS specification, there are two access methods defined for the SMBIOS structures. The first method, defined in v2.0 of SMBIOS specification, provides the SMBIOS structures through a Plug-and-Play function interface. A table-based method, defined in v2.1 of the SMBIOS specification, provides the SMBIOS structures as a packed list of data referenced by a table entry point.

A BIOS compliant with v2.1 of the SMBIOS specification can provide one or both methods. A BIOS compliant with v2.2 and later of this specification must provide the table-based method and can optionally provide the Plug-and-Play function interface. EFI uses the second method.

In EFI, SMBIOS core driver provides table-based information. SMBIOSVIEW gets the information and translates it to users. The table includes a table header, a structure table, and other data objects. See the SMBIOS specification at http://www.dmtf.org/standards/smbios/ for more information on the table entries.

SMBIOS Structure Table Entry Point

The information of SMBIOS is organized as the SMBIOS structure, and the SMBIOS structure is accessed by the means of the SMBIOS structure table Entry Point Structure (EPS).

Table Organization Graph

The table organization graph shown in Figure 8.2 is used to make the SMBIOS table more understandable. The SMBIOS table includes a table header and a structure table.

The table header contains the general information of the table and the necessary information to access the structure table.

The structure table contains a serial of structures. The type of the last structure is 127, which indicates End-of-table.

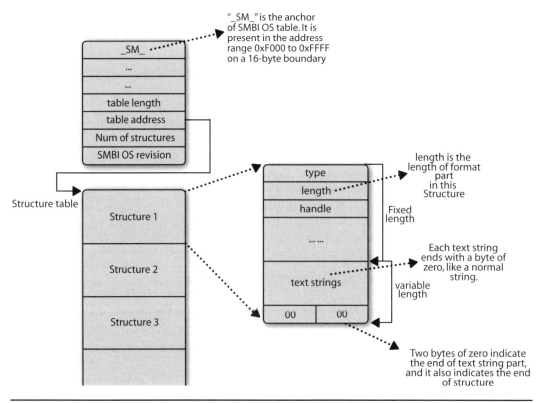

Figure 8.2   SMBIOS Table Organization

The EPS (Entry Point Structure) has information about the structure table:

- *Table-Address* points to the structure table starting address.
- *Table-Length* is the length of the structure table.
- *Num-of-Structures* is the number of structures in the structure table.

The first structure begins with the Table-Address. The second structure begins with the next byte of the end of the first one, and so on.

The type of the last structure is 127. The last structure is also indicated by the Num-of-Structures in the EPS.

The structures between the first and last are of random type. In other words, the structures are packed neither increasing type nor decreasing type, but random.

Each Structure has a common header. The header contains three fields:

- *Type* – type of this structure, following data is organized according to this type.
- *Length* – number of bytes of format part, it does *not* include the text string length.
- *Handle* – Uniquely identifies the structure in the structure table.

The format part follows the header. Text strings follow the format part. In text string parts, two bytes of 0x00 identify the end of structure. It also identifies the end of the structure table header.

Structure Standards

Each SMBIOS structure has a formatted section and an optional unformed section. The formatted section of each structure begins with a 4-byte header. Remaining data in the formatted section is determined by the structure type, as is the overall length of the formatted section.

Structure Evolution and Usage Guidelines

As the industry evolves, the structures defined in this specification will evolve. To ensure that the evolution occurs in a nondestructive fashion, the following guidelines must be followed.

If a new field is added to an existing structure, that field is added at the end of the formatted area of that structure and the structure's *Length* field is increased by the new field's size.

Any software that interprets a structure shall use the structure's *Length* field to determine the formatted area size for the structure rather than hard-coding or deriving the *Length* from a structure field.

Each structure shall be terminated by a double-null (0x0000), either directly following the formatted area (if no strings are present) or directly following the last string. This includes system- and OEM-specific structures and allows upper-level software to easily traverse the structure table. See below for structure-termination examples.

The unformed section of the structure is used for passing variable data such as text strings, see *3.4.3 Text Strings* of the SMBIOS specification for more information.

When an enumerated field's values are controlled by the DMTF, new values can be used as soon as they are defined by the DMTF without requiring an update to this specification.

Starting with v2.3, each SMBIOS structure type has a *minimum* length—enabling the addition of new, but optional, fields to SMBIOS structures. In no case shall a structure's length result in a field being less than fully populated. For example, a Voltage Probe structure with *Length* of 0x15 is invalid since the *Nominal Value* field would not be fully specified.

Software that interprets a structure field must verify that the structure's length is sufficient to encompass the optional field; if the length is insufficient, the optional field's value as *Unknown*. For example, if a Voltage Probe structure has a *Length* field of 0x14, the probe's *Nominal Value* is *Unknown*. A Voltage Probe structure with Length greater than 0x14 *always* includes a Nominal Value field.

Text Strings

Text strings associated with a given SMBIOS structure are returned in the *dmiStrucBuffer*, appended directly after the formatted portion of the structure. This method of returning string information eliminates the need for application software to deal with pointers embedded in the SMBIOS structure. Each string is terminated with a null (0x00) UINT8 and the set of strings is terminated with an additional null (0x00) UINT8. When the formatted portion of a SMBIOS structure references a string, it does so by specifying a nonzero string number within the structure's string-set. For example, if a string field contains 0x02, it references the second string following the formatted portion of the SMBIOS structure. If a string field references no string, a null (0) is placed in that string field. If the formatted portion of the structure contains string-reference fields and all the string fields are set to 0 (no string references), the formatted section of the structure is followed by two null (0x00) BYTES. See *3.4.1 Structure Evolution and Usage Guidelines* on page 8 of the SMBIOS specification for a string-containing example.

Note: Each text string is limited to 64 significant characters due to system MIF limitations.

Required Structures and Data

Beginning with SMBIOS v2.3, compliant SMBIOS implementations include the following base set of required structures and data within those structures. These structures include the BIOS information, system information, processor information, and several tables describing the system information.

Features

SMBIOSVIEW allows users to display SMBIOS structure information with different detail options. Its main goal is to provide a user-friendly interface of the SMBIOS structure. SMBIOSVIEW allows users to:

- Display structure table statistics information
- Display structure information with different level:
  - SHOW_NONE - Don't interpret just dump the structure
  - SHOW_OUTLINE - Only display header information
  - SHOW_NORMAL - Display header information and element value
  - SHOW_DETAIL - Display header and element detail information (default)
- Display all structures' information of certain Type

  ■ Display structure's information of certain Handle

  ■ Display structures' information one by one or all at once

  ■ Controls (such as change display option) in application

  ■ Use a simple help guide (>SmbiosView -?).

User Interface Design

This section describes the details of the user interface (UI) to the SMBIOS-VIEW shell command.

Design Guide

 1. Command line arguments determine what action the SMBIOS View tool should perform.

 2. In SMBIOSVIEW, change the options to determine how to display the respective SMBIOS table contents.

 1. SmbiosView [-t type] | [-h handle] | [-s] | [-a]

```
-t     - View structures of certain type
-h     - View structure of certain handle
-s     - View statistics of whole SMBIOS table

-a     - View all structures once a time
```

 2. Internal commands:
```
:q     - Quit SmbiosView
:0     - SmbiosView display NONE info
:1     - SmbiosView display OUTLINE info
:2     - SmbiosView display NORMAL info
:3     - SmbiosView display DETAIL info
/?     - Show help
```

Note: Internal commands provide optional controls to users and they are got from users' input after a prompt '$'. Users can also press Enter skip internal commands.The following command allows for describing the various portions of the SMBIOS table. The various actions that can occur with respect to the table manipulation are encoded via various input command line parameters. These options include a description of the options via '-?.'

Usage

>SmbiosView -?   - Show help page

>SmbiosView   - Show structures as default

>SmbiosView -s   - Show statistics information, as shown in Figure 8.3

>SmbiosView -t 8   - Show all structures of type=8, as shown in Figure 8.4

>SmbiosView -h 25   - Show structure of handle=0x25

>SmbiosView -a > 1.log - Show all structures and output to file of 1.log

Examples

fs0:\>SmbiosView -s

```
█ "Bus Driver Console Window"                                    _ □ ×

=====================================================================
Index=0001  Type=000  Handle=0x0000  Offset=0x0035  Len=0x0035
Index=0002  Type=001  Handle=0x0001  Offset=0x0071  Len=0x003C
Index=0003  Type=002  Handle=0x0002  Offset=0x00A0  Len=0x002F
Index=0004  Type=003  Handle=0x0003  Offset=0x00E0  Len=0x0040
Index=0005  Type=126  Handle=0x0004  Offset=0x0120  Len=0x0040
Index=0006  Type=126  Handle=0x0005  Offset=0x0160  Len=0x0040
Index=0007  Type=004  Handle=0x0006  Offset=0x01A2  Len=0x0042
Index=0008  Type=005  Handle=0x0007  Offset=0x01B8  Len=0x0016
Index=0009  Type=006  Handle=0x0008  Offset=0x01D1  Len=0x0019
Index=0010  Type=006  Handle=0x0009  Offset=0x01EA  Len=0x0019
Index=0011  Type=007  Handle=0x000A  Offset=0x0210  Len=0x0026
Index=0012  Type=007  Handle=0x000B  Offset=0x0236  Len=0x0026
Index=0013  Type=008  Handle=0x000C  Offset=0x0255  Len=0x001F
Index=0014  Type=008  Handle=0x000D  Offset=0x0276  Len=0x0021
Index=0015  Type=008  Handle=0x000E  Offset=0x0297  Len=0x0021
Index=0016  Type=008  Handle=0x000F  Offset=0x02C0  Len=0x0029
Index=0017  Type=008  Handle=0x0010  Offset=0x02E3  Len=0x0023
Index=0018  Type=126  Handle=0x0011  Offset=0x0309  Len=0x0026
Index=0019  Type=126  Handle=0x0012  Offset=0x0339  Len=0x0030
Index=0020  Type=008  Handle=0x0013  Offset=0x035E  Len=0x0025
Press Enter to continue. .

Enter to continue, :q to exit, :[0-3] to change mode, /? for help. .
$
```

Figure 8.3 SmbiosView Statistics

fs0:\>SmbiosView -t 8

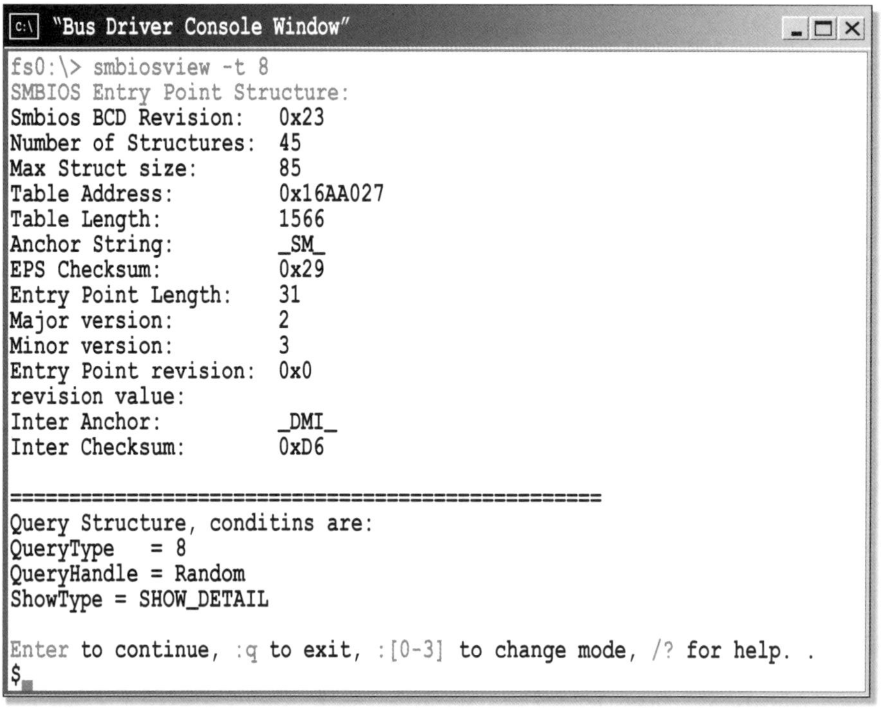

```
┌──────────────────────────────────────────────────────────┐
│ [c:\] "Bus Driver Console Window"              [_][□][×]  │
├──────────────────────────────────────────────────────────┤
│ fs0:\> smbiosview -t 8                                    │
│ SMBIOS Entry Point Structure:                            │
│ Smbios BCD Revision:    0x23                             │
│ Number of Structures:   45                              │
│ Max Struct size:        85                              │
│ Table Address:          0x16AA027                       │
│ Table Length:           1566                            │
│ Anchor String:          _SM_                            │
│ EPS Checksum:           0x29                            │
│ Entry Point Length:     31                              │
│ Major version:          2                               │
│ Minor version:          3                               │
│ Entry Point revision:   0x0                             │
│ revision value:                                         │
│ Inter Anchor:           _DMI_                           │
│ Inter Checksum:         0xD6                            │
│                                                          │
│                                                          │
│ ==========================================               │
│ Query Structure, conditins are:                          │
│ QueryType   = 8                                         │
│ QueryHandle = Random                                    │
│ ShowType = SHOW_DETAIL                                  │
│                                                          │
│ Enter to continue, :q to exit, :[0-3] to change mode, /? for help. . │
│ $                                                        │
└──────────────────────────────────────────────────────────┘
```

Figure 8.4   SmbiosView User Interface

Architecture Design

The SMBIOS utility components architecture is illustrated in Figure 8.5 (the arrows indicate the calling of another module), and can be described as follows:

Init Module Gets the SMBIOS table and initializes the environment of the SMBIOS utility.

Dispatch Module Gets and transacts the shell command parameters and user input.

User Input   The user inputs the internal commands such as changing a display option or quitting the program.

SMBIOS Info Access Module   Provides a set of APIs to access the SMBIOS table or structures.

Element Info Interpret Module   Translates packed data to understandable text according to specification.

Data Unpack Module   Translates packed data to understandable information.

Display Module   Displays information as required options.

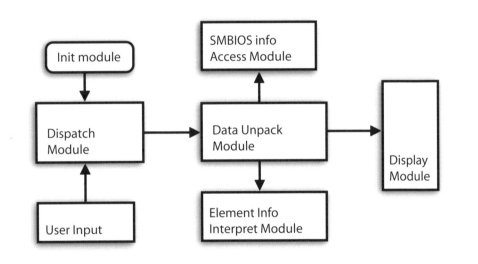

Figure 8.5   Smbios Utility Components Architecture

Data Structure

There are four key data structures in the editor implementation, as listed in Table 8.1.

Table 8.1 Key Data Structures

Data Structure Name	Header File Name
SMBIOS_STRUCTURE_TABLE	LibSmbios.h
SMBIOS_HEADER	LibSmbios.h
SMBIOS_STRUCTURE_POINTER	LibSmbios.h
STRUCTURE_STATISTICS	SmbiosView.h

SMBIOS_STRUCTURE_TABLE

The structure of the SMBIOS_STRUCTURE_TABLE is as follows:

```
#pragma pack(1)
typedef struct {
    UINT8    AnchorString[4];
    UINT8    EntryPointStructureChecksum;
    UINT8    EntryPointLength;
    UINT8    MajorVersion;
    UINT8    MinorVersion;
    UINT16   MaxStructureSize;
    UINT8    EntryPointRevision;
    UINT8    FormattedArea[5];
    UINT8    IntermediateAnchorString[5];
    UINT8    IntermediateChecksum;
    UINT16   TableLength;
    UINT32   TableAddress;
    UINT16   NumberOfSmbiosStructures;
    UINT8    SmbiosBcdRevision;
} SMBIOS_STRUCTURE_TABLE;
#pragma pack()
```

Descriptions:

This structure is defined as the EPS (Entry Point Structure) of the SMBIOS table. Access to SMBIOS table information is by this structure. For detailed information refer to Chapter 3.

Note: Because SMBIOS table uses a byte alignment data structure, this structure is also using #pragma pack(1) to configure structure data alignment of one byte.   This is necessary because a general C declaration would be naturally aligned, but the present utility needs to map the data structure to an external specification.

Members

Table 8.2 lists the members of the SMBIOS_STRUCTURE_TABLE data structure. These tables are going to be manipulated by the utility.

The description below explicates the specific entries and meaning.

Table 8.2   Members of SMBIOS_STRUCTURE_TABLE

Member	Description
AnchorString	_SM_, specified as (5F 53 4D 5F)
EntryPointStructureChecksum	Checksum of the Entry Point Structure (EPS)
EntryPointLength	Length of the Entry Point Structure
MajorVersion	Identifies the major version of SMBIOS specification implemented in the table structures.
MinorVersion	Identifies the minor version of SMBIOS specification implemented in the table structures.
MaxStructureSize	Size of the largest SMBIOS structure, in bytes, encompasses the structure's formatted area and text strings.
EntryPointRevision	Identifies the EPS revision implemented in this structure and identifies the formatting of offsets 0Bh to 0Fh.
FormattedArea[5]	The value present in the Entry Point Revision field defines the interpretation to be placed upon these 5 bytes.
IntermediateAnchorString[5]	_DMI_, specified as five ASCII characters (5F 44 4D 49 5F).
IntermediateChecksum	Checksum of Intermediate Entry Point Structure (IEPS)
TableLength	Total length of SMBIOS Structure Table, pointed to by the Structure Table Address, in bytes.
TableAddress	Total length of SMBIOS Structure Table, pointed to by the Structure Table Address, in bytes.
NumberOfSmbiosStructures	Total number of structures present in the SMBIOS Structure Table.
SmbiosBcdRevision	Indicates compliance with a revision of SMBIOS specification.

SMBIOS_HEADER

The structure of SMBIOS_HEADER is as follows:

```
#pragma pack(1)
typedef struct {
    UINT8   Type;
    UINT8   Length;
    UINT16  Handle;
} SMBIOS_HEADER;
#pragma pack()
```

Members

Table 8.3 lists the members of SMBIOS_HEADER.

Table 8.3   Members of SMBIOS_HEADER

Member	Description
Type	Structure type
Length	Format part length of structure
Handle	Unique identifier of structure in structure table

SMBIOS_STRUCTURE_POINTER

The structure of SMBIOS_STRUCTURE_POINTER is as follows:

```
typedef union {
    SMBIOS_HEADER    *Hdr;
    SMBIOS_TYPE0     *Type0;
    SMBIOS_TYPE1     *Type1;
    SMBIOS_TYPE2     *Type2;
    SMBIOS_TYPE3     *Type3;
    SMBIOS_TYPE4     *Type4;
    SMBIOS_TYPE5     *Type5;
    SMBIOS_TYPE6     *Type6;
    SMBIOS_TYPE7     *Type7;
    SMBIOS_TYPE8     *Type8;
    SMBIOS_TYPE9     *Type9;
    SMBIOS_TYPE10    *Type10;
    SMBIOS_TYPE11    *Type11;
    SMBIOS_TYPE12    *Type12;
    SMBIOS_TYPE13    *Type13;
```

```
        SMBIOS_TYPE14    *Type14;
        SMBIOS_TYPE15    *Type15;
        SMBIOS_TYPE16    *Type16;
        SMBIOS_TYPE17    *Type17;
        SMBIOS_TYPE18    *Type18;
        SMBIOS_TYPE19    *Type19;
        SMBIOS_TYPE20    *Type20;
        SMBIOS_TYPE21    *Type21;
        SMBIOS_TYPE22    *Type22;
        SMBIOS_TYPE23    *Type23;
        SMBIOS_TYPE24    *Type24;
        SMBIOS_TYPE25    *Type25;
        SMBIOS_TYPE26    *Type26;
        SMBIOS_TYPE27    *Type27;
        SMBIOS_TYPE28    *Type28;
        SMBIOS_TYPE29    *Type29;
        SMBIOS_TYPE30    *Type30;
        SMBIOS_TYPE31    *Type31;
        SMBIOS_TYPE32    *Type32;
        SMBIOS_TYPE33    *Type33;
        SMBIOS_TYPE34    *Type34;
        SMBIOS_TYPE35    *Type35;
        SMBIOS_TYPE36    *Type36;
        SMBIOS_TYPE37    *Type37;
        SMBIOS_TYPE38    *Type38;
        SMBIOS_TYPE39    *Type39;
        SMBIOS_TYPE126   *Type126;
SMBIOS_TYPE127   *Type127;
UINT8            *Raw;
} SMBIOS_STRUCTURE_POINTER;
```

Descriptions:

This structure is defined as a union. Each field in the union is a method of organizing the data of the structure, such as structure header, a structure type, or simply a byte raw array.

Members

Table 8.4 lists the members of SMBIOS_STRUCTURE_POINTER.

Table 8.4 Members of SMBIOS_STRUCTURE_POINTER

Members	Description
Hdr	Points to Structure header, common part of all structure types
Type(n)	Interprets the structure as certain structure type format
Raw	Interprets the Structure as simple bytes packet

STRUCTURE_STATISTICS

The structure of STRUCTURE_STATISTICS is as follows:

```
typedef struct {
    UINT16    Index;
    UINT8     Type;
    UINT16    Handle;
    UINT16    Addr;
    UINT16    Len;
} STRUCTURE_STATISTICS;
```

Members

Table 8.5 lists the members of STRUCTURE_STATISTICS.

Table 8.5 Members of STRUCTURE_STATISTICS

Member	Description
Index	Index in the SMBIOS structure table
Type	Structure type identified in the structure header
Handle	Structure handle unique identified structure in the table
Addr	Structure offset from structure table start address
Len	Structure whole length including format part and text format

Source Code for the Utility

To bring the SMBIOS overview and design discussions together, the SMBIOS view command is described next. Various portions of this UEFI Shell utility are presented and decomposed in order to show how the theory of SMBIOS can be married to a particular UEFI practice.

```
256 #include "EfiShellLib.h"
257 #include "LIbSmbios.h"
258 #include "LibSmbiosView.h"
259 #include "smbiosview.h"
260 #include "smbios.h"
```

Lines 1–5

These lines contain the include files for the application.

```
261 STATIC  UINT8                    mInit         = 0;
262 STATIC  SMBIOS_STRUCTURE_TABLE   *mSmbiosTable = NULL;
263 STATIC  SMBIOS_STRUCTURE_POINTER m_SmbiosStruct;
264 STATIC  SMBIOS_STRUCTURE_POINTER *mSmbiosStruct =
265                                  &m_SmbiosStruct;
```

Lines 6–10

These lines contain the module globals for the application.

```
266 EFI_STATUS
267 LibSmbiosInit (
268   VOID
269   )
270 /*++
271 Routine Description:
272    Init the SMBIOS VIEW API's environment.
273   Arguments:
274     None
275 Returns:
276    EFI_SUCCESS        - Successful to init the SMBIOS
277 VIEW Lib\
278     Others            - Cannot get SMBIOS Table
279 --*/
280 {
281   EFI_STATUS   Status;
282
283   //
284   // Init only once
```

```
285   //
286   if (mInit == 1) {
287     return EFI_SUCCESS;
288   }
289   //
290   // Get SMBIOS table from System Configure table
291   //
292   Status = LibGetSystemConfigurationTable
293           (&gEfiSmbiosTableGuid, &mSmbiosTable);
294
295   if (mSmbiosTable == NULL) {
296     PrintToken (STRING_TOKEN
297       (STR_SMBIOSVIEW_LIBSMBIOSVIEW_CANNOT_GET_TABLE),
298       HiiHandle);
299
300     return EFI_NOT_FOUND;
301   }
302
303   if (EFI_ERROR (Status)) {
304     PrintToken (STRING_TOKEN
305       (STR_SMBIOSVIEW_LIBSMBIOSVIEW_GET_TABLE_ERROR),
306        HiiHandle, Status);
307     return Status;
308   }
309   //
310   // Init SMBIOS structure table address
311   //
312   mSmbiosStruct->Raw  = (UINT8 *) (UINTN) (mSmbiosTable-
313                                   >TableAddress);
314
315    mInit               = 1;
316    return EFI_SUCCESS;
317 }
318
```

Lines 11–63

These lines contain an initialization routine for the application, including logic to discover the SMBIOS data in memory.

```
319 VOID
320 LibSmbiosGetEPS (
321   SMBIOS_STRUCTURE_TABLE **pEntryPointStructure
322   )
```

```
323 {
324   //
325   // return SMBIOS Table address
326   //
327   *pEntryPointStructure = mSmbiosTable;
328 }
```

Lines 64–73

These lines contain code to discover the entry point structure.

```
329 VOID
330 LibSmbiosGetStructHead (
331   SMBIOS_STRUCTURE_POINTER *pHead
332   )
333 {
334   //
335   // return SMBIOS structure table address
336   //
337   pHead = mSmbiosStruct;
338 }
339
```

Lines 74–84

These lines contain code to discover the head structure.

```
340 EFI_STATUS
341 LibGetSmbiosInfo (
342   OUT CHAR8    *dmiBIOSRevision,
343   OUT UINT16   *NumStructures,
344   OUT UINT16   *StructureSize,
345   OUT UINT32   *dmiStorageBase,
346   OUT UINT16   *dmiStorageSize
347   )
348 /*++
349 Routine Description:
350     Get SMBIOS Information.
351
352   Arguments:
353     dmiBIOSRevision   - Revision of the SMBIOS
354                         Extensions.
355     NumStructures     - Max. Number of Structures the
356                         BIOS will return.
357     StructureSize     - Size of largest SMBIOS Structure.
358     dmiStorageBase    - 32-bit physical base address for
```

```
359                               memory mapped SMBIOS data.
360     dmiStorageSize    - Size of the memory-mapped SMBIOS
361                         data.
362
363   Returns:
364     DMI_SUCCESS                - successful.
365     DMI_FUNCTION_NOT_SUPPORTED  - Does not support SMBIOS
366 calling interface capability.
367   --*/
368 {
369   //
370   // If no SMIBOS table, unsupported.
371   //
372   if (mSmbiosTable == NULL) {
373     return DMI_FUNCTION_NOT_SUPPORTED;
374   }
375
376   *dmiBIOSRevision  = mSmbiosTable->SmbiosBcdRevision;
377   *NumStructures    = mSmbiosTable
378                       ->NumberOfSmbiosStructures;
379   *StructureSize    = mSmbiosTable->MaxStructureSize;
380   *dmiStorageBase   = mSmbiosTable->TableAddress;
381   *dmiStorageSize   = mSmbiosTable->TableLength;
382
383   return DMI_SUCCESS;
384 }
```

Lines 85–129

These lines contain code to set various fields of the SMBIOS information.

```
385
386 EFI_STATUS
387 LibGetSmbiosStructure (
388   IN  OUT UINT16   *Handle,
389   IN  OUT UINT8    *Buffer,
390   OUT UINT16       *Length
391   )
392 /*++
393    Routine Description:
394      Get SMBIOS structure given the Handle,copy data to
395 the Buffer, Handle is changed to the next handle or
396 0xFFFF when the end is reached or the handle is not
397 found.
398
```

```
399    Arguments:
400      Handle:    - 0xFFFF: get the first structure
401                 - Others: get a structure according to this
402                   value.
403      Buffter:   - The pointer to the caller's memory
404                   buffer.
405      Length:    - Length of return buffer in bytes.
406    Returns:
407      DMI_SUCCESS - Buffer contains the required
408                    structure data
409                  - Handle is updated with next structure
410                    handle or
411                    0xFFFF(end-of-list).
412
413      DMI_INVALID_HANDLE  - Buffer not contain the
414                            requiring structure data
415  --*/
416  {
417    SMBIOS_STRUCTURE_POINTER  Smbios;
418    SMBIOS_STRUCTURE_POINTER  SmbiosEnd;
419    UINT8                     *Raw;
420
421    if (*Handle == INVALIDE_HANDLE) {
422      *Handle = mSmbiosStruct->Hdr->Handle;
423      return DMI_INVALID_HANDLE;
424    }
425
426    if (Buffer == NULL) {
427      PrintToken (STRING_TOKEN
428  (STR_SMBIOSVIEW_LIBSMBIOSVIEW_NO_BUFF_SPEC), HiiHandle);
429      return DMI_INVALID_HANDLE;
430    }
431    *Length      = 0;
432    Smbios.Hdr   = mSmbiosStruct->Hdr;
433    SmbiosEnd.Raw = Smbios.Raw + mSmbiosTable->TableLength;
434    while (Smbios.Raw < SmbiosEnd.Raw) {
435      if (Smbios.Hdr->Handle == *Handle) {
436        Raw = Smbios.Raw;
437        //
438        // Walk to next structure
439        //
440        LibGetSmbiosString (&Smbios, (UINT16) (-1));
441
```

```
442        //
443        // Length = Next structure head - this structure
444        // head
445        //
446        *Length = (UINT16) (Smbios.Raw - Raw);
447        CopyMem (Buffer, Raw, *Length);
448        //
449        // update with the next structure handle.
450        //
451        if (Smbios.Raw < SmbiosEnd.Raw) {
452          *Handle = Smbios.Hdr->Handle;
453        } else {
454          *Handle = INVALIDE_HANDLE;
455        }
456        return DMI_SUCCESS;
457      }
458    //
459    // Walk to next structure
460    //
461    LibGetSmbiosString (&Smbios, (UINT16) (-1));
462  }
463
464  *Handle = INVALIDE_HANDLE;
465  return DMI_INVALID_HANDLE;
466 }
467
```

Lines 130–211

These lines contain code to discover specific SMBIOS structures.

Summary

This chapter has described how the UEFI Shell can be used for an important action in the platform development and deployment space, namely diagnostics. The discussion has ranged from some basic background on prior art in diagnostics, a few use-cases, and then a detailed elaboraation on a particular usage, namely SMBIOS. For the detailed example, extant industry standards, such as SMBIOS, can be comprehended by UEFI and then assessed/managed via a UEFI Shell application. Again, this is just one instance where the UEFI Shell with its rich application library can assist in real-world platform deployment and management activities.

Chapter 9

UEFI Shell Scripting

I honestly have no strategy whatsoever. I'm waiting for that script to pop through the letterbox and completely surprise me.

—Ben Kingsley

UEFI Shell scripts are interpreted programs (usually with the extension `.nsh`) written in a text-based language supported directly by the UEFI Shell. Similar to many shell scripts, (most notably the Windows command prompt) it also includes features unique to the pre-OS environment, such as standardized command output and redirection to and from environment variables.

The UEFI Shell searches for shell scripts first in the current directory and then in the directories specified by the path environment variable. Shell scripts are carriage-return delimited lists of shell commands that are executed (by default) from first to last. Shell scripts also support several additional commands that change the flow of control in a script or control the output:

- `echo` Outputs text to the standard output device.

- `exit` Terminates the currently executing script.

- `for...endfor` Repeatedly executes a block of script commands.

- `goto` Continues execution with the specified label.

- **if…else…endif** Conditionally executes a block of script commands.
- **shift** Shifts positional command-line parameters.

These are described in detail in Appendix B.

Using shell scripts, complex tasks can be performed simply. The following sections take on successively more difficult tasks using scripts and explain how they work, line by line:

- **HelloWorld.nsh** The simplest script outputs "Hello, World" to the screen.
- **Echo1.nsh** Echoes 3 shell parameters to the screen.
- **Echo2.nsh** Echoes all shell parameters to the screen.
- **Echo3.nsh** Echoes all shell parameters to the screen with a count.
- **Concat1.nsh** Creates a new text file by joining together the contents of one or more user-specified text files.
- **Lsgrep.nsh** Asks the user for which file information (from the ls command) to output and then output just that information to the screen.
- **InstallCmd.nsh** Example script file that installs a new shell command and updates all of the necessary environment variables.

After these examples, we will demonstrate how to create a UEFI boot option that invokes a shell script.

Hello, World

The simplest script is shown in Figure 9.1.

```
256 1    @echo "Hello, World!"
```

Figure 9.1   HelloWorld.nsh

Line 1

The echo command copies the remainder of the line to standard output. The "@" prevents the script line itself from being displayed.

If you run this script, you will see:

```
Shell> HelloWorld
Hello, World!
```

Echo

This script simply echoes the first three arguments to the screen, as shown in Figure 9.2.

```
256 @echo First : %1
256 @echo Second: %2
257 @echo Third : %3
```

Figure 9.2   Echo1.nsh

Lines 1–3

This will print out the first three command-line parameters. The first command-line parameter is %1, the second is %2, all the way up to (theoretically) %9. What happens if there are more than 9? Well, that is the subject of our next script.

If you run this script using *abra*, *cadab*, and *ra* as your parameters, you will see:

```
Shell> Echo1 abra cadab ra
First : abra
Second: cadab
Third : ra
```

Normally, any whitespace character will separate one command-line parameter from the next. However, quotation marks can be used to break the rules. For example:

```
Shell> Echo1 "abra cadab" ra1 ra2
First : "abra cadab"
Second: ra1
Third : ra2
```

The quotation marks caused the space between abra cadab to be ignored. Also, the quotation marks were retained, rather than being discarded. Now try:

```
Shell> Echo1 ^"abra cadab^" ra
First : "abra
Second: cadab"
Third : ra
```

The "^" caret character forces the next character to be treated as a normal character.

Echo All Parameters

This script shown in Figure 9.3 echoes all of the command-line parameters, no matter how many there are.

```
256 :start
257 if not %1 == ""
258     @echo Parameter: %1
259     shift
260     goto start
261 endif
```

Figure 9.3   Echo2.nsh

Line 1

The word *start* is a label that can be referenced later in a goto command.

Line 2

Check to see whether or not the command-line parameter is empty. The only way a command-line parameter can be empty is if it is not present. So this is really a check to see whether there are any more command-line parameters. If it is the last parameter, then execution starts after the `endif`.

Line 3

If the parameter was present (see line 1), then display it.

Line 4

The `shift` command moves all of the command-line parameters over by one. So, %2 is moved to %1, %3 to %2, and so on. If the command line contains more than 9 parameters, the tenth will go to %9.

Line 5

The `goto` command causes execution to continue with the label specified after the command. In this case, execution continues after line 1.

If you execute this command, you might see:

```
Shell> Echo2
Shell> Echo2 abc
Parameter: abc
Shell> Echo2 1 2 3 4 5 6 7 8 9 20
Parameter: 1
Parameter: 2
Parameter: 3
Parameter: 4
Parameter: 5
Parameter: 6
Parameter: 7
Parameter: 8
Parameter: 9
Parameter: 20
```

Echo All Parameters (Improved Version)

The script shown in Figure 9.4 is an enhanced version of the previous script. Instead of just printing the static text "Parameter" before the text of each parameter, it actually prints "Parameter 1", "Parameter 2", and so on. Most of it is identical to the previous version, but it takes advantage of the `for...endfor` command's ability to iterate through a series of integers.

```
256 #
262 # echo3.nsh
263 #
264
265 for %a run 1 100
266   if %1 == " "
267     exit /b
268   endif
269   @echo Parameter %a: %1
270   shift
271 endfor
```

Figure 9.4   Echo3.nsh

Line 5

The for…endfor script command repeatedly executes a block of script commands until the list of possible index values has been exhausted. The block of script commands on lines 6–10 would execute 100 times.

Acting as an index variable, %a will be updated each time through the loop. There are 26 possible index variable names (a through z).

The keyword run indicates that the index variable will be initialized with the first value (1) during the first time through the loop and that it will be incremented by 1 each time through the loop. The loop will terminate when the index variable's value exceeds the second value (100). An optional third value indicates the amount to increment or decrement the index variable. If it is not present, then it is assumed to be 1 if the initial value is less than the ending value or -1 if the initial value is greater than the ending value.

Instead of run, the keyword in can be used to step through a list of space-delimited strings. This is demonstrated in the next example.

Linc 6

This line checks to see if the next command-line parameter is blank. The command-line parameter can only be blank if there are no more command-line parameters present.

Line 7

The `exit` command, when used with the `/b` parameter, terminates the processing of the current script. The exit code may also be specified, but, if not present, 0 is assumed.

Line 9

As in the previous example, the parameter is output. But, in this example, `%a` is added. When the script is executed, the `%a` will be replaced with the actual contents of the index variable created in line 5.

If you execute this command, you might see:

```
Shell> Echo3
Shell> Echo3 abc
Parameter 1: abc
Shell> Echo3 1 2 3 4 5 6 7 8 9 20
Parameter 1: 1
Parameter 2: 2
Parameter 3: 3
Parameter 4: 4
Parameter 5: 5
Parameter 6: 6
Parameter 7: 7
Parameter 8: 8
Parameter 9: 9
Parameter 10: 20
```

Concatenate Text Files

This script, shown in Figure 9.5 creates a new text file that consists of the contents of zero or more other text files. The syntax is:

```
concat1 output-file [input-file1...]
```

Just to make things interesting, we will allow any of the input files to contain wildcard characters.

```
256 #
272 # concat1.nsh
273 #
274
275 if %1 == ""
276   @echo Error: missing output file name
277   exit /b 1
278 endif
279
280 set -v outputfile %1
281
282 :nextparm
283 if not %2 == ""
284   for %a in %2
285     type %a >> %outputfile%
286   endfor
287   shift
288   goto nextparm
289 endif
```

Figure 9.5   Concat1.nsh

Lines 5–8

> Check to see whether the output file name is specified. If not, an error message is generated and the script exits with the return code of "1". If the /b were not specified, then the entire instance of the shell would be exited.

Line 10

> Saves the output file name to a volatile environment variable. The name needs to be saved because, after the shift statement on line 17, it would be lost. If the -v were missing, the value of 'outputfile' would be saved across system reset or system power-cycle.

Lines 12–13, 18

> The label 'nextparm', along with the `if` and the `goto` create a loop that exits only when there are no more command-line parameters after the first.

Lines 14–16

> The for…endfor commands create a loop, with one iteration for each file name that matches the pattern specified by %2. Inside the loop, %a is initialized with the actual file name. The type command outputs the contents to standard output. The >> redirects standard output so that it is appended to the specified file "outputfile".

Line 17

> This moves all the command-line parameters by one so that %2 becomes the next input file name (if any).

List Only Selected "ls" Information

This script, shown in Figure 9.6, accepts the same syntax as "ls",, but it prompts the user to specify information about the files to display. Using echo and the getkey command from the previous chapter, it asks the user to select one of seven pieces of information about the file:

1. Full Name
2. Logical Size
3. Physical Size
4. Attributes
5. File Access Date
6. File Creation Date
7. File Modification Date

Then it pipes the standard-format output of the ls command to the parse command to extract the desired field. Many of the UEFI Shell commands have a special mode (-sfo) where the output is formatted in a well-defined, easy to parse format. Except for this special mode, the output of UEFI Shell commands is not standardized.

Standard format output consists of rows of information, with each row taking up one line. Each row is divided into columns by a comma. The first column contains an identifier that describes the type of information that appears in the other columns. All columns except the first are quoted.

The `ls` command produces three different row types: ShellCommand, VolumeInfo, and FileInfo. The ShellCommand row type must be the first row produced by any shell command that produces standard-format output. The VolumeInfo row type describes such information as the volume name and how much free space is available. The FileInfo row type describes an individual file, with each column giving the information listed above.

The `parse` command can go through a file and extract any single column from standard-format output from a specified row type and display it.

```
256 #
290 # lsgrep.nsh
291 #
292
293 @echo 1) Full Name
294 @echo 2) Logical Size
295 @echo 3) Physical Size
296 @echo 4) Attributes
297 @echo 5) File Access Date
298 @echo 6) File Creation Date
299 @echo 7) File Modification Date
300 @echo
301 :wait_for_key
302 @getkey "Select The File Data To Display" _key
303
304 if %_key% lt 1 or %_key% gt 7
305   @echo %_key% is not between 1 and 7
306   goto wait_for_key
307 endif
308
309 math %_key% + 1 >e _key
310 ls %1 %2 %3 %4 %5 %6 %7 %8 %9 | parse FileInfo %_key%
```

Figure 9.6   Lsgrep.nsh

Lines 5–14

Display all of the possible fields on the screen for the user to select from and then wait for a key. The resulting key press is stored in the environment variable _key.

Lines 16–19

> Check to see whether the user input is valid. If not, display an error message and go back to wait again for a key.

Line 21

> Add one to the value entered by the user. The standard-format output for the ls command puts the full name in column 2, the logical size in column 3, and so on. The resulting value goes into the _key environment variable again.

Line 22

> List all of the files, using the same command-line options passed to the script itself. Up to 9 command-line options can be passed without doing some additional work. Even if 9 weren't specified, the remaining options will be blanks. The output is redirected to a text file.
>
> The parse command searches through the specified file for lines that begin with the tag "FileInfo", extracts the column number specified by %_key% and displays it.

Install Script

The script shown in Figure 9.7 acts as an installation script for the GetKey sample application from the previous chapter. It demonstrates how to:

1. Detect whether or not the UEFI Shell supports the features that are required to support the GetKey sample application.

2. Detect errors during installation and display error messages.

3. Install the executable and help files to the correct directory.

4. Update the path to point to the target directory.

5. Create a new UEFI Shell profile called "_shellbook"

The script has the following syntax:

```
InstallCmd command-name target-directory
```

where `command-name` is the name of the shell command (such as GetKey) and `target-directory` is the directory where the command should be installed.

```
256 #
256 # InstallCmd.nsh — Install a new UEFI Shell Command
257 #
258 # InstallCmd command-name target-directory
259 #
260
261 #
262 # Validate the UEFI Shell support level
263 #
264
265 if %shellsupport% ult 3
266   exit /b 2
267 endif
268
269 #
270 # Make sure that the command isn't already installed.
271 #
272
273 if exists(%2/%1.efi)
274   @echo %1.efi already exists at %2.
275   exit /b 1
276 endif
277
278 if available(%1.efi)
279   @echo %1.efi already exists in the path.
280   exit /b 1
281 endif
282
283 #
284 # Create the target directory
285 #
286
287 md %2
288 if not exists(%2)
289   @echo Could not create target directory %2
290   exit /b 1
291 endif
292
293 #
294 # Copy the executable and help file to the target directory
295 #
296
```

```
297 cp —q %1.efi %2
298 if not %lasterror" == 0
299   @echo Could not copy %1.efi to the target directory.
300   exit /b 1
301 endif
302
303 cp —q %1.man %2
304 if not %lasterror" == 0
305   @echo Could not copy %1.man to the target directory.
306   del %2/%1.efi
307   exit /b 1
308 endif
309
310 #
311 # Create the profile _shellbook, if it doesn't exist
312 #
313
314 if not profile(_shellbook)
315   set profiles %profiles";_shellbook
316 endif
317
318 #
319 # If necessary, add the target directory to the path
320 #
321
322 if not available(%1.efi)
323   set path %path%;%2
324 endif
```

Figure 9.7   InstallCmd.nsh

258

Lines 11–13

These lines check the `%shellsupport%` environment variable to determine which UEIF Shell features are present. If the support level is too low, then the script exits with error code 2. No error message is displayed, since shell support levels less than 3 have no standard output support.

The UEFI Shell is very configurable and many of the features, APIs, and shell commands described in the UEFI Shell specification may or may not be present. However, the various standard support levels can be detected by a UEFI Shell script by examining `shellsupport`. The various valid values are described in Chapter 3 of the UEFI Shell specification. They are briefly summarized in Table 9.1.

Table 9.1   UEFI Shell Support Levels

Level	Name	Execute()/ Scripting/ startup.nsh	Interactive?	Commands
0	Minimal	No	No	None
1	Scripting	Yes	No	`for`, `endfor`, `goto`, `if`, `else`, `endif`, `shift`, `exit`
2	Basic	Yes	No	`attrib`, `cd`, `cp`, `date*`, `time*`, `del`, `load`, `ls`, `map`, `mkdir`, `mv`, `rm`, `reset`, `set`, `timezone*`
3	Interactive	Yes	Yes	`alias`, `date`, `echo`, `help`, `pause`, `time`, `touch`, `type`, `ver`, `cls`, `timezone`

Level 0 (Minimal) isn't very interesting in the context of this chapter, since even scripting is not supported. Level 1 (Scripting) adds the basic scripting support described in this chapter, except for echo. Level 2 (Basic) adds basic file handling, date/time, and environment variable commands, which do not rely on standard input or standard output. Level 3 (Interactive) adds those commands that rely on standard input and/or standard output.

Lines 19–22

This section checks to see whether or not the specified shell command already exists in the target directory. The `exists` operator returns nonzero if the specified file does not exist in the specified directory (or in the current working directory, if no directory is specified). If the file already exists, then the script exits with an error message and an error code of 1.

Lines 24–27

This section checks to see whether the specified shell command already exists in the current path. If the current shell command was installed and there was already a shell command in the path, it is confusing to the user, since they aren't sure which would be executed. The `available` operator returns nonzero if the specified file does not exist in the current directory or in any directory listed in the `path` environment variable. If the file already exists, then the script exits with an error message and an error code of 1.

Lines 33–37

This section creates the target directory using the `md` (a built-in alias of `mkdir`) command. The `cp` command used in later sections of this script will fail if the target directory does not already exist, so it must be created first. The script does not check the error code to see whether there has been an error, but rather checks to see if the directory exists after trying to create it. Directories can be checked in the same way as files, using the `exists` operator.

Lines 43–47

This section copies the executable from the current directory to the target directory. It then checks to see whether there has been an error by examining the %lasterror% environment variable. Any nonzero value indicates one of the errors listed in Appendix C of the UEFI Shell Specification. If there has been an error, a message is displayed and the script is terminated with an error code.

Lines 49–54

This section copies the help file from the current directory to the target directory. The UEFI Shell automatically searches for help files in the same directory as the executable. If an error has occurred when copying, an error message is displayed and the script is terminated with an error code.

Lines 60–62

This section installs our custom UEFI Shell profile, with the name "_shellbook". UEFI Shell profiles are collections of related UEFI Shell applications. Each UEFI Shell profile has a unique name. Standard profiles are described in Chapter 5 of the UEFI Shell Specification. Custom profile names must begin with an underscore ("_") character.

The list of currently installed shell profiles is stored in the nonvolatile environment variable with the name `profiles`, separated by a semicolon (";") character. A profile name should not be added to `profiles` unless all of the commands are present, since other scripts may rely on the information.

The profiles operator is a Boolean operator that can be used to detect whether a specific profile is installed in the UEFI Shell. This section first checks to see whether the _shellbook profile exists and then, if not, adds it to the profiles environment variable using the set shell command.

The example given here assumes there is only one shell command in the profile. If there were more than one shell command in the profile, then there should be additional "if available" script commands to ensure that all other shell commands in the profile were present before adding the profile name.

Lines 68–70

This section makes sure that the target directory is in the path, which is a list of directories that the shell searches for executables and scripts. The path is stored in the path environment variable. Since the script has already copied the script executable to the target directory, the available operator should return nonzero if the target directory is already in the path. If it returns zero, then the path environment variable is updated with the target-directory.

How to Make a Shell Script Appear as a Boot Option

UEFI Shell scripts and shell executables can be launched directly from the boot manager. The UEFI boot manager relies on the contents of several EFI variables to determine the boot order. The bcfg command can add new boot options easily. The UEFI Shell itself is a standard UEFI application that can take command-line arguments that are encoded as part of the boot option. First, let's create a small script, shown in Figure 9.8, that just prints a message and then waits for a key to be pressed.

```
256 #
311 # HelloWorld2.nsh
312 #
313
314 @echo "Hello, World, Again!"
315 @pause
```

Figure 9.8   HelloWorld2.nsh

Now, let's add the HelloWorld2.nsh script so that it will be launched as a boot option.

```
bcfg boot addp 1 shell.efi "Hello World Script" —opt "hel-
loworld2.nsh"
```

This adds a new boot option that will show up as "Hello World Script". When selected, it will launch the UEFI Shell, display "Hello, World, Again!", wait for a keypress, and then exit back to the UEFI boot manager.

Chapter **10**

UEFI Shell Programming

Right now it's only a notion, but I think I can get the money to make it into a concept, and later turn it into an idea.

—Woody Allen

This chapter provides an overview of the techniques used when creating UEFI Shell applications. The UEFI Shell provides additional capabilities beyond those available to normal UEFI applications. First, the `EFI_SHELL_PARAMETERS_PROTOCOL` protocol is installed on the image handle. This protocol provides access to the command-line parameters, as well as the handle of the standard input, standard output, and standard error capabilities of the shell. Second, the `EFI_SHELL_PROTOCOL` provides access to the file system, the environment variables, and the device mappings.

The full source of four basic UEFI Shell applications is presented, along with detailed notes. The notes are designed to help understand what the applications are doing and how the shell resources are being used.

For information on setting up the build environment, see "Setting Up the Build Environment" later in this chapter.

A Simple UEFI Shell Application

The simplest of UEFI Shell applications requires source files, a component information file, and a build description file. The source files are those files that have a compiler associated with them, such as C source code. The component description file describes how to build a single driver or application. The build description file describes how to put together several drivers or applications, such as when creating a BIOS.

The Source File

The simplest source file requires only a few lines, as shown in Figure 10.1.

```
256 //
257 // Simple Hello World Application
258 //
259
260 #include <tiano.h>
261 #include <uefishellib.h>
262
263 EFI_APPLICATION_ENTRY_POINT (EfiMain);
264
265 EFI_STATUS
266 EfiMain(
267   IN EFI_HANDLE        ImageHandle
268   IN EFI_SYSTEM_TABLE *SystemTable,
269   )
270 {
271       EFI_SHELL_APP_INIT (ImageHandle, SystemTable);
272
273       Print(L"Hello, World!\n");
274       return SHELL_SUCCESS;
275 }
```

Figure 10.1   Simple UEFI Shell Application Source Code

Lines 5–6

The header file tiano.h contains all of the basic UEFI type definitions. The header file uefishelllib.h contains the definitions for the EDK's UEFI Shell Library functions.

Line 8

The macro `EFI_APPLICATION_ENTRY_POINT` marks the entry point for the function.

Lines 10–14

The standard entry point for UEFI Shell applications looks like the entry point for a standard UEFI application. It contains a pointer to the standard EFI System Table and the image handle of the UEFI Shell application itself.

Line 16

The macro EFI_SHELL_APP_INIT performs the initialization for the UEFI Shell Library. The standard initialization sets up pointers to commonly used UEFI and UEFI Shell features, as described in Table 10.1. References to external symbols, such as the names of these pointers are part of uefishelllib.h.

Table 10.1 UEFI Shell Library Commonly Used Pointers

Pointer	Description
gST	Points to EFI_SYSTEM_TABLE
gBS	Points to EFI_BOOT_SERVICES
gRT	Points to EFI_RUNTIME_SERVICES
gSP	Points to EFI_SHELL_PROTOCOL
gSPP	Points to EFI_SHELL_PARAMETERS_PROTOCOL

Line 18

The `Print()` function is one of the standard functions provided by the EDK's UEFI Shell Library.

Line 19

Returning SHELL_SUCCESS (0) indicates that there was no error. A non-zero value would indicate an error.

The INF File

The component description (.INF) file shown in Figure 10.2 describes information necessary for building a single application, driver or library, such as the source files and build options.

```
1376256  #
276    # HelloWorld.inf
277    #
278
279    [defines]
280      BASE_NAME = HelloWorld
281      FILE_GUID = a215e049-88dc-4b64-9198-fbb6065a9fed
282      COMPONENT_TYPE = APPLICATION
283
284    [sources.common]
285      HelloWorld.c
286
287    [includes.common]
288      $(EDK_SOURCE)\Foundation
289      $(EDK_SOURCE)\Foundation\Efi
290      $(EDK_SOURCE)\Foundation\Efi\Include
291      $(EDK_SOURCE)\Foundation\Framework
292      $(EDK_SOURCE)\Foundation\Framework\Include
293      $(EDK_SOURCE)\Foundation\Include
294      $(EDK_SOURCE)\Foundation\Include\IndustryStandard
295      $(EDK_SOURCE)\Shell\UefiInclude
296      $(EDK_SOURCE)\Shell\UefiLibrary
297
298    [libraries.common]
299      EfiShellLib
300
301    [nmake.common]
302      IMAGE_ENTRY_POINT = EfiMain
```

Figure 10.2   Simple Component Description File

Line 5

The [defines] section lists various attributes of the component being built. The BASE_NAME attribute gives the name of the output executable. The FILE_GUID attribute specifies the GUID associated with the UEFI Shell application. The COMPONENT_TYPE attribute specifies that this is a UEFI application.

Line 10

The [sources.common] section lists all of the source files that are part of the application.

Line 13

The [includes.common] section lists all of the paths that will be searched for include files. The $(EDK_SOURCE) references the environment variable that contains the root directory of the EDK source code. The include files listed here are typical.

Line 24

The [libraries.common] section lists all of the libraries to be linked with the application.

Line 27

The [nmake.common] section contains compiler flags. The IMAGE_ENTRY_POINT specifies the entry point to the application and must match the one specified in the EFI_APPLICATION_ENTRY_POINT macro.

The DSC File

Modify the file build.dsc to include the lines shown in Figure 10.3.

```
256 [libraries.platform]
303   ...other libraries...
304   Shell\UefiLibrary\uefishelllib.inf
305
306 [components]
307   ...other components...
308   Sample\App\HelloWorld\HelloWorld.inf FV=NULL
```

Figure 10.3 Updated Build Description File for Simple Application

Line 1

In the [libraries.platform] section, add the directory of the UEFI Shell library, relative to $(EDK_SOURCE).

Line 5

In the [components] section, add the directory of the HelloWorld.inf file, relative to $(EDK_SOURCE).

Graphics Device Information Display Application

The next example is another simple application that displays something to the console. But the example goes one step further by querying the UEFI services for information about the graphics devices in the system.

UEFI operates in two phases: boot and runtime. The boot phase lasts until the operating system (OS) is ready to take over the control of the various hardware devices in the system. At that point, the OS calls ExitBootServices() to tell the firmware that it is taking control. Most of the UEFI drivers are unloaded and the UEFI core itself only continues to provide a small subset of the services, known as the runtime services.

The UEFI Shell executes in the boot phase. It has access to a wealth of information about the system and can use a wide array of services to control the system and its devices, including the graphics devices. The EFI_GRAPHICS_OUTPUT_PROTOCOL is the UEFI-standard way for graphics devices to expose services during the boot phase.

This little utility dumps information about each of the graphics devices in the system, what modes they support, and the current modes.

Entry Point Source Code

The EFI_APPLICATION_ENTRY_POINT macro, the EFI_SHELL_APP_INIT macro, and the EfiMain() function in this example are nearly identical to the simple HelloWorld application. The differences are highlighted in bold type in Figure 10.4.

```
256 /*++
309
310 Module Name:
311
312    gopdump.c
313
314 Abstract:
315    Shell command to dump out information about installed
316    instances of the Graphics Output Protocol
317
318 Revision History
319
320 --*/
321
322 #include <tiano.h>
323 #include <uefishelllib.h>
324
325 #include EFI_PROTOCOL_CONSUMER(GraphicsOutput)
326 #include EFI_PROTOCOL_CONSUMER(DevicePath)
327 #include EFI_PROTOCOL_CONSUMER(DevicePathToText)
328
329 EFI_APPLICATION_ENTRY_POINT (EfiMain);
330
331 EFI_STATUS
332 GopDump (
333    VOID
334    );
335
336 EFI_STATUS
337 EfiMain (
338    IN EFI_HANDLE        ImageHandle,
339    IN EFI_SYSTEM_TABLE *SystemTable
340    )
341 {
342    EFI_SHELL_APP_INIT (ImageHandle, SystemTable);
343
344    return GopDump();
345 }
```

Figure 10.4   UEFI Graphics Device Information Display Application, Part 1

Lines 18-20

The standard headers included by tiano.h provide macros for using the protocols defined in the UEFI specification. The `EFI_PROTOCOL_CONSUMER(protocol-name)` macro indicates that this application consumes the specified UEFI protocol protocol-name. The macro includes the correct header file. The header declares the protocol's data structure and provides a global variable for the protocol's GUID.

For example, if protocol-name is GraphicsOutput, then the file $(EDK_SOURCE)\Efi\Protocol\GraphicsOutput\GraphicsOutput.h. is included and the global variable gEfiGraphicsOutputProtocolGuid can be used in the project.

The `EFI_GRAPHICS_OUTPUT_PROTOCOL` controls a single graphics device. It provides information about the current mode (Mode) and all supported modes (QueryMode()). It can also change the current mode (SetMode()) and perform various bitmap operations (Blt()). See the UEFI Specification, Chapter 11, for more information on output in UEFI.

The `EFI_DEVICE_PATH_PROTOCOL` is a data structure that describes how a device is connected to the system. In this case, the program show which graphics device the information is related to. The `EFI_DEVICE_PATH_TO_TEXT_PROTOCOL` provides services for rendering the contents of an `EFI_DEVICE_PATH_PROTOCOL` as text. See the UEFI Specification, Chapter 9, for more information on device paths.

Line 35

The shell initialization library functions set up pointers to commonly used UEFI and UEFI Shell features, as described earlier in Table 10.1. References to common external symbols, such as the names of these pointers are part of uefishelllib.h.

Lines 25-27, 37

The `GopDump()` function does the actual work, which we will examine later.

GopDump() Source Code

This function, shown in Figure 10.5, locates all instances of the `EFI_GRAPHICS_OUTPUT_PROTOCOL` and then processes each in turn.

```
346 EFI_DEVICE_PATH_TO_TEXT_PROTOCOL *gDevicePathToText = NULL;
347
348 EFI_STATUS
349 GopDumpHandle(
350   IN UINTN      Index,
351   IN EFI_HANDLE GopDeviceHandle
352   );
353
354 EFI_STATUS
355 GopDump (
356   VOID
357   )
358 {
359   EFI_STATUS Status;          // temp. to hold EFI function
 status
360   UINTN      HandleCount;    // number of handles
361   EFI_HANDLE *HandleBuffer;  // array of handles
362   UINTN      HandleIndex;    // current handle
363
364   //
365   // Find the single instance of EFI_DEVICE_PATH_TO_TEXT_
 PROTOCOL
366   //
367   Status = gBS->LocateProtocol (
368                    &gEfiDevicePathToTextProtocolGuid,
369                    NULL,
370                    &gDevicePathToText
371                    );
372   if (Status != SHELL_SUCCESS) {
373     Print(L"error: Unable to find \
374       EFI_DEVICE_PATH_TO_TEXT_PROTOCOL\n");
375     return 1;
376   }
377
378   //
379   //  Find all handles with EFI_GRAPHICS_OUTPUT_PROTOCOL.
380   //
381   Status = gBS->LocateHandleBuffer (
382                    ByProtocol,
383                    &gEfiGraphicsOutputProtocolGuid,
384                    NULL,
385                    &HandleCount,
```

```
386                           &HandleBuffer
387                           );
388  if (Status != SHELL_SUCCESS) {
389    Print(L"error: Unable to find an instance \
390      of EFI_GRAPHICS_OUTPUT_PROTOCOL\n");
391    return 1;
392  }
393
394  //
395  // For each handle, dump out information about it.
396  //
397  for (HandleIndex = 0;
398       HandleIndex < HandleCount;
399       HandleIndex++) {
400    Status = GopDumpHandle(
401             HandleIndex,
402             HandleBuffer[HandleIndex]
403             );
404    if (Status != SHELL_SUCCESS) {
405      break;
406    }
407  }
408
409  FreePool(HandleBuffer);
410  return Status;
411 }
```

Figure 10.5   UEFI Graphics Device Information Display Application, Part 2

Lines 39, 57–69

The global variable gDevicePathToText points to the instance of the
EFI_DEVICE_PATH_TO_TEXT_PROTOCOL. Like many other UEFI service
protocols, there can only be once instance. The LocateProtocol() boot
service function is useful for finding this sort of UEFI service protocol.

Lines 41–45

The function GopDumpHandle() displays the information about a single
instance of the EFI_GRAPHICS_OUTPUT_PROTOCOL.

Lines 74–80

The `LocateHandleBuffer()` boot service finds all handles which have a specified protocol installed on them and places all of those handles in an allocated buffer. It is the application's responsibility to later free the handle (see Line 102).

Lines 87–100

Walk through each of the handles found and call `GopDumpHandle()` to display the information about it. If there is any trouble, break out of the loop.

Lines 102–103

Clean up and exit.

GopDumpHandle() Source Code

This function, shown in Figure 10.6, dumps all of the information about a specific graphics device.

```
412 EFI_STATUS
413 GopDumpHandle(
414    IN UINTN       Index,
415    IN EFI_HANDLE GopDeviceHandle
416    )
417 {
418    EFI_STATUS                          Status;
419    EFI_GRAPHICS_OUTPUT_PROTOCOL        *Gop;
420    EFI_DEVICE_PATH_PROTOCOL            *DevicePath;
421    CHAR16                              *Text;
422    UINT32                              Mode;
423    EFI_GRAPHICS_OUTPUT_MODE_INFORMATION *Info;
424    UINTN                               SizeOfInfo;
425
426    //
427    // Get instance of EFI_GRAPHICS_OUTPUT_PROTOCOL on the
    handle.
428    //
429    Gop = NULL;
430    Status = gBS->HandleProtocol(
431                    GopDeviceHandle,
432                    &gEfiGraphicsOutputProtocolGuid,
```

```
433                          (VOID**) &Gop
434                          );
435    if (Status != SHELL_SUCCESS) {
436      return 1;
437    }
438
439    //
440    // Get the instance of EFI_DEVICE_PATH_PROTOCOL on the
 handle.
441    //
442    DevicePath = NULL;
443    Status = gBS->HandleProtocol(
444                    GopDeviceHandle,
445                    &gEfiDevicePathProtocolGuid,
446                    (VOID**) &DevicePath
447                    );
448
449    //
450    // Print out either the device path or else 'no device
 path'
451    //
452    if (DevicePath == NULL) {
453      Print (L"GOP %d: No device path\n", Index+1);
454    } else {
455      Text = mDevicePathToText->
456              ConvertDevicePathToText(DevicePath,TRUE,FALSE);
457      Print (L"GOP %d: %s\n", Index+1, Text);
458      FreePool(Text);
459    }
460    Print(L"-------\n");
461
462    //
463    // Print out the current mode information
464    //
465    if (Gop->Mode == NULL) {
466      Print (L"Current Mode:    Not set\n");
467    } else {
468      Print (L"Current Mode:      %d\n",
469              Gop->Mode->Mode);
470      Print (L"Number Of Modes:   %d\n",
471              Gop->Mode->MaxMode);
472      Print (L"Frame Buffer:      %x\n",
473              Gop->Mode->FrameBufferBase);
```

```
474        Print (L"Frame Buffer Size: %x\n",
475                Gop->Mode->FrameBufferSize);
476
477        GopDumpModeInfo(
478          Gop->Mode->Info,
479          sizeof(EFI_GRAPHICS_OUTPUT_MODE_INFORMATION)
480          );
481
482        //
483        // Display the information about each supported mode
484        //
485        Print(L"\nSupported Mode Information\n");
486        for (Mode = 0; Mode < Gop->Mode->MaxMode; Mode++) {
487          Status = Gop->QueryMode (
488            Gop,
489            Mode,
490            &SizeOfInfo,
491            &Info
492            );
493          if (Status != SHELL_SUCCESS || Info == NULL)  {
494            continue;
495          }
496
497          Print (L"-->Mode %d\n", Mode);
498          GopDumpModeInfo(Info,SizeOfInfo);
499          Print (L"\n");
500        }
501      }
502
503    return SHELL_SUCCESS;
504 }
```

Figure 10.6   UEFI Graphics Device Information Display Application, Part 3

Lines 119–130

Finds the pointer to the instance of the EFI_GRAPHICS_OUTPUT_PROTOCOL installed on the handle passed in.

Lines 132–140

> Finds the pointer to the instance of the `EFI_DEVICE_PATH_PROTOCOL` installed on the handle passed in. It is possible that no device path is associated with the graphics device in the case of software-emulated graphical displays such as the Framework's console splitter.

Lines 142–153

> Display the device path (if any) and the instance.

Lines 155–168

> Display the information about the current mode, the maximum number of modes, and the address and size of the frame buffer.

Lines 170–173

> The other information about the current mode is the same as that returned for each of the supported modes. In both cases, `GopDumpModeInfo()` is used.

Lines 175–194

> The `QueryMode()` function returns information about each of the supported graphics mode.

GopDumpModeInfo() Source Code

This function, shown in Figure 10.7, dumps the information about a single graphics mode. The structure can be different sizes, depending on the version of the specification, so the size of the structure is necessary.

```
505 EFI_STATUS
506 GopDumpModeInfo (
507   IN CONST EFI_GRAPHICS_OUTPUT_MODE_INFORMATION *Info,
508   IN UINTN                                       InfoSize
509   )
510 {
511   if (Info == NULL ||
512       InfoSize < sizeof(EFI_GRAPHICS_OUTPUT_MODE_
  INFORMATION)) {
513     Print(L"No Mode Information\n");
514   } else {
515     Print(L"Resolution:          %d x %d pixels\n",
```

```
516        Info->HorizontalResolution,
517        Info->VerticalResolution);
518     Print(L"Scan Line Size:      %d pixels\n",
519        Info->PixelsPerScanLine);
520
521     Print(L"Pixel Format:           ");
522     switch(Info->PixelFormat) {
523       case PixelRedGreenBlueReserved8BitPerColor:
524         Print(L"RGBr\n");
525         break;
526
527       case PixelBlueGreenRedReserved8BitPerColor:
528         Print(L"BGRr\n");
529         break;
530
531       case PixelBitMask:
532         Print(L"Mask (R: %x, G: %x, B: %x, r: %x\n",
533           Info->PixelInformation.RedMask,
534           Info->PixelInformation.GreenMask,
535           Info->PixelInformation.BlueMask,
536           Info->PixelInformation.ReservedMask
537           );
538         break;
539
540       case PixelBltOnly:
541         Print(L"Blt Only\n");
542         break;
543
544       default:
545         Print(L"Unknown Format (%d)\n",
546           Info->PixelFormat);
547         break;
548     }
549   }
550
551   return SHELL_SUCCESS;
552 }
```

Figure 10.7   UEFI Graphics Device Information Display Application, Part 4

The INF (Component Description) File

The component description (.INF) file in Figure 10.8 describes information necessary for building the GopDump application. This is very similar to the HelloWorld example.

```
256   #/*++
553   #
554   #   Module Name:
555   #
556   #     GopDump.inf
557   #
558   #   Abstract:
559   #
560   #     Graphics device information dump utility.
561   #
562   --*/
563
564   [defines]
565   BASE_NAME              = GopDump
566   FILE_GUID              = 53b84969-af53-42ac-add9-f91d18f07936
567   COMPONENT_TYPE         = APPLICATION
568
569   [sources.common]
570     GopDump.c
571
572   [includes.common]
573     .
574     $(EDK_SOURCE)\Shell\UefiInclude
575     $(EDK_SOURCE)\Shell\UefiLibrary
576     $(EDK_SOURCE)\Foundation
577     $(EDK_SOURCE)\Foundation\Include
578     $(EDK_SOURCE)\Foundation\Include\IndustryStandard
579     $(EDK_SOURCE)\Foundation\Efi
580     $(EDK_SOURCE)\Foundation\Efi\Include
581     $(EDK_SOURCE)\Foundation\Framework\Include
582     $(DEST_DIR)\
583
584   [libraries.common]
585     UefiShellLib
```

```
586       EdkProtocolLib
587       EfiProtocolLib
588       EdkGuidLib
589       EfiGuidLib
590
591    [nmake.common]
592       IMAGE_ENTRY_POINT=EfiMain
```

Figure 10.8　Component Description File for the GopDump Application

GetKey Script Helper Application

This application is a common script helper application that reads a key and changes a specified environment variable. The application has the syntax:

```
getkey -?
getkey prompt-string env-var-name
```

The first usage causes GetKey to display the application's command-line syntax.

The second usage displays the string prompt-string and then waits for a key. If Ctrl-C is pressed, it exits with SHELL_ABORTED. Otherwise, a text representation of the key is placed in the environment variable env-var-name. Table 10.2 shows the text that is returned based on the key pressed.

Table 10.2 Text Representations of Keys Pressed

Key Pressed	Text
Printable Characters	The actual character (example: "A", "!")
Control Characters	"^" followed by the uppercase printable character. That is, Ctrl-A becomes ^A, Ctrl-Q becomes ^Q, and so on.
F1-F12	"f1" – "f12"
Escape	"esc"
Up Arrow	"up"
Down Arrow	"down"
Left Arrow	"left"
Right Arrow	"right"
Page Up	"pageup"
Page Down	"pagedown"
Insert	"insert"
Delete	"delete"
Home	"home"
End	"end"
Other Characters	"unknown"

This small application uses several UEFI Shell features. Many of the features are provided through two protocols (EFI_SHELL_PROTOCOL, EFI_SHELL_PARAMETERS_PROTOCOL) installed on the image handle of the application by the UEFI Shell prior to passing control to the application's entry point. This application illustrates:

■ Command-Line Processing. GetKey examines and processes command-line options. The EFI_SHELL_PARAMETERS_PROTOCOL describes the number of command-line arguments (Argc) and an array of pointers to the text for each argument (Argv). Any double quotation marks (") have been stripped. The first command-line option is always present and contains the volume, directory, and file name of the application itself (for example: fs0:\path\myapp.efi).

- Help Text. GetKey uses the built-in shell help support to handle the "-?" command-line option. Help text is provided in a separate file (GetKey.man) that is automatically located by the UEFI Shell when the `GetHelpText()` function is called.

- Console Input. GetKey reads console input from a user keyboard or a redirected file. Console input can be read as a key (using `ConIn` in the `EFI_SYSTEM_TABLE`) or as a file (using `StdIn` in the `EFI_SHELL_PARAMETERS_PROTOCOL`). GetKey waits for a key to be pressed using the `WaitForKey()` member of `ConIn` and then `ReadKeyStroke()` to get the key pressed.

- Execution Break Detection. GetKey detects when the user presses Ctrl-C and exits early by waiting for the `ExecutionBreak` member of the `EFI_SHELL_PROTOCOL` to be signaled.

- Environment Variables. GetKey changes the UEFI Shell's environment variables using the `SetEnv()` member of the `EFI_SHELL_PROTOCOL`. Since GetKey is designed for use inside of scripts, it only uses volatile environment variables.

Entry Point Source Code

The basics of the GetKey entry point, shown in Figure 10.9, are the same as the previous examples. The overall flow for the application can be broken into six steps:

1. Initialize the application
2. Parse the command-line options
3. Display the prompt string
4. Wait for the user to press a key
5. Convert the key to text
6. Change the environment variable.

```
256 EFI_APPLICATION_ENTRY_POINT (EfiMain);
593
594 EFI_STATUS
595 EfiMain (
596   IN EFI_HANDLE        ImageHandle,
597   IN EFI_SYSTEM_TABLE *SystemTable
598   )
599 {
600   EFI_STATUS    Status;
601   EFI_INPUT_KEY Key;
602
603   EFI_SHELL_APP_INIT (ImageHandle, SystemTable);
604
605   Status = ParseCommandLine();
606   if (Status != SHELL_SUCCESS || gHelpUsage) {
607     return Status;
608   }
609
610   Print(gPrompt);
611
612   Status = ReadKey(&Key);
613   if (!Status != SHELL_SUCCESS) {
614     Status = gSP->SetEnv(gEnvVar, ConvertKeyToText(&Key),
 TRUE);
615   }
616
617   Print(L"\n");
618   return Status;
619 }
```

Figure 10.9   GetKey Script Helper Application, Part 1

Line 12

The shell initialization library functions set up pointers to commonly used UEFI and UEFI Shell features, as described earlier in Table 10.1. References to standard external symbols, such as these pointers, are part of uefishelllib.h.

Lines 14–17

> When parsing the command line, there are three cases:
> - There was an error. Status returns with the error code.
> - The user asked for help using the -? syntax. The gHelpUsage variable is set to TRUE in this case.
> - The user specified a prompt string (gPrompt) and environment variable (gEnvVar).

Line 19

> Display the prompt string using the library function Print(). The cursor will be to the right of the last character in the prompt string.

Lines 21-22

> Wait for the user to press a key using ReadKey(). If the user presses Ctrl-C, then SHELL_ABORTED is returned and the program exits immediately. For all other keys, SHELL_SUCCESS is returned.

Line 23

> First, the keystroke is converted to a text representation using ConvertKey-ToText(). Then, the environment variable is changed.

Line 26

> Print out an extra carriage-return/line-feed so that the cursor will be on the next line.

The ParseCommandLine() Source Code

The ParseCommandLine() function shown in Figure 10.10 checks the command-line arguments for common usage errors and initializes the command-line related global variables.

```
620 CONST CHAR16 *gPrompt    = NULL;
621 CONST CHAR16 *gEnvVar    = NULL;
622 BOOLEAN       gHelpUsage = FALSE;
623
624 EFI_STATUS
625 ParseCommandLine(
626   VOID
627   )
628 {
629   if (gSPP->Argc < 3) {
630     Print(L"%s: too few command-line options\n", gSPP-
    >Argv[0]);
631     return SHELL_INVALID_PARAMETER;
632   }
633
634   if (gSPP->Argc == 2 && EfiStrCmp(gSPP->Argv[1],L"-?") == 0)
    {
635     CHAR16 *HelpText;
636
637     gSP->GetHelpText(L"GetKey", NULL, &HelpText);
638     Print(L"GetKey — Wait for key and put in environment
    var\n");
639     Print(HelpText);
640     gHelpUsage = TRUE;
641     return SHELL_SUCCESS;
642   }
643
644   gPrompt = gSPP->Argv[1];
645   gEnvVar = gSPP->Argv[2];
646   return SHELL_SUCCESS;
647 }
```

Figure 10.10 GetKey Script Helper Application, Part 2

Line 29

Global variable that holds the prompt string specified on the command line.

Line 30

Global variable that holds the environment variable name specified on the command line.

Line 31

Global variable that indicates whether the user wants help information.

Lines 38–41

Check to make sure that there are at least two arguments on the command line. If not, print an error and return an error.

Lines 43–52

If -? was specified, then print out the help text and then call the UEFI Shell to print out all of the help text for this command. Setting gHelpUsage tells the caller not to do anything more.

Lines 53–54

Copy the shell parameters into the global variables.

The ReadKey() Source Code

The ReadKey() function shown in Figure 10.11 waits for the user to either type in a key or press Ctrl-C. UEFI Shell applications can read input from standard input using two methods:

1. Polling. The application can poll for a key using the ReadKeyStroke() console input function.

2. Waiting. The application can pause and wait for a key using the UEFI Boot Services WaitForEvent() in combination with the WaitForKey console input event, which will be signaled when the user presses a key.

For more information on these console input features, see EFI_SIMPLE_TEXT_INPUT_PROTOCOL in the UEFI Specification, Chapter 11.

The UEFI Shell provides special handling for Ctrl-C. There are three ways a UEFI Shell application can detect that Ctrl-C was pressed by the user:

1. Many of the EFI_SHELL_PROTOCOL functions can return the status code SHELL_ABORTED, which indicates that Ctrl-C was detected during the function's execution.

2. The application can poll to see if Ctrl-C was detected by the UEFI Shell by using the UEFI Boot Service CheckEvent() in combination with the ExecutionBreak member of the EFI_SHELL_PROTOCOL. If CheckEvent() returns EFI_SUCCESS, then Ctrl-C has been pressed.

3. The application can wait for Ctrl-C to be pressed by using the UEFI Boot Service `WaitForEvent()` in combination with the ExecutionBreak member of the `EFI_SHELL_PROTOCOL`.

Since GetKey needs to monitor both user input and Ctrl-C, it uses `Wait-ForEvent()` for both `ExecutionBreak` and `WaitForKey` to simplify implementation.

```
648 EFI_STATUS
649 ReadKey(
650   IN EFI_INPUT_KEY *Key
651   )
652 {
653   EFI_STATUS      Status;
654   UINTN           EventIndex;
655   EFI_EVENT       Events[2];
656
657   Events[0] = gST->ConIn->WaitForKey;
658   Events[1] = gSP->ExecutionBreak;
659
660   Status = gBS->WaitForEvent(2, Events, &EventIndex);
661   if (EventIndex == 1 || Status != SHELL_SUCCESS) {
662     return SHELL_ABORTED;
663   }
664
665   return gST->ConIn->ReadKeyStroke(gST->ConIn,Key);
666 }
```

Figure 10.11   GetKey Script Helper Application, Part 3

Lines 57–60

This function returns back the key pressed in the `EFI_INPUT_KEY` structure, which is defined in the UEFI Specification, Chapter 11.

Lines 66–67

The Events array holds two `EFI_EVENT`s: one that indicates a normal key press and one that indicates an execution break with Ctrl-C.

Line 69

The UEFI Boot Service `WaitForEvent()` will wait until one or the other event is signaled and place the zero-based index into `EventIndex`.

Line 70–72

If there is an error or Ctrl-C is detected, return with `SHELL_ABORTED`.

Line 74

Otherwise, read the key and return.

The ConvertKeyToText() Source Code

The `ConvertKeyToText()` function shown in Figure 10.12 provides a text representation for a console keystroke. Console keystrokes are represented by the UEFI data structure `EFI_INPUT_KEY`, which describes three classes of valid keystrokes:

- Printable Unicode. Character values that can have a glyph associated with them. These all have character values greater than or equal to 32.

- Non-Printable Unicode. Character values that cannot have a glyph associated with them. Certain keystrokes (Backspace, Tab, Enter) are returned as non-printable Unicode.

- Special Keys. These include the function keys, Escape, the arrow keys, Page Up, Page Down, Home, End, Insert and Delete.

The `EFI_INPUT_KEY` structure has two members: `UnicodeChar` and `ScanCode`. If `UnicodeChar` is zero, then `ScanCode` describes the special key code. If `UnicodeChar` is non-zero, then it contains the printable or non-printable character.

```
667 CONST CHAR16 *KeyName[] = {
668    L"null",
669    L"up",      L"down",    L"right",   L"left",
670    L"home",    L"end",     L"insert",  L"delete",
671    L"pageup",  L"pagedown",
672    L"f1",      L"f2",      L"f3",      L"f4",
673    L"f5",      L"f6",      L"f7",      L"f8",
674    L"f9",      L"f10",     L"f11",     L"f12",
```

```
675   L"esc"
676 };
677
678 STATIC
679 CHAR16
680 KeyChar[3];
681
682 CONST CHAR16 *
683 ConvertKeyToText (
684   IN EFI_INPUT_KEY *Key
685   )
686 {
687   CONST CHAR16 *KeyStr;
688
689   if (Key->UnicodeChar == L'\00') {
690     if (Key->ScanCode >= sizeof(KeyName)/sizeof(KeyName[0]))
  {
691       KeyStr = L"unknown";
692     }
693     else {
694       KeyStr = KeyName[Key->ScanCode];
695     }
696   }
697   else if (Key->UnicodeChar < L' ') {
698     KeyChar[0] = L'^';
699     KeyChar[1] = Key->UnicodeChar + L'@';
700     KeyChar[2] = L'\00';
701     KeyStr = KeyChar;
702   }
703   else {
704     KeyChar[0] = Key->UnicodeChar;
705     KeyChar[1] = L'\00';
706     KeyStr = KeyChar;
707   }
708   return KeyStr;
709 }
```

Figure 10.12 GetKey Script Helper Application, Part 4

Lines 76–85

This array contains the names returned if the keystroke is a special key.

Lines 87–89

> This small array is used when returning Unicode keystrokes.

Lines 98–105

> If this is a special keystroke (UnicodeChar = 0), then use ScanCode as an index into the array of key names. If ScanCode is too large, return "unknown".

Lines 106–111

> If this is a non-printable character, then create a small string consisting of ^ and the character value shifted up to a capital letter character value.

Lines 112–116

> Otherwise, if this is printable, create a small string consisting of just the Unicode character value.

The INF (Component Description) File

The component description file for the GetKey application is shown in Figure 10.13.

```
256 #/*++
710 #
711 #   Module Name:
712 #
713 #      GetKey.inf
714 #
715 #   Abstract:
716 #
717 #   Display a prompt, get a key from the user and set an
718 #   enviroment variable with the result.
719 #
720 #
721 --*/
722
723 [defines]
724 BASE_NAME          = GetKey
725 FILE_GUID          = f4094ff7-bcd6-4466-a1d8-2d52bf296051
726 COMPONENT_TYPE     = APPLICATION
727
728 [sources.common]
```

```
729    GetKey.c
730
731 [includes.common]
732    .
733    $(EDK_SOURCE)\Shell\UefiInclude
734    $(EDK_SOURCE)\Shell\UefiLibrary
735    $(EDK_SOURCE)\Foundation
736    $(EDK_SOURCE)\Foundation\Include
737    $(EDK_SOURCE)\Foundation\Include\IndustryStandard
738    $(EDK_SOURCE)\Foundation\Efi
739    $(EDK_SOURCE)\Foundation\Efi\Include
740    $(EDK_SOURCE)\Foundation\Framework\Include
741    $(DEST_DIR)\
742
743 [libraries.common]
744    UefiShellLib
745    EdkProtocolLib
746    EfiProtocolLib
747    EdkGuidLib
748    EfiGuidLib
749
750
751 [nmake.common]
752    IMAGE_ENTRY_POINT=EfiMain
753
```

Figure 10.13   Component Description File for the GetKey Application

The MAN (Component Help) File

The file GetKey.man is a standard UEFI Shell help file. The help file is a text file with a title and zero or more sections. The title is specified by a line beginning with:

```
.TH command-name 0 "short-description"
```

Each section begins with a line:

```
.SH section-name
```

There are several standard section names, such as NAME, SYNOPIS, and
DESCRIPTION.   Others can be found in Appendix B of the UEFI Shell
specification. Figure 10.14 shows the help file for GetKey.

```
256 .TH GetKey 0 "Get user key into environment variable"
754
755 .SH NAME
756 GetKey
757 Prompt user, wait for a key, store key in environment vari-
able.
758
759 .SH SYNOPSIS
760 GetKey -?
761 GetKey prompt-string env-variable
762
763 .SH DESCRIPTION
764 GetKey displays the prompt string and waits for a user key-
press.
765 The user keypress is converted to a text string and stored
in the
766 environment variable env-variable.
767
768 The following table describes the conversion:
769
770 Key Pressed             Text
771 Printable Characters    The actual character (e.g. "A", "!")
772 Control Characters      "^" followed by upper-case character.
That
773                         is, Ctrl-A becomes ^A, Ctrl-Q becomes
^Q,
774                         and so on.
775 F1-F12                  "f1" - "f12"
776 Escape                  "esc"
777 Up Arrow                "up"
778 Down Arrow              "down"
779 Left Arrow              "left"
780 Right Arrow             "right"
781 Page Up                 "pageup"
782 Page Down               "pagedown"
783 Insert                  "insert"
784 Delete                  "delete"
785 Home                    "home"
```

```
786 End                       "end"
787 Other Characters          "unknown"
788
789 .SH OPTIONS
790 -?                        Display help.
791
792 .SH RETURN VALUES
793 0                           Success
794 SHELL_ABORTED              Ctrl-C detected
795 SHELL_INVALID_PARAMETER Invalid command-line arguments.
```

Figure 10.14   Component Help File for the GetKey Application

Line 1

> This is the help title. The name and the short description will be displayed at the top of each page of help.

Lines 3–5

> The name of the utility followed by a one-line summary.

Lines 7–9

> The usage summary for the utility.

Lines 11–35

> The description of the utility.

Lines 37–38

> The description of the different command-line options for the utility, one per line.

Lines 40–43

> The list of all possible exit values for the utility.

UniCodeDecode Sample Application

The UniCodeDecode application converts to and from ASCII and the Unicode UCS-2 encoded files. It supports explicit control by the user as to the file formats and also employs various forms of auto-detection, using either the Unicode-defined file marker or some heuristics.

The application has the syntax:

```
ucd -?
ucd input-file output-file [-a2u|-u2a]
```

This application demonstrates several key shell capabilities:

■ File Handling. This application shows how to create, open, and write files.

■ Command-Line Handling. This application shows more advanced command-line handling, including defaulting and error checking.

■ Help Text. This application shows how to use the built-in help text support.

■ Unicode. This application delves into some of the Unicode handling aspects of UEFI applications, including file markers. The UEFI specification uses Unicode's UCS-2 (little-endian) extensively. UCS-2 differs from UTF-16 in that it does not handle surrogate pairs. For more information, see www.unicode.org.

Entry Point Source Code

The entry point source code shown in Figure 10.15 performs the basic initialization and then walks through the four basic steps: parsing the command-line, opening the input and output files, converting the file, and then closing the files.

```
256 BOOLEAN       gHelpUsage = FALSE;
796 BOOLEAN       gAscii2Ucs = FALSE;
797 BOOLEAN       gUcs2Ascii = FALSE;
798
799 CONST CHAR16    *InputFileName = NULL;
800 CONST CHAR16    *OutputFileName = NULL;
801
```

```
802 EFI_APPLICATION_ENTRY_POINT (EfiMain);
803
804 EFI_STATUS
805 EfiMain (
806   IN EFI_HANDLE        ImageHandle,
807   IN EFI_SYSTEM_TABLE *SystemTable
808   )
809 {
810   EFI_STATUS     Status;
811
812   EFI_SHELL_APP_INIT (ImageHandle, SystemTable);
813
814   Status = ParseCommandLine();
815   if (Status != SHELL_SUCCESS || gHelpUsage) {
816     return Status;
817   }
818
819   Status = OpenFiles();
820   if (Status != SHELL_SUCCESS) {
821     return Status;
822   }
823
824   if (gAscii2Ucs) {
825     ConvertAsciiToUcs2();
826   }
827   else if (gUcs2Ascii) {
828     ConvertUcs2ToAscii();
829   }
830
831   Status = CloseFiles();
832   if (Status != SHELL_SUCCESS) {
833     return Status;
834   }
835
836   return SHELL_SUCCESS;
837 }
```

Figure 10.15   UniCodeDecode Application, Part 1

Lines 1–6

> These are global variables, set based on the command-line options, that control the flow of the program. They are initialized to default values.

Line 8–18

> This is the standard initialization code for UEFI Shell applications.

Line 20–23

> Here all of the command-line options are parsed into the global variables. Upon return, if there is an error *or* the user wants to view the help information, the application exits immediately.

Line 25–28

> The main body of the application opens the input file, converts the text, and writes it to the output file.

Parsing the Command Line

The startup code called by the EFI_SHELL_APP_INIT macro initializes the gSPP macro to point to the EFI_SHELL_PARAMETERS_PROTOCOL instance installed on the application's image handle. This protocol gives the handle of the standard input, standard output and standard error devices.

It also contains the number of command-line options and a pointer to the text of each option. The first option is always the full path and file name of the application itself. This is modeled after the C programming language's argv and argc parameters for main(). One difference is that all parameters are encoded using 16-bit Unicode (UCS-2) characters.

This section, shown in Figure 10.16, reads the command-line options and the file names and checks for errors.

```
838 EFI_STATUS
839 ParseCommandLine(
840   VOID
841   )
842 {
843   for (UINTN n = 1; n < gSPP->Argc; n++) {
844     if (gSPP->Argv[n][0] == L'-') {
845       if (EfiStrCmp(gSPP->Argv[n], L"-?") == 0) {
```

```
846            gHelpUsage = TRUE;
847          }
848        else if (EfiStrCmp(gSPP->Argv[n], L"a2u") == 0) {
849          gAscii2Ucs = TRUE;
850          gUcs2Ascii = FALSE;
851        }
852        else if (EfiStrCmp(gSPP->Argv[n], L"u2a") == 0) {
853          gAscii2Ucs = FALSE;
854          gUcs2Ascii = TRUE;
855        }
856        else {
857          Print(L"%s: unknown command-line argument '%s'\n",
858              gSPP->Argv[0], gSPP->Argv[n]);
859          return SHELL_INVALID_PARAMETER;
860        }
861      }
862      else if (InputFileName == NULL) {
863        InputFileName = gSPP->Argv[n];
864      }
865      else if (OutputFileName == NULL) {
866        OutputFileName = gSPP->Argv[n];
867      }
868      else {
869        Print(L"%s: unexpected command-line argument '%s'\n",
870            gSPP->Argv[0], gSPP->Argv[n]);
871        return SHELL_INVALID_PARAMETER;
872      }
873    }
874
875    if (gHelpUsage) {
876      CHAR16 *HelpText;
877
878      gSP->GetHelpText(L"Ucd", L"NAME", &HelpText);
879      Print(HelpText);
880      FreePool(HelpText);
881
882      gSP->GetHelpText(L"Ucd", L"SYNOPSIS", &HelpText);
883      Print(HelpText);
884      FreePool(HelpText);
885
886      gSP->GetHelpText(L"Ucd", L"DESCRIPTION", &HelpText);
887      Print(HelpText);
888      FreePool(HelpText);
```

```
889   }
890   else {
891     if (InputFileName == NULL) {
892       Print(L"%s: missing input file name\n", gSPP->Argv[0]);
893       return SHELL_INVALID_PARAMETER;
894     }
895     if (OutputFileName == NULL) {
896       Print(L"%s: missing output file name\n", gSPP-
>Argv[0]);
897       return SHELL_INVALID_PARAMETER;
898     }
899   }
900
901   return SHELL_SUCCESS;
902 }
```

Figure 10.16   UniCodeDecode Application, Part 2

Lines 44–49, 79

> To begin command-line processing, the function goes through all of the options, except option 0 (which is the application's path and file name).

Lines 50–67

> If the option begins with a "-" then the option should be one of the options -? (for help), -a2u (force ASCII to Unicode), or –u2a (force Unicode to ASCII). If it is one of these, the appropriate flag is set and processing continues to the next option. If it is not any of these, then an error is displayed and returned.

Lines 68–70

> If there is no "-" at the beginning of the option, it must be a file name of some sort. If no input file name has been discovered so far, then assign the current option's text to the input file name. At this point, we don't do any error checking on the file path/name itself. Instead, we'll leave that until we try to open the file.

Lines 71–73

> At this point, if no output file name has been discovered, then assign the current option's text to the output file name.

Lines 74–78

> Whoops! There was something more on the command-line that wasn't recognized, so generate an error and return.

Lines 81–95

> If the user requested help using -?, then this function uses the shell API function `GetHelpText()` to display the NAME, SYNOPSIS, and DESCRIPTION sections of the help text for this application. The shell automatically processes the manual (.MAN) file (described below) and gets the specified sections.

Lines 96–105

> If the user did not specify the -?, then the user must have specified both input and output file names. Otherwise, an error is generated.

Opening and Closing Files

This section, shown in Figure 10.17, demonstrates standard file activities, such as creating files, opening files, closing files and setting the file position.

```
903 EFI_FILE_HANDLE InputFileHandle = NULL;
904 EFI_FILE_HANDLE OutputFileHandle = NULL;
905
906 EFI_STATUS
907 OpenFiles(
908   VOID
909   )
910 {
911   EFI_STATUS Status;
912
913   Status = gSP->OpenFileByName(
914                   InputFileName,
915                   &InputFileHandle,
916                   EFI_FILE_MODE_READ
917                   );
918   if (Status != SHELL_SUCCESS) {
919     Print(L"%s: unable to open input file %s\n",
920       gSPP->Argv[0],
921       InputFileName
922       );
```

```
923    return SHELL_INVALID_PARAMETER;
924  }
925
926  if (!gAscii2Ucs2 && !gUcs2Ascii) {
927    CHAR16 ch;
928    UINTN  sch = sizeof(ch);
929
930    Status = gSP->ReadFile(InputFileHandle, &sch, &ch);
931    if (Status != SHELL_SUCCESS) {
932      Print(L"%s: unable to read from input file\n",
933        gSPP->Argv[0]);
934      gSP->CloseFile(InputFileHandle);
935      return SHELL_INVALID_PARAMETER;
936    }
937    gSP->SetFilePosition(InputFileHandle, 0);
938
939    if (ch == UNICODE_BYTE_ORDER_CHAR ||
940        ch == UNICODE_ZERO_WIDTH_NON_BREAKING_SPACE) {
941      gUcs2Ascii = TRUE;
942    }
943    else if (ch & 0xFF00 == 0 ||
944             ch & 0xFF == 0) {
945      gUcs2Ascii = TRUE;
946    }
947    else {
948      gAscii2Ucs2 = TRUE;
949    }
950  }
951
952  Status = gSP->OpenFileByName(
953                 OutputFileName,
954                 &OutputFileHandle,
955                 EFI_FILE_MODE_CREATE|EFI_FILE_MODE_WRITE
956                 );
957  if (Status != SHELL_SUCCESS) {
958    Print(L"%s: unable to open output file %s\n",
959      gSPP->Argv[0],
960      OutputFileName
961      );
962    gSP->CloseFile(InputFileHandle);
963    return SHELL_INVALID_PARAMETER;
964  }
965
```

```
966   return SHELL_SUCCESS;
967 }
968
969 EFI_STATUS
970 CloseFiles(
971   VOID
972   )
973 {
974   EFI_STATUS Status;
975
976   Status = gSP->CloseFile(InputFileHandle);
977   if (Status != SHELL_SUCCESS) {
978     return SHELL_DEVICE_ERROR;
979   }
980
981   Status = gSP->CloseFile(OutputFileHandle);
982   if (Status != SHELL_SUCCESS) {
983     return SHELL_DEVICE_ERROR;
984   }
985
986   return SHELL_SUCCESS;
987 }
```

Figure 10.17 UniCodeDecode Application, Part 3

Lines 119–130

> Opens the input file for reading and saves the handle for later usage. If the file
> can't be opened, display an error.

Lines 132–156

> If the user didn't explicitly specify whether to do ASCII-to-Unicode or
> Unicode-to-ASCII conversion, try to auto-detect by reading the first two
> bytes of the input file. If it is the Unicode byte-order mark, convert from
> Unicode-to-ASCII. If either byte is a zero, then convert from Unicode-to-
> ASCII. Otherwise, assume it must be ASCII to Unicode. After reading the
> two bytes, reset the file position to the start of the file.

Lines 158–170

> Creates the output file and opens it for writing, saving the handle for later usage. If the file can't be created, close the input file and display an error. If EFI_FILE_MODE_CREATE is not specified, then the file must already exist.

Lines 175–193

> When closing files, just call CloseFiles() twice, once with each handle.

Convert to/from Unicode

These functions, shown in Figure 10.18, use a very simple algorithm, reading one character at a time from the input file, converting it, and then writing the converted character to the output file. The GetFileSize() function returns the file's entire size and ReadFile() and WriteFile() write n characters to the specified file.

In general, the translation between the two character sets is straightforward, since the first 256 characters in the UCS-2 (and UTF-16) Unicode character sets match those in the ISO-Latin-1 ASCII character set. However, there are a several places where there is more than one Unicode character value that can be translated to a single ASCII character. In particular, the small and wide forms of letters and punctuation.

```
988  VOID
989  ConvertAsciiToUcs2(
990    VOID
991    )
992  {
993    EFI_STATUS Status;
994    UINT64     FileSize;
995    CHAR8      ch;
996    CHAR16     uch;
997    UINTN      ReadSize;
998    UINTN      WriteSize;
999
1000   Status = gSP->GetFileSize(InputFileHandle, &FileSize);
1001   if (Status != SHELL_SUCCESS || FileSize == 0) {
1002     Print(L"%s: unable to get input file size\n", gSPP->Argv[0]);
1003     return;
```

```
1004  }
1005
1006  do {
1007    ReadSize = sizeof(ch);
1008    Status = gSP->ReadFile(InputFileHandle, &ReadSize, &ch);
1009    if (Status != SHELL_SUCCESS) {
1010      Print(L"%s: trouble reading from input file\n",
1011        gSPP->Argv[0]);
1012      return;
1013    }
1014
1015    uch = ch;
1016    WriteSize = sizeof(uch);
1017    Status = gSP->WriteFile(OutputFileHandle, &WriteSize, &uch);
1018    if (Status != SHELL_SUCCESS) {
1019      Print(L"%s: trouble writing to output file\n",
1020        gSPP->Argv[0]);
1021      return;
1022    }
1023
1024    FileSize -= ReadSize;
1025  } while (FileSize > 0);
1026 }
1027
1028 VOID
1029 ConvertUcs2ToAscii(
1030   VOID
1031   )
1032 {
1033   EFI_STATUS  Status;
1034   UINT64      FileSize;
1035   CHAR8       ch;
1036   CHAR16      uch;
1037   UINTN       ReadSize;
1038   UINTN       WriteSize;
1039
1040   Status = gSP->GetFileSize(InputFileHandle, &FileSize);
1041   if (Status != SHELL_SUCCESS || FileSize == 0) {
1042     Print(L"%s: unable to get input file size\n", gSPP->Argv[0]);
1043     return;
1044   }
1045
1046   do {
```

```
1047    ReadSize = sizeof(uch);
1048    Status = gSP->ReadFile(InputFileHandle, &ReadSize, &uch);
1049    if (Status != SHELL_SUCCESS) {
1050      Print(L"%s: trouble reading from input file\n",
1051        gSPP->Argv[0]);
1052      return;
1053    }
1054
1055    switch (uch) {
1056    case UNICODE_FULLWIDTH_CENT_SIGN:            ch = 0xa2; break;
1057    case UNICODE_FULLWIDTH_POUND_SIGN:           ch = 0xa3; break;
1058    case UNICODE_FULLWIDTH_NOT_SIGN:             ch = 0xac; break;
1059    case UNICODE_FULLWIDTH_MACRON:               ch = 0xaf; break;
1060    case UNICODE_FULLWIDTH_BROKEN_BAR:           ch = 0xa6; break;
1061    case UNICODE_FULLWIDTH_YEN_SIGN:             ch = 0xa5; break;
1062
1063    case UNICODE_SMALL_COMMA:                    ch = ','; break;
1064    case UNICODE_SMALL_FULL_STOP:                ch = '.'; break;
1065    case UNICODE_SMALL_SEMICOLON:                ch = ';'; break;
1066    case UNICODE_SMALL_COLON:                    ch = ':'; break;
1067    case UNICODE_SMALL_QUESTION_MARK:            ch = '?'; break;
1068    case UNICODE_SMALL_EXCLAMATION_MARK:         ch = '!'; break;
1069    case UNICODE_SMALL_LEFT_PARENTHESIS:         ch = '('; break;
1070    case UNICODE_SMALL_RIGHT_PARENTHESIS:        ch = ')'; break;
1071    case UNICODE_SMALL_LEFT_CURLY_BRACKET:       ch = '{'; break;
1072    case UNICODE_SMALL_RIGHT_CURLY_BRACKET:      ch = '}'; break;
1073    case UNICODE_SMALL_NUMBER_SIGN:              ch = '#'; break;
1074    case UNICODE_SMALL_AMPERSAND:                ch = '&'; break;
1075    case UNICODE_SMALL_ASTERISK:                 ch = '*'; break;
1076    case UNICODE_SMALL_PLUS_SIGN:                ch = '+'; break;
1077    case UNICODE_SMALL_HYPHEN_MINUS:             ch = '-'; break;
1078    case UNICODE_SMALL_LESS_THAN_SIGN:           ch = '<'; break;
1079    case UNICODE_SMALL_GREATER_THAN_SIGN:        ch = '>'; break;
1080    case UNICODE_SMALL_EQUALS_SIGN:              ch = '='; break;
1081    case UNICODE_SMALL_REVERSE_SOLIDUS:          ch = '\\'; break;
1082    case UNICODE_SMALL_DOLLAR_SIGN:              ch = '$'; break;
1083    case UNICODE_SMALL_PERCENT_SIGN:             ch = '%'; break;
1084    case UNICODE_SMALL_COMMERCIAL_AT:            ch = '@'; break;
1085
1086    case UNICODE_ZERO_WIDTH_NON_BREAKING_SPACE: continue;
1087    case UNICODE_BYTE_ORDER_CHAR:                continue;
1088
1089    default:
```

```
1090        if (uch > 0xff00 && uch < 0xff5f) {
1091          ch = (CHAR8) ((uch & 0xff) + ' ');
1092        }
1093        else if (uch < 0x100) {
1094          ch = (uch & 0xff);
1095        }
1096        else {
1097          ch = '?';
1098        }
1099        break;
1100      }
1101
1102      WriteSize = sizeof(ch);
1103      Status = gSP->WriteFile(OutputFileHandle, &WriteSize, &ch);
1104      if (Status != SHELL_SUCCESS) {
1105        Print(L"%s: trouble writing to output file\n",
1106          gSPP->Argv[0]);
1107        return;
1108      }
1109
1110      FileSize -= ReadSize;
1111    } while (FileSize > 0);
1112 }
```

Figure 10.18 UniCodeDecode Application, Part 4

Lines 206–210, 246–250

> Get the file size using GetFileSize(). If the file size can't be read or the file size is zero, exit with an error message.

Lines 212–219, 252–259

> Read a single character using ReadFile().

Line 221

> Convert the character from ASCII to UCS-2 by zero-extending to 16-bits.

Lines 261–306

> Convert the character from UCS-2 to ASCII. Except for some exceptional characters, just trim off the upper 8 bits. However, if there is no 1-to-1 conversion, substitute the "?" character instead.

Lines 222–228, 308–314

Write a single character using WriteFile().

Lines 230–231, 316–317

Keep reading until there is no space left.

INF File

Figure 10.19 shows the component description file (INF) for the UniCodeDecode utility.

```
 256 #/*++
1113#
1114#  Module Name:
1115#
1116#    UniCodeDecode.inf
1117#
1118#  Abstract:
1119#
1120#    Convert file to/from ASCII, UCS-2
1121#
1122#
1123#--*/
1124
1125[defines]
1126BASE_NAME            = Ucd
1127   FILE_GUID          = 498c2e0b-6f05-4158-89e5-a2ec57cb8a36
1128   COMPONENT_TYPE     = APPLICATION
1129
1130[sources.common]
1131   UniCodeDecode.c
1132
1133[includes.common]
1134   .
1135   $(EDK_SOURCE)\Shell\UefiInclude
1136   $(EDK_SOURCE)\Shell\UefiLibrary
1137   $(EDK_SOURCE)\Foundation
1138   $(EDK_SOURCE)\Foundation\Include
1139   $(EDK_SOURCE)\Foundation\Include\IndustryStandard
1140   $(EDK_SOURCE)\Foundation\Efi
1141   $(EDK_SOURCE)\Foundation\Efi\Include
```

```
1142    $(EDK_SOURCE)\Foundation\Framework\Include
1143    $(DEST_DIR)\
1144
1145 [libraries.common]
1146    UefiShellLib
1147    EdkProtocolLib
1148    EfiProtocolLib
1149    EdkGuidLib
1150    EfiGuidLib
1151
1152
1153 [nmake.common]
1154    IMAGE_ENTRY_POINT=EfiMain
```

Figure 10.19   Component Description File for the UniCodeDecode Application

Math Script Helper Application

The math helper application is used by scripts to calculate the result of a mathematical expression on the command line and output it to standard output. The syntax is:

```
math -?
math expression
```

Currently expression only handles decimal integers and the four basic operators (*, /, +, -), but it does handle operator precedence correctly. Other operators could be easily added.

Entry Point Source Code

Figure 10.20 shows the entry point source code for the Math script helper application.

```
256 BOOLEAN gHelpUsage = FALSE;
1155
1156 VOID
1157 DisplayHelp()
1158 {
```

```
1159   CHAR16 *HelpText;
1160
1161   gSP->GetHelpText(L"Math", NULL, &HelpText);
1162   Print(L"Math - Display math operation on the command-line\n");
1163   Print(HelpText);
1164   gHelpUsage = TRUE;
1165 }
1166
1167 EFI_STATUS
1168 ParseExpr(
1169   INT32   Parm,
1170   UINT64 *Result
1171   );
1172
1173 EFI_APPLICATION_ENTRY_POINT (EfiMain);
1174
1175 EFI_STATUS
1176 EfiMain (
1177   IN EFI_HANDLE       ImageHandle,
1178   IN EFI_SYSTEM_TABLE *SystemTable
1179   )
1180 {
1181   EFI_STATUS    Status;
1182   UINT64        Result;
1183   UINTN         n;
1184
1185   EFI_SHELL_APP_INIT (ImageHandle, SystemTable);
1186
1187   for (n = 1; n < gSPP->Argc; n++) {
1188     if (gSPP->Argv[n][0] == L'-') {
1189       if (EfiStrCmp(gSPP->Argv[n], L"-?") == 0) {
1190         gHelpUsage = TRUE;
1191       }
1192       else {
1193         Print(L"%s: unknown command-line argument '%s'\n",
1194             gSPP->Argv[0], gSPP->Argv[n]);
1195         return SHELL_INVALID_PARAMETER;
1196       }
1197     }
1198   }
1199   if (gHelpUsage) {
1200     DisplayHelp();
1201     return SHELL_SUCCESS;
```

```
1202  }
1203
1204  Status = ParseExpr(1, &Result);
1205  if (Status == SHELL_SUCCESS) {
1206    Print(L"%d", Result);
1207  }
1208
1209  return Status;
1210 }
```

Figure 10.20   Math Script Helper Application, Part 1

Lines 14–18

> This utility uses a very simple recursive descent expression parser with opera-
> tor precedence. It assumes that all of the operators and operands are separated
> by whitespace, thus making them into separate command-line options.

Lines 34–45

> This utility uses very simple command-line processing in order to see whether
> -? is specified.

Lines 46–49

> If -? is specified, then `DisplayHelp()` displays the help text and exits.

Lines 51–54

> Starting with the first parameter, start the process of parsing the command
> line into operands. If there is no error, then print the result.

Expression Handling Source Code

The code in Figure 10.21 is the code that actually processes through the different command-line arguments, evaluating them either as a number or as an
operator.

```
1211 EFI_STATUS
1212 ParseExprTerm(
1213   IN  INT32  Parameter,
1214   OUT UINT64 *Result
1215   )
1216 {
1217   if (gSPP->Argc > (UINTN) Parameter) {
1218     return EfiStringToValue(Result, gSpp->Argv[Parameter], NULL);
1219   }
1220   return SHELL_INVALID_PARAMETER;
1221 }
1222
1223 EFI_STATUS
1224 ParseExpr1(
1225   IN  INT32  Parameter,
1226   OUT UINT64 *Result
1227   )
1228 {
1229   EFI_STATUS Status;
1230   UINT64     Left;
1231   UINT64     Right;
1232
1233   Status = ParseExprTerm(Parameter, &Left);
1234   if (Status != SHELL_SUCCESS) {
1235     return Status;
1236   }
1237
1238   if (gSPP->Argc > )UINTN) Parameter + 2) {
1239     if (EfiStrCmp(gSPP->Argv[Parameter + 1], L"*") == 0) {
1240       Status = ParseExpr1(Parameter + 2, &Right);
1241       if (Status != SHELL_SUCCESS) {
1242         return Status;
1243       }
1244       *Result = Left * Right;
1245       return SHELL_SUCCESS;
1246     }
1247     else if (EfiStrCmp(gSPP->Argv[Parameter + 1], L"/") == 0) {
1248       Status = ParseExpr1(Parameter + 2, &Right);
1249       if (Status != SHELL_SUCCES) {
1250         return Status;
1251       }
1252       if (Right == 0) {
```

```
1253           return EFI_INVALID_PARAMETER;
1254       }
1255
1256     *Result = Left / Right;
1257       return SHELL_SUCCESS;
1258   }
1259 }
1260
1261   *Result = Left;
1262   return SHELL_SUCCESS;
1263 }
1264
1265 EFI_STATUS
1266 ParseExpr(
1267   IN   INT32  Parameter,
1268   OUT UINT64 *Result
1269   )
1270 {
1271   EFI_STATUS Status;
1272   UINT64     Left;
1273   UINT64     Right;
1274
1275   Status = ParseExpr1(Parameter, &Left);
1276   if (Status != SHELL_SUCCESS) {
1277     return Status;
1278   }
1279
1280   if (gSPP->Argc > (UINTN) Parameter + 2) {
1281     if (EfiStrCmp(gSPP->Argv[Parameter + 1], L"+") == 0) {
1282       Status = ParseExpr(Parameter + 2, &Right);
1283       if (Status != SHELL_SUCCESS) {
1284         return Status;
1285       }
1286       *Result = Left + Right;
1287       return SHELL_SUCCESS;
1288     }
1289     else if (EfiStrCmp(gSPP->Argv[Parameter + 1], L"-") == 0) {
1290       Status = ParseExpr(Parameter + 2, &Right);
1291       if (Status != SHELL_SUCCESS) {
1292         return Status;
1293       }
1294       *Result = Left - Right;
1295       return SHELL_SUCCESS;
```

```
1296     }
1297   }
1298
1299   *Result = Left;
1300   return SHELL_SUCCESS;
1301 }
```

Figure 10.21   Math Script Helper Application, Part 2

Lines 58–68

> This function parses integers. There is no environment variable handling, since the shell will have expanded them all prior to calling the utility entry point. If it is not an integer at this point, then it must be an error.

Lines 76–109

> This function handles the multiplication "*" and division "/" operations. First, it calls to `ParseExprTerm()` to get the integers, then checks for the operator and, if it finds one, handles the right side of the expression by recursively calling itself. If neither * nor / are found, then the `ParseExprTerm()` value is passed back.

Lines 118–147

> This function handles the addition "+" and subtraction "-" operations. First it calls to `ParseExpr1()` to handle higher-priority operators, then checks for an operator and, if it finds one, handles the right side of the expression by recursively calling itself. If neither * nor / are found, then the `ParseExpr1()` value is passed back.

Setting Up the Build Environment

The standard build environment recommended here is used for building individual applications, which can then later be integrated into a master EDK build as necessary. In order to do that:

1. Set the EDK_SOURCE environment variable to wherever the EDK was installed on your system (for example: C:\EDK)

2. Set the PROCESSOR environment variable to the processor target (such as Ia32, X64, Ia64)

App.Dsc

The App.Dsc file shown in Figure 10.22 is the common build directory for all of the applications in this chapter. It is not attached to specific build platform, but rather generates standalone shell applications. It goes in $(EDK_SOURCE)\Sample\Platform\App.

```
256 #/*++
1302#
1303#  Module Name:
1304#
1305#    App.dsc
1306#
1307#  Abstract:
1308#
1309#    Simple build file for UEFI Shell applications.
1310#
1311#--*/
1312
1313
1314[defines]
1315PLATFORM                 = $(PROJECT_NAME)
1316
1317!include "$(EDK_SOURCE)\Sample\Platform\Common.dsc"
1318!include "$(EDK_SOURCE)\Sample\Platform\Common$(PROCESSOR).dsc"
1319
1320[libraries]
1321DEFINE EDK_PREFIX=
1322
1323!include "$(EDK_SOURCE)\Sample\Platform\EdkLibAll.dsc"
1324
1325[libraries.platform]
1326Shell\UefiLibrary\UefiShellLib.inf
1327
1328[components]
1329DEFINE PACKAGE=Default
1330Sample\App\HelloWorld\HelloWorld.inf FV=NULL
1331Samplc\App\GopDump\GopDump.inf FV=NULL
1332Sample\App\GetKey\GetKey.inf FV=NULL
1333Sample\App\UniCodeDecode\UniCodeDecode.inf FV=NULL
```

Figure 10.22 Common Build Directory for Chapter 10 Sample Applications

Chapter 11

Managing UEFI Drivers Using the Shell

He has half the deed done who has made a beginning.

—Horace

Several UEFI Shell commands can be used to help debug UEFI drivers. These UEFI Shell commands are already documented in the UEFI 2.0 Shell Specification, so the full capabilities of the UEFI Shell commands are not discussed here. There is also a built-in UEFI Shell command called `help` that provides a detailed description of an UEFI Shell command. Figure 11.1 below shows the results of issuing the "help –b" command.

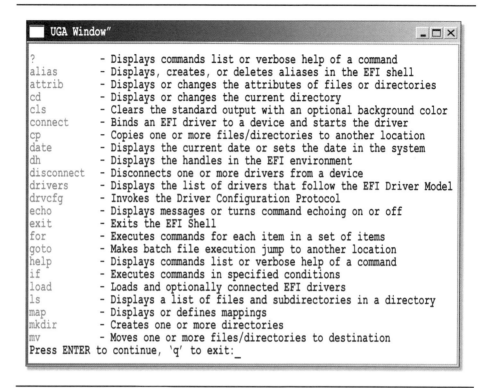

```
UGA Window"                                                    _ □ ×
?               - Displays commands list or verbose help of a command
alias           - Displays, creates, or deletes aliases in the EFI shell
attrib          - Displays or changes the attributes of files or directories
cd              - Displays or changes the current directory
cls             - Clears the standard output with an optional background color
connect         - Binds an EFI driver to a device and starts the driver
cp              - Copies one or more files/directories to another location
date            - Displays the current date or sets the date in the system
dh              - Displays the handles in the EFI environment
disconnect      - Disconnects one or more drivers from a device
drivers         - Displays the list of drivers that follow the EFI Driver Model
drvcfg          - Invokes the Driver Configuration Protocol
echo            - Displays messages or turns command echoing on or off
exit            - Exits the EFI Shell
for             - Executes commands for each item in a set of items
goto            - Makes batch file execution jump to another location
help            - Displays commands list or verbose help of a command
if              - Executes commands in specified conditions
load            - Loads and optionally connected EFI drivers
ls              - Displays a list of files and subdirectories in a directory
map             - Displays or defines mappings
mkdir           - Creates one or more directories
mv              - Moves one or more files/directories to destination
Press ENTER to continue, 'q' to exit:_
```

Figure 11.1 The help –b Command

Testing Specific Protocols

Table 11.1 lists UEFI Shell commands that can be used to test and debug UEFI drivers along with the protocol and/or service exercised.

Table 11.1. UEFI Shell Commands

Command	Protocol Tested	Service Tested
Load −nc		DriverEntryPoint Supported()
Load		DriverEntryPoint
	Driver Binding	Supported()
	Driver Binding	Start()
Unload	Loaded Image	Unload()
Connect	Driver Binding	Supported()
	Driver Binding	Start()
Disconnect	Driver Binding	Stop()
Reconnect	Driver Binding	Supported()
	Driver Binding	Start()
	Driver Binding	Stop()
Drivers	Component Name	GetDriverName()
Devices	Component Name	GetDriverName()
	Component Name	GetControllerName()
DevTree	Component Name	GetControllerName()
Dh −d	Component Name	GetDriverName()
	Component Name	GetControllerName()
DrvCfg −s	Driver Configuration	SetOptions()
DrvCfg −f	Driver Configuration	ForceDefaults()
DrvCfg −v	Driver Configuration	OptionsValid()
DrvDiag	Driver Diagnostics	RunDiagnostics()

Other tests can be performed from within the UEFI Shell, as listed in Table 11.2. These are not testing a specific protocol, but are testing for other coding practices.

Table 11.2 Other Shell Testing Procedures

Shell Command sequence	What it tests
Shell> Memmap Shell> Dh Shell> Load DriverName.efi Shell> Memmap Shell> Dh Shell> Unload DriverHandle Shell> Memmap Shell> Dh	Tests for incorrectly matched up `DriverEntryPoint` and `Unload()` functions. This will catch memory allocation that is not unallocated, protocols that are installed and not uninstalled, and so on.
Shell> Memmap Shell> Connect DeviceHandle DriverHandle Shell> Memmap Shell> Disconnect DeviceHandle DriverHandle Shell> Memmap Shell> Reconnect DeviceHandle Shell> Memmap	Tests for incorrectly matched up DriverBinding `Start()` and `Stop()` functions. This will catch memory allocation that is not unallocated.
Shell> dh Shell> Connect DeviceHandle DriverHandle Shell> dh Shell> Disconnect DeviceHandle DriverHandle Shell> dh Shell> Reconnect DeviceHandle Shell> dh	Tests for incorrectly matched up *DriverBinding* `Start()` and `Stop()` functions. This will catch protocols that are installed and not uninstalled.
Shell> OpenInfo DeviceHandle Shell> Connect DeviceHandle DriverHandle Shell> OpenInfo DeviceHandle Shell> Disconnect DeviceHandle DriverHandle Shell> OpenInfo DeviceHandle Shell> Reconnect DeviceHandle Shell> OpenInfo DeviceHandle	Tests for incorrectly matched up DriverBinding `Start()` and `Stop()` functions. This will catch protocols that are opened and not closed.

Loading and Unloading UEFI Drivers

Two UEFI Shell commands are available to load and start UEFI drivers, Load and LoadPciRom. The UEFI Shell command that can be used to unload an UEFI driver if it is unloadable is Unload.

Load

The `Load` command loads an UEFI driver from a file. UEFI driver files typically have an extension of .efi. This command has one important option, the `-nc` ("No Connect") option, for UEFI driver developers. When the `Load` command is used without the `-nc` option, the loaded driver is automatically connected to any devices in the system that it is able to manage. This means that the UEFI driver's entry point is executed and then the EFI Boot Service `ConnectController()` is called. If the UEFI driver produces the Driver Binding Protocol in the driver's entry point, then the `ConnectController()` call exercises the `Supported()` and `Start()` services of Driver Binding Protocol that was produced.

If the `-nc` option is used with the `Load` command, then this automatic connect operation is not performed. Instead, only the UEFI driver's entry point is executed. When the `-nc` option is used, the UEFI Shell command `Connect` can be used to connect the UEFI driver to any devices in the system that it is able to manage. The `Load` command can also take wild cards, so multiple UEFI drivers can be loaded at the same time.

The following are some examples of the `Load` command.

Example 1 loads and does not connect the UEFI driver image `EfiDriver.efi`. This example exercises only the UEFI driver's entry point:

```
fs0:> Load -nc EfiDriver.efi
```

Example 2 loads and connects the UEFI driver image called `EfiDriver.efi`. This example exercises the UEFI driver's entry point and the `Supported()` and `Start()` functions of the Driver Binding Protocol:

```
fs0:> Load EfiDriver.efi
```

Example 3 loads and connects all the UEFI drivers with an `.efi` extension from `fs0:`, exercising the UEFI driver entry points and their `Supported()` and `Start()` functions of the Driver Binding Protocol:

```
fs0:> Load *.efi
```

LoadPciRom

The LoadPciRom command simulates the load of a PCI option ROM by the PCI bus driver. This command parses a ROM image that was produced with the EfiRom build utility. Details on the EfiRom build utility can be found at www.tianocore.org. The LoadPciRom command finds all the UEFI drivers in the ROM image and attempts to load and start all the UEFI drivers. This command helps test the ROM image before it is burned into a PCI adapter's ROM. No automatic connects are performed by this command, so only the UEFI driver's entry point is exercised by this command. The UEFI Shell command Connect must be used for the loaded UEFI drivers to start managing devices. The example below loads and calls the entry point of all the UEFI drivers in the ROM file called MyAdapter.ROM:

```
fs0:> LoadPciRom MyAdapter.ROM
```

Unload

The Unload command unloads an UEFI driver if it is unloadable. This command takes a single argument that is the image handle number of the UEFI driver to unload. The Dh -p Image command and the Drivers command can be used to search for the image handle of the driver to unload. Once the image handle number is known, an unload operation can be attempted. The Unload command may fail for one of the following two reasons:

1. The UEFI driver may not be unloadable, because UEFI drivers are not required to be unloadable.

2. The UEFI driver might be unloadable, but it may not be able to be unloaded right now.

Some UEFI drivers may need to be disconnected before they are unloaded. They can be disconnected with the Disconnect command. The following example unloads the UEFI driver on handle 27. If the UEFI driver on handle 27 is unloadable, it will have registered an Unload() function in its Loaded Image Protocol. This command exercises the UEFI driver's Unload() function.

```
Shell> Unload 27
```

Connecting UEFI Drivers

Three UEFI Shell commands can be used to test the connecting of UEFI drivers to devices: Connect, Disconnect, and Reconnect. These commands have many options. A few are described in the following sections.

Connect

The `Connect` command can be used to connect all UEFI drivers to all devices in the system or connect UEFI drivers to a single device. The following are some examples of the `Connect` command.

Example 1 connects all drivers to all devices:

```
fs0:> Connect -r
```

Example 2 connects all drivers to the device that is abstracted by handle 23:

```
fs0:> Connect 23
```

Example 3 connects the UEFI driver on handle 27 to the device that is abstracted by handle 23:

```
fs0:> Connect 23 27
```

Disconnect

The `Disconnect` command stops UEFI drivers from managing a device. The following are some examples of the `Disconnect` command.

Example 1 disconnects all drivers from all devices. However, the use of this command is not recommended, because it also disconnects all the console devices.

```
fs0:> Disconnect -r
```

Example 2 disconnects all the UEFI drivers from the device represented by handle 23:

```
fs0:> Disconnect 23
```

Example 3 disconnects the UEFI driver on handle 27 from the device represented by handle 23:

```
fs0:> Disconnect 23 27
```

Example 4 destroys the child represented by handle 32. The UEFI driver on handle 27 produced the child when it started managing the device on handle 23.

```
fs0:> Disconnect 23 27 32
```

Reconnect

The `Reconnect` command is the equivalent of executing the `Disconnect` and `Connect` commands back to back. The `Reconnect` command is the best command for testing the Driver Binding Protocol of UEFI drivers. This command tests the `Supported()`, `Start()`, and `Stop()` services of the Driver Binding Protocol. The `Reconnect -r` command tests the Driver Binding Protocol for every UEFI driver that follows the UEFI Driver Model. Use this command before an UEFI driver is loaded to verify that the current set of drivers pass the `Reconnect -r` test, and then load the new UEFI driver and rerun the `Reconnect -r` test. An UEFI driver is not complete until it passes this interoperability test with the UEFI core and the full set of UEFI drivers. The following are some examples of the `Reconnect` command.

Example 1 reconnects all the UEFI drivers to the device handle 23:

```
fs0:> Reconnect 23
```

Example 2 reconnects the UEFI driver on handle 27 to the device on handle 23:

```
fs0:> Reconnect 23 27
```

Example 3 reconnects all the UEFI drivers in the system:

```
fs0:> Reconnect -r
```

Driver and Device Information

Five UEFI Shell commands can be used to dump information about the UEFI drivers that follow the UEFI Driver Model. Each of these commands shows information from a slightly different perspective.

Drivers

The `Drivers` command lists all the UEFI drivers that follow the UEFI Driver Model. It uses the `GetDriverName()` service of the Component Name protocol to retrieve the human-readable name of each UEFI driver if it is available. It also shows the file path from which the UEFI driver was loaded. As UEFI drivers are loaded with the `Load` command, they will appear in the list of drivers produced by the `Drivers` command. The `Drivers` command can also show the name of the UEFI driver in different languages. The following are some examples of the `Drivers` command.

Example 1 shows the `Drivers` command being used to list the UEFI drivers in the default language:

```
fs0:> Drivers
```

Example 2 shows the driver names in Spanish:

```
fs0:> Drivers -lspa
```

Devices

The `Devices` command lists all the devices that are being managed or produced by UEFI drivers that follow the UEFI Driver Model. This command uses the `GetControllerName()` service of the Component Name protocol to retrieve the human-readable name of each device that is being managed or produced by UEFI drivers. If a human-readable name is not available, then the EFI device path is used. The following are some examples of the `Devices` command.

Example 1 shows the `Devices` command being used to list the UEFI drivers in the default language:

```
fs0:> Devices
```

Example 2 shows the device names in Spanish:

```
fs0:> Devices -lspa
```

DevTree

Similar to the `Devices` command. the `DevTree` command lists all the devices being managed by UEFI drivers that follow the UEFI Driver Model. This command uses the `GetControllerName()` service of the Component Name Protocol to retrieve the human-readable name of each device that is being managed or produced by UEFI drivers. If the human-readable name is not available, then the EFI device path is used. This command also shows the parent/child relationships between all of the devices visually by displaying them in a tree structure. The lower a device is in the tree of devices, the more the device name is indented. The following are some examples of the `DevTree` command.

Example 1 displays the device tree with the device names in the default language:

```
fs0:> DevTree
```

Example 2 displays the device tree with the device names in Spanish:

```
fs0:> DevTree -lspa
```

Example 3 displays the device tree with the device names shown as EFI device paths:

```
fs0:> DevTree -d
```

Dh –d

The `Dh -d` command provides a more detailed view of a single driver or a single device than the `Drivers`, `Devices`, and `DevTree` commands. If a driver binding handle is used with the `Dh -d` command, then a detailed description of that UEFI driver is provided along with the devices that the driver is managing and the child devices that the driver has produced. If a device handle is used with the `Dh -d` command, then a detailed description of that device is provided along with the drivers that are managing that device, that device's parent controllers, and the device's child controllers. If the `Dh -d` command is used without any parameters, then detailed information on all of the drivers and devices is displayed. The following are some examples of the `Dh -d` command.

Example 1 displays the details on the UEFI driver on handle 27:

```
fs0:> Dh -d 27
```

Example 2 displays the details for the device on handle 23:

```
fs0:> Dh -d 23
```

Example 3 shows details on all the drivers and devices in the system:

```
fs0:> Dh -d
```

OpenInfo

The `OpenInfo` command provides detailed information about a device handle that is being managed by one or more UEFI drivers that follow the UEFI Driver Model. The `OpenInfo` command displays each protocol interface installed on the device handle and the list of agents that have opened that protocol interface with the `OpenProtocol()` Boot Service. This command can be used in conjunction with the `Connect`, `Disconnect`, and `Reconnect` commands to verify that an UEFI driver is opening and closing protocol interfaces correctly. The following example shows the `OpenInfo` command being used to display the list of protocol interfaces on device handle 23 along with the list of agents that have opened those protocol interfaces:

```
fs0:> OpenInfo 23
```

Testing the Driver Configuration and Driver Diagnostics Protocols

The UEFI Shell provides a command that can be used to test the Driver Configuration Protocol, DrvCfg, and one that can be used to test the Driver Diagnostics Protocol, DrvDiag.

DrvCfg

The `DrvCfg` command provides the services that are required to test the Driver Configuration Protocol implementation of an UEFI driver. This command can show all the devices that are being managed by UEFI drivers that support the Driver Configuration Protocol. The `Devices` and `Drivers` commands also show the drivers that support the Driver Configuration Protocol and the devices that those drivers are managing or have produced.

Once a device has been chosen, the `DrvCfg` command can be used to invoke the `SetOptions()`, `ForceDefaults()`, or `OptionsValid()` services of the Driver Configuration Protocol. The following are examples of the `DrvCfg` command.

Example 1 displays all the devices that are being managed by UEFI drivers that support the Driver Configuration Protocol:

```
fs0:> DrvCfg
```

Example 2 forces defaults on all the devices in the system:

```
fs0:> DrvCfg -f
```

Example 3 validates the options on all the devices in the system:

```
fs0:> DrvCfg -v
```

Example 4 invokes the `SetOptions()` service of the Driver Configuration Protocol for the driver on handle 27 and the device on handle 23:

```
fs0:> DrvCfg -s 23 27
```

DrvDiag

The `DrvDiag` command provides the ability to test all the services of the Driver Diagnostics Protocol that are produced by an UEFI driver. This command shows the devices that are being managed by UEFI drivers that support the Driver Diagnostics Protocol. The `Devices` and `Drivers` commands also show the drivers that support the Driver Diagnostics Protocol and the devices that those drivers are managing or have produced. Once a device has been chosen, the `DrvDiag` command can be used to invoke the `RunDiagnostics()` service of the Driver Diagnostics Protocol. The following are some examples of the `DrvDiag` command.

Example 1 displays all the devices that are being managed by UEFI drivers that support the Driver Diagnostics Protocol:

```
fs0:> DrvDiag
```

Example 2 invokes the `RunDiagnostics()` service of the Driver Diagnostics Protocol in standard mode for the driver on handle 27 and the device on handle 23:

```
fs0:> DrvDiag -s 23 27
```

Example 3 invokes the `RunDiagnostics()` service of the Driver Diagnostics Protocol in manufacturing mode for the driver on handle 27 and the device on handle 23:

```
fs0:> DrvDiag -m 23 27
```

Debugging Code Statements

Every module has a debug (check) build and a clean build. The debug build includes code for debug that will not be included in normal clean production builds. A debug build is enabled when the identifier `EFI_DEBUG` exists. A clean build is defined as when the `EFI_DEBUG` identifier does not exist.

The following debug macros can be used to insert debug code into a checked build. This debug code can greatly reduce the amount of time it takes to root cause a bug. These macros are enabled only in a debug build, so they do not take up any executable space in the production build. Table 11.3 describes the debug macros that are available.

Table 11.3 Available Debug Macros

Debug Macro	Description
ASSERT (Expression)	For check builds, if Expression evaluates to FALSE, a diagnostic message is printed and the program is aborted. Aborting a program is usually done via the EFI_BREAKPOINT () macro. For clean builds, Expression does not exist in the program and no action is taken. Code that is required for normal program execution should never be placed inside an ASSERT macro, because the code will not exist in a production build.
ASSERT_EFI_ERROR (Status)	For check builds, an assert is generated if Status is an error. This macro is equivalent to ASSERT (!EFI_ERROR (Status)) but is easier to read.
DEBUG ((ErrorLevel, String, ...))	For check builds, String and its associated arguments will be printed if the ErrorLevel of the macro is active. See Table 11.4 for a definition of the ErrorLevel values.
DEBUG_CODE (Code)	For check builds, Code is included in the build. DEBUG_CODE (is on its own line and indented like normal code. All the debug code follows on subsequent lines and is indented an extra level. The) is on the line following all the code and indented at the same level as DEBUG_CODE (.
EFI_BREAKPOINT ()	On a check build, inserts a break point into the code.
DEBUG_SET_MEM (Address, Length)	For a check build, initializes the memory starting at Address for Length bytes with the value BAD_POINTER. This initialization is done to enable debug of code that uses memory buffers that are not initialized.
CR (Record, TYPE, Field, Signature)	The containing record macro returns a pointer to TYPE when given the structure's Field name and a pointer to it (Record). The CR macro returns the TYPE pointer for check and production builds. For a check build, an ASSERT () is generated if the Signature field of TYPE is not equal to the Signature in the CR () macro.

The `ErrorLevel` parameter referenced in the `DEBUG()` macro allows an UEFI driver to assign a different error level to each debug message. Critical errors should always be sent to the standard error device. However, informational messages that are used only to debug a driver should be sent to the standard error device only if the user wants to see those specific types of messages. The UEFI Shell supports the `Err` command that allows the user to set the error level. The UEFI Boot Maintenance Manager allows the user to enable and select a standard error device. It is recommended that a serial port be used as a standard error device during debug so the messages can be logged to a file with a terminal emulator. Table 11.4 contains the list of error levels that are supported in the UEFI Shell. Other levels are usable, but not defined for a specific area.

Note `DEBUG ((ErrorLevel, String, …))` is not universally supported. Some EFI-compliant systems may not print out the message.

Table 11.4 Error Levels

Mnemonic	Value	Description
EFI_D_INIT	0x00000001	Initialization messages
EFI_D_WARN	0x00000002	Warning messages
EFI_D_LOAD	0x00000004	Load events
EFI_D_FS	0x00000008	EFI file system messages
EFI_D_POOL	0x00000010	EFI pool allocation and free messages
EFI_D_PAGE	0x00000020	EFI page allocation and free messages
EFI_D_INFO	0x00000040	Informational messages
EFI_D_VARIABLE	0x00000100	EFI variable service messages
EFI_D_BM	0x00000400	UEFI boot manager messages
EFI_D_BLKIO	0x00001000	EFI Block I/O Protocol messages
EFI_D_NET	0x00004000	EFI Simple Network Protocol, PXE base code, BIS messages
EFI_D_UNDI	0x00010000	UNDI driver messages
EFI_D_LOADFILE	0x00020000	Load File Protocol messages
EFI_D_EVENT	0x00080000	EFI Event Services messages
EFI_D_ERROR	0x80000000	Critical error messages

POST Codes

If an UEFI driver is being developed that cannot make use of the DEBUG() and ASSERT() macros, then a different mechanism must be used to help in the debugging process. Under these conditions, it is usually sufficient to send a small amount of output to a device to indicate what portions of an UEFI driver have executed and where error conditions have been detected. A few possibilities are presented below, but many others are possible depending on the devices that may be available on a specific platform. It is important to note that these mechanisms are useful during driver development and debug, but they should never be present in production versions of UEFI drivers because these types of devices are not present on all platforms.

The first possibility we will describe here is to use a POST card.

Post Card Debug

A POST card is an add-in card adapter that displays the hex value of an 8-bit I/O write cycle to address 0x80 (and sometimes 0x81 also). If an UEFI driver can depend on the PCI Root Bridge I/O Protocol being present, then the driver can use the services of the PCI Root Bridge I/O Protocol to send an 8-bit I/O write cycle to address 0x80. A driver can also use the services of the PCI I/O Protocol to write to address 0x80, as long as the pass-through BAR value is used. Figure 11.2 shows how the PCI Root Bridge I/O and PCI I/O Protocols can be used to send a value to a POST card.

```
EFI_STATUS                          Status;
EFI_PCI_ROOT_BRIDGE_IO_PROTOCOL     *PciRootBridgeIo;
EFI_PCI_IO_PROTOCOL                 *PciIo;
UINT8                               Value;

Value = 0xAA;
Status = PciRootBridgeIo->Io.Write (
                            PciRootBridgeIo,
                            EfiPciWidthUint8,
                            0x80,
                            1,
                            &Value
                            );

Value = 0xAA;
Status = PciIo->Io.Write (
                    PciIo,
                    EfiPciIoWidthUint8,
                    EFI_PCI_IO_PASS_THROUGH_BAR,
                    0x80,
                    1,
                    &Value
                    );
```

Figure 11.2   POST Code Examples

Text-Mode VGA Frame Buffer

The next possibility is a text-mode VGA frame buffer. If a system initializes the text-mode VGA display by default before the UEFI driver executes, then the UEFI driver can make use of the PCI Root Bridge I/O or PCI I/O Protocols to write text characters to the text-mode VGA display directly. Figure 11.3 shows how the PCI Root Bridge I/O and PCI I/O Protocols can be used to send the text message "ABCD" to the text-mode VGA frame buffer. Some systems do not have a VGA controller, so this solution will not work on all systems.

```
EFI_STATUS                              Status;
EFI_PCI_ROOT_BRIDGE_IO_PROTOCOL   *PciRootBridgeIo;
EFI_PCI_IO_PROTOCOL               *PciIo;
UINT8                             *Value;

Value = {'A',0x0f,'B',0x0f,'C',0x0f,'D',0x0f};

Status = PciRootBridgeIo->Mem.Write (
                              PciRootBridgeIo,
                              EfiPciWidthUint8,
                              0xB8000,
                              8,
                              Value
                              );

Status = PciIo->Mem.Write (
                  PciIo,
                  EfiPciIoWidthUint8,
                  EFI_PCI_IO_PASS_THROUGH_BAR,
                  0xB8000,
                  8,
                  Value
                  );
```

Figure 11.3   VGA Display Examples

Other Options

Another option that can be used if the UEFI driver being developed cannot make use of the DEBUG() and ASSERT() macros is to use some type of byte-stream-based device. This device could include a UART or a SMBus, for example. Like the POST card, the idea is to use the services of the PCI Root Bridge I/O or PCI I/O Protocols to initialize and send characters to the byte-stream device.

Many EFI-compliant implementations allow for the use of a COM cable to send debug information to another system. This allows the developer or tester to see debug code statements and other output from a separate system.

Appendix A

Security Considerations

We will bankrupt ourselves in the vain search for absolute security.
—Dwight D. Eisenhower

This appendix describes some options for hardening the integrity of the UEFI Shell.

UEFI Shell Binary Integrity

Recall that the UEFI Shell can be stored in the platform ROM, on disk, or across the network. For the latter two scenarios, the integrity of the UEFI Shell may be a concern in that a possibly hostile agent in the operating system may corrupt the UEFI system partition or a man-in-the-middle (MITM) attack may occur during the network download of the UEFI Shell.

Signing of the UEFI Shell is one option to handle this case of ensuring integrity of code introduced into the platform, especially from a mutable disk or across the network.

Overview

The UEFI specification provides a standard format for executables. These executables may be located on unsecured media (such as a hard driver or unprotected flash device) or may be delivered via a unsecured transport layer (such as a network) or originate from a unsecured port (such as an Express Card device or USB device). In each of these cases, the system provider may decide to authenticate either the origin of the executable or its integrity (that is, that it has not been tampered with).

The UEFI specification describes a means of generating a digital signature for a UEFI executable, embedding that digital signature within the UEFI executable, and automatically verifying that the digital signature is from the authorized source. It is to allay concerns of the BIOS vendors regarding the wide availability of the firmware image construction tools and documentation. The firmware tools and the encoding can be made public, as would the security scheme used in the UEFI specification. The privacy would only involve the private key used by the OEM in his factory to sign the image.

One of the main goals for pre-operating system security is to ensure various integrity goals. These goals include protecting the platform firmware from possibly errant or malicious third-party content. One way to meet this goal is to ensure that binary executable content, such as a shell not built into the platform firmware itself, comes from a well-known source. Cryptographic signatures applied to the binary with the platform firmware perform the verification action prior to performing the LoadImage/StartImage action on the executable.

The platform construction and integrity precepts used to evaluate the system can be derived from a more formal, commercial integrity model, such as Clark-Wilson. More information can found in Clark, David D. and Wilson, David R. "A Comparison of Commercial and Military Computer Security Policies" in *Proceedings of the 1987 IEEE Symposium on Research in Security and Privacy* (SP'87), May 1987, Oakland, CA, IEEE Press, pp. 184–193.

Signed Executable Overview

Figure A.1 shows the format of an original sample UEFI executable. The UEFI executable format is compatible with *Microsoft Portable Executable (PE) and Common Object File Format (COFF) Specification, Version 8.0.*

An executable primarily consists of file header, section table, and section data. See Chapters 3, 4, 5, and 6 in the PE and COFF Specification for more detailed executable structure description.

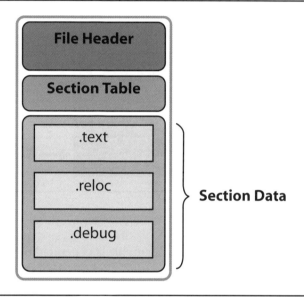

Figure A.1   Sample UEFI Executable Format

A signed UEFI executable encapsulates a certificate, which is used during the executable load process to detect unauthorized tamper or ensure its origination. The certificate may contain a digital signature used for validating the driver. Figure A.2 illustrates how a certificate is embedded in the PE/COFF file.

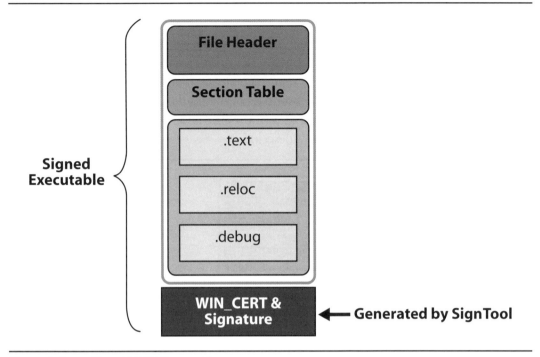

Signed Executable

Figure A.2   Signed UEFI Executable

The signature of the executable is generated by a sign tool, which appends the `WIN_CERT` data and signature information of the whole executable to the end of the original file.

Digital Signature

As a rule, digital signatures require two pieces: the *data* (often referred to as the *message*) and a *public/private key pair*. In order to create a digital signature, the message is processed by a hashing algorithm to create a hash value. The hash value is, in turn, encrypted using a signature algorithm and the private key to create the digital signature. Figure A.3 illustrates the process to create a digital signature.

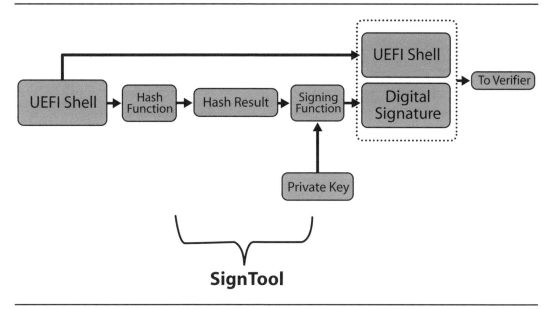

Figure A.3   Creating a digital signature

In order to verify a signature, two pieces of data are required: the *original message* and the *public key*. First, the hash must be calculated exactly as it was calculated when the signature was created. Then the digital signature is decoded using the public key and the result is compared against the computed hash. If the two are identical, then you can be sure that message data is the one originally signed and it has not been tampered with. Figure A.4 illustrates the process of verifying a digital signature.

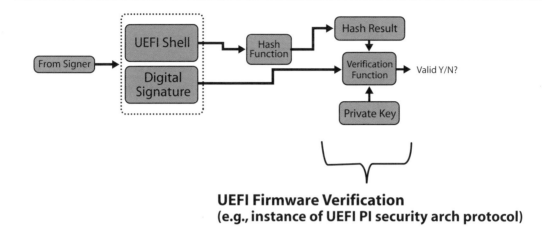

UEFI Firmware Verification
(e.g., instance of UEFI PI security arch protocol)

Figure A.4   Verifying a digital signature

Therefore, the signature process dealing with the UEFI executable can be described briefly as follows:

```
Hash = SHA-256 (Executable File contents)
Signature = RSA_SIGN (Private_Key, Hash)
```

Signed Executable Processing

Signed executable processing is accomplished by an OS-present application (SignTool.exe) that calculates the signature of a UEFI executable file (SHA-256 and PKCS1V15 RSA_Sign) and then embeds that signature into the executable. The following subsections define the responsibilities at each stop along the signed executable processing path.

Signed Executable Generation Application (SignTool)

The SignTool application is an OS-present application that is responsible for locating the executable and output a signed executable. SignTool locates an existing well formed TIANO executable file that forms the basis of the resultant firmware image.

To calculate the executable digital signature that loaded into memory, SignTool must:

1. For PE/COFF headers and sections, align them on the appropriate section alignment for the architecture, as stipulated in the *SectionAlignment* field of header. Pad inter-section regions (that is, in case file alignment and section alignment are not the same) with zeroes. Some sections, like debug and security may be ignorable.

2. Skip the following fields in the calculation:

   ■ CheckSum

   ■ *Certificate Data Directory* (the fifth entry in data directory)

As SignTool's input, the whole well-formatted executable is hashed and signed by SignTool. The final signature is appended to the original executable file to generate a signed executable file. Figure A.5 illustrates the layout of a signed executable.

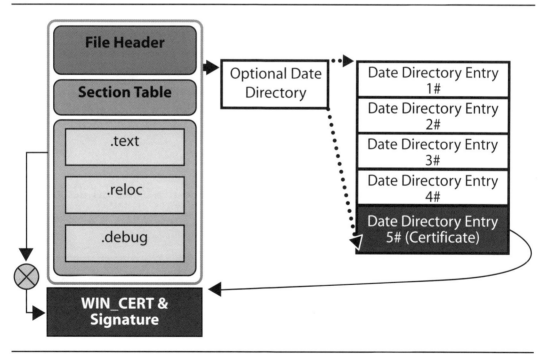

Figure A.5   Layout of signed executable

UEFI Load Image

During the processing of UEFI images, the UEFI driver verification is processed in the UEFI implementation, such as a UEFI PI core. One of the UEFI core's responsibilities is to load UEFI executables into physical memory; it may utilize an instance of the Security Architectural Protocol (SAP) to verify their signatures in order to ensure they are not tampered with and that they come from an authorized source.

SignTool

SignTool is a command-line application that digitally signs a UEFI executable (.efi file) and generates a signed executable (.signed). This section describes the command-line arguments, design, and their expected effect on the behavior of the utility.

Build Environment

The sign utility is built in the standard EDK tool build environment. This environment is closely tied to the EDK source development environment. The utility developer should only provide source code specific to the utility. All generic structures, macros, and equates should be referenced from an EFI 2.0 library so as to be consistent. The utility may make use of standard C libraries.

Command Line Design

The SignTool application provides some key features. Table A.1 describes the feature requirements in brief.

Table A.1   SignTool Feature Requirements

Feature	Requirement Description
Sign Executable	Digitally sign the UEFI executable with given private key.
Executable Verification	Verify the signatures of the UEFI signed executable
Key Generation	Generate RSA key pair to be used in signing.
Information Dump	Dump key and signature information

Command Line

Usage:

```
SignTool [command] [options [parameter(s)]]
```

[command] is one of the command flags that specify an operation to perform on a executable; The commands listed in Table A.2 are supported by Sign-Tool.

Table A.2 Commands Supported by SignTool

Command	Description
sign	Generates a signed executable
verify	Verifies a given signed executable
keygen	Generates a new key pair and writes it to the specified file.
-h or -?	For help and usage information

[options[parameters]] describes one or more command options and/or its desired parameters.

Options for Sign, Verify, and KeyGen commands are described in Table A.3.

Table A.3 The Sign, Verify, and KeyGen Command Options

Command	Options	Description
Sign	-a HashAlg	Specifies the hash algorithms for signing, which must be either SHA-1 or SHA-256 (default value)
	-i ExecutableFile	Name of an existing well-formatted UEFI executable file that forms the basis of the resultant signed executable.
	-s SignedExeFile	To write result signed executable file to file SignedExeFile
	-k KeyFile	Specifies the private key file name (.pvk), which provides key information for signature generation
Verify	-s SignedExeFile	Specifies a signed executable file name to be verified
	-dump	Dumps public key and signature from an existing signed executable file
KeyGen	-k KeyFile	Specifies the private key file name (.pvk), which provides RSA key information for signature generation
	-l keylength	Designates key length with 1024 or 2048 (default)

Examples

The following command creates a new, random RSA key pair and stores it in mykey.pvk.

```
SignTool KeyGen —l 2048 —k mykey.pvk
```

To sign a given UEFI executable file with given key information from described file, the following command will work:

```
SignTool Sign —a SHA256 —i driver.efi —s driver.signed —k
mykey.pvk
```

SignTool can help to verify given signed-capsule and output its verification information (and dump key and signature information from it):

```
SignTool Verify —s driver.signed -dump
```

Signing Operation

This section provides a high level overview of the signing operations performed by SignTool.

Inputs/Outputs

SignTool takes as input the following when generating a signed capsule:

- Well-formatted UEFI executable file (normally .efi file) (required)
- RSA key pair file (required)
- Designated hash algorithm (optional)

A signed capsule is written to .signed file (required). Figure A.6 shows the SignTool input and outputs pictorially.

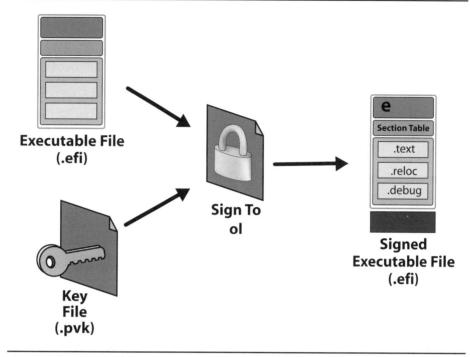

Figure A.6 SignTool Inputs and Outputs

Processing

All writes by the SignTool utility are done to the output file name specified on the command line. Following is the execution flow of SignTool when executed with valid Sign command line arguments for create a signed capsule image:

1. Read UEFI executable file (.efi) to memory;

2. Parse the RSA private key from key description file (.pvk);

3. Locate the image according CAPSULE_HEADER's information;

4. Calculate the HASH value of File Headers (skip CheckSum and Certificate Data Directory) by using given hash algorithms (SHA-1 or SHA-256);

5. Align all sections on the appropriate section alignment for the architecture, as stipulated in the *SectionAlignment* field of header. Pad inter-section regions (that is, in case file alignment and section alignment are

not the same) with zeroes. Calculate the HASH value of these sections in incremental mode.

6. Generate a PKCS1v1.5 RSA signature for the final HASH value with parsed RSA private key;

7. Update Header's Certificate Data Directory and CheckSum information and write header and section data to new signed executable, then append the certificate in the end of new created file;

8. Close the output file, which is a signed capsule.

Returned Status Code

SignTool detects the error conditions described in Table A.4. It returns a distinct Status Code for each error condition. SignTool displays the error text to the console using STDOUT. SignTool may return additional text to further clarify the specific error condition detected.

Table A.4 SignTool Error Descriptions

Error Condition	Returned Status Code
No error conditions detected.	EFI_SUCCESS
One or more of the input parameters is invalid.	EFI_INVALID_PARAMETER
A resource required by SignTool was unavailable. Most commonly this will be memory allocation or file creation.	EFI_OUT_OF_RESOURCES
Error generating the signed executable file, such as errors in Disk I/O or an invalid executable file.	EFI_ABORTED
Unsupported operations.	EFI_UNSUPPORTED

Command Reference

This appendix enumerates the commands that are part of the UEFI Shell standard and provide insight into what commands are associated with a given shell level or profile.

Command Profiles and Levels

The UEFI Shell has associated with it two concepts which assist the user or program in determining what capabilities a given shell environment has. Since each shell implementation allows for a vast amount of differentiation, the concepts of shell levels and shell profiles were introduced.

- *Shell Levels.* The level associated with a given shell environment is derived by analyzing the "shellsupport" environment variable. This variable reflects the current support level provided by the currently running shell environment. Table B1 shows a series of commands that would potentially correspond to a particular shell level value.

- *Shell Profiles.* Shell command profiles are groups of shell commands that are identified by a profile name. The profile(s) supported by a given shell environment is derived by analyzing the "profiles" environment variable. Profile names that begin with the underscore character (_) are reserved for individual implementations.

Command List

Table B.1 provides a list of commands in the UEFI Shell standard.

Table B.1 Commands in the UEFI Shell Standard

Command	Description	Required at Shell Level or Profile
Alias	Displays, creates, or deletes aliases in the UEFI Shell environment	3
Attrib	Displays or changes the attributes of files or directories	2
Bcfg	Manipulates boot order and driver order	Debug1, Install1
Cd	Displays or changes the current directory	2
Cls	Clears the standard output and optionally changes the background color	3
Comp	Compares the contents of two files on a byte-for-byte basis	Debug1
Connect	Binds a driver to a specific device and starts the driver	Driver1
cp	Copies one or more source files or directories to a destination	2
date	Displays and sets the current date for the system	2/3
dblk	Displays the contents of one or more blocks from a block device	Debug1
del	Deletes one or more files or directories	2
devices	Displays the list of devices managed by UEFI drivers	Driver1
devtree	Displays the tree of devices compliant with the UEFI Driver Model	Driver1
dh	Displays the device handles in the UEFI environment	Driver1
dir	Lists directory contents or file information	2
disconnect	Disconnects one or more drivers from the specified devices	Driver1
dmem	Displays the contents of system or device memory	Debug1
dmpstore	Manages all UEFI NVRAM variables	Debug1
Drivers	Displays a list of information for drivers that follow the EFI Driver Model in the EFI environment	Driver1

Table B.1   Commands in the UEFI Shell Standard (continued)

Command	Description	Required at Shell Level or Profile
Drvcfg	Configures the driver using the UEFI Configuration Access Protocol	Driver1
Drvdiag	Invokes the Driver Diagnostics Protocol	Driver1
Echo	Controls whether or not script commands are displayed as they are read from the script file and prints the given message to the display	3
Edit	Provides a full-screen editor for ASCII or UCS-2 files	Debug1
eficompress	Compresses a file using EFI Compression Algorithm	Debug1
Efidecompress	Decompresses a file using EFI Decompression Algorithm	Debug1
Else	Conditionally executes commands if a previous if condition was false	1
Endfor	Ends a loop stated with for in a script	1
Endif	Ends a conditional block started with if	1
Exit	Exits the UEFI Shell environment and returns control to the parent that launched the UEFI Shell	1
For	Starts a loop in a script	1
Getmtc	Returns current monotonic count	3
Goto	Gos to a label in a script	1
Guid	Displays all registered EFI GUIDs	Debug1
Help	Displays the list of commands that are built into the UEFI Shell	3
Hexedit	Provides a full-screen hex editor for files, block devices, or memory	Debug1
If	Conditionally executes script statements	1
Ifconfig	Displays or modifies the current IP configuration	Network1
Ipconfig	Displays or modifies the current IP configuration	Network1
Load	Loads a UEFI driver into memory	2
loadpcirom	Loads a PCI Option ROM from the specified file	Debug1
Ls	Lists a directory's contents or file information	2
map	Defines a mapping between a user-defined name and a device handle	2

Table B.1   Commands in the UEFI Shell Standard (continued)

Command	Description	Required at Shell Level or Profile
mem	Displays the contents of system or device memory	Debug1
memmap	Displays the memory map maintained by the EFI environment	Debug1
mkdir	Creates one or more new directories	2
mm	Displays or modifies MEM/MMIO/IO/PCI/PCIE address space	Debug1
mode	Displays or changes the console output device mode	Debug1
mv	Moves one or more files to a destination within a file system	2
openinfo	Displays the protocols and agents associated with a handle	Driver1
parse	Parses data returned from standard formatted output	2
pause	Pauses script execution and waits for a keypress	3
pci	Displays PCI device list or PCI function configuration space	Debug1
ping	Checks response of an IP address	Network1
reconnect	Reconnects drivers to the specific device	Driver1
reset	Resets the system	2
rm	Deletes one or more files or directories	2
sermode	Sets serial port attributes	Debug1
set	Is used to maintain the environment variables that are available from the EFI environment	2
setsize	Sets the size of a file	Debug1
setvar	Changes value of UEFI variable	Debug1
shift	Shifts to the second set of positional parameters	1
smbiosview	Displays SMBIOS information	Debug1
time	Displays or sets the current time for the system	2/3
timezone	Displays or sets time zone information	2/3
touch	Updates the time and date on a file to the current time and date	3
type	Sends the contents of a file to the standard output device	3

Table B.1 Commands in the UEFI Shell Standard (continued)

Command	Description	Required at Shell Level or Profile
Unload	Unloads a driver image that has already been loaded	Driver1
Ver	Displays the version information for this EFI firmware	3

Standardizing Command Output

A goal of UEFI-based specifications is to clearly describe the required components while leaving room for implementation-specific differentiation. Yet there was a strong desire to standardize the output of shell commands so that tools could clearly operate on the output of these commands.

The standardized format produces content using rows and columns of column-delimited data. The first column always contains a C-style identifier that describes the type of data on the row. The details of how to interpret the subsequent columns would be defined by the table name definition that is contained in the UEFI Shell specification. If the identifier name begins with the "_" character, it is an implementation-specific table not covered by the UEFI Shell standard.

To facilitate both implementation-specific differentiation and standardized output, some commands had support for an "-sfo" parameter added to them.

Shell commands that implement the –sfo parameter implement the following standard formatting methodology:

■ *First Column Defines the Table Name.* The standardized format produces content using rows and columns of column-delimited data. The first column always contains a C-style identifier that describes the type of data on the row. The details of how to interpret the subsequent columns would be defined by the table name definition that is contained in the UEFI Shell specification. If the identifier name begins with the "_" character, it is an implementation-specific table not covered by the UEFI Shell standard.

■ *Format for -SFO.* The –sfo output follows these formatting guidelines:

```
sfo-format       := sfo-row
                    sfo-row  <EOL>  <sfo-row>
sfo-row          := sfo-table-name, sfo-columns
sfo-table-name   := identifier
sfo-columns      := sfo-column |
                    sfo-columns, sfo-column
sfo-column       := quoted-string |        <empty>
```

■ Examples of this formatted output

```
VolumeInfo,"MikesVolume","136314880","False",
"1024","512"

FileInfo,"fs0:/efi/boot/timsfile.txt","1250","a"

FileInfo,"fs0:/efi/boot/BOOTx64.EFI","1250","arsh"
```

Command Details

This section gives a brief overview of each command and its parameters.
It is intended as a quick reference for purposes of understanding the basic
command capabilities. For full details on each of the commands, refer to
the UEFI Shell Specification, which gives much more detail.

alias

This command displays, creates, or deletes aliases in the UEFI Shell
environment. An alias provides a new name for an existing UEFI Shell command or UEFI application. Once the alias is created, it can be used to run the
command or launch the UEFI application.

```
alias [-d|-v] [alias-name] [command-name]
```

alias-name Alias name

command-name   Original command's name or original command's file name/directory.

-d Delete an alias; command-name should not be present.

-v Make the alias volatile.

attrib

This command displays and sets the attributes of files or directories. The following four attribute types are supported in the UEFI file system: archive, system, hidden, and read only.

attrib [+a|-a] [+s|-s] [+h|-h] [+r|-r] [file...] [directory...]

+a|-a Set or clear the archive attribute

+s|-s Set or clear the system attribute

+h|-h Set or clear the hidden attribute

+r|-r Set or clear the read-only attribute

file File name (wild cards are permitted)

directory Directory name (wildcards are permitted)

bcfg

This command manages the boot and driver options stored in NVRAM. The bcfg command can display the Boot#### or Driver#### environment variables by using the dump option. The add option can be used to add a new Boot#### or Driver#### environment variable. The rm option can be used to delete a Boot#### or Driver#### environment variable. The mv option can be used to reorder the Boot#### and Driver#### environment variables. The add, rm, and mv options also update the BootOrder or DriverOrder environment variables as appropriate.

bcfg driver|boot [dump [-v]] [add # file "desc"] [addp # file "desc"] [addh # handle "desc"] [rm #] [mv # #] [-opt # [[filename]|["data"]] | [KeyData <ScanCode UnicodeChar>*]]

driver Display/modify the driver option list.

boot Display/modify the boot option list.

dump Display the option list.

-v Display the option list with extra information including the optional data.

add Add an option. The # is the number of options to add in hexadecimal. The `file` is the file name of the UEFI application/driver for the option. The quoted parameter is the description of the option being added.

addh Add an option that refers to the driver specified by `handle`. The # is the number of options to add, in hexadecimal. The `handle` is the driver handle, in hexadecimal. The device path for the option is retrieved from the handle. The quoted parameter is the description of the option being added.

addp Add an option that refers to a specific file. Only the portion of the device path starting with the hard drive partition is placed in the option. The # is the number of options to add, in hexadecimal. The quoted parameter is the description of the added option.

rm Remove an option. The parameter lists the number of the options to remove in hexadecimal.

mv Move an option. The first numeric parameter is the number of the option to move in hexadecimal. The second numeric parameter is the new number of the option being moved.

-opt Display/modify the optional data associated with a driver or boot option. Followed either by the file name of the file that contains the binary data to be associated with the driver or boot option optional data or else the quote-delimited data that will be associated with the driver or boot option optional data.

KeyData The packed value associated with a hot-key. This is the equivalent of the EFI_KEY_DATA value in the UEFI specification.

ScanCode This is the UEFI-defined ScanCode portion of the EFI_INPUT_KEY struction. This value is directly associated with the preceding KeyData value and there may be 1 to 4 entries per the UEFI specification. When one instance of this parameter has a nonzero value, the paired UnicodeChar value will have a zero-based value.

UnicodeChar   This is the Unicode value for the character associated with the preceding KeyData value. There may be 1 to 4 entries per the UEFI specification. When one instance of this parameter has a nonzero value, the paired ScanCode value will have a zero-based value.

Examples are provided due to the abundance of parameters and to avoid confusion in the utilization of the command.

To display driver options:

```
Shell> bcfg driver dump
```

To display boot options:

```
Shell> bcfg boot dump
```

To display verbosely of boot options:

```
Shell> bcfg boot dump —v
```

To add a driver option #5

```
Shell> bcfg driver add 5 mydriver.efi "My Driver"
```

To add a boot option #3

```
Shell> bcfg boot add 3 osloader.efi "My OS"
```

To remove boot option #3

```
Shell> bcfg boot rm 3
```

To move boot option #3 to boot option #7

```
Shell> bcfg boot mv 3 7
```

To assign a Ctrl-B hot-key to boot option #3.

```
Shell> bcfg boot —opt 3 0x40000200 0 0x42
```

cd

This command changes the current working directory that is used by the UEFI Shell environment. If a file system mapping is specified, then the current working directory is changed for that device. Otherwise, the current working directory is changed for the current device.

Some predefined directory names are intended to have a special meaning. These are:

.   Refers to current directory

..   Refers to parent directory

\   Refers to the root of the current file system

```
cd [path]
```

path The relative or absolute directory path.

cls

This command clears the standard output device with an optional background color attribute. If `color` is not specified, then the background color does not change.

```
cls [color]
```

color New background color:

0 - Black

1 - Blue

2 - Green

3 - Cyan

4 - Red

5 - Magenta

6 - Yellow

7 - Light gray

comp

This command compares the contents of two files in binary mode. It displays up to 10 differences between the two files. For each difference, up to 32 bytes from the location where the difference starts is dumped. It will exit immediately if the lengths of the compared files are different.

`comp [-b] file1 file2`

-b Display one screen at a time

file1 First file name (directory name or wildcards not permitted)

file2 Second file name (directory name or wildcards not permitted)

connect

This command binds a driver to a specific device and starts the driver. If the -r flag is used, then the connection is done recursively until no further connections between devices and drivers are made. If the -c flag is used, then the connect command binds the proper drivers to the console devices that are described in the EFI environment variables.

If no parameters are specified, then the command will attempt to bind all proper drivers to all devices without recursion. Each connection status will be displayed.

`connect [[DeviceHandle] [DriverHandle] | [-c] | [-r]]`

-r Recursively scan all handles and check to see if any loaded or embedded driver can match the specified device. If so, the driver will be bound to the device. Additionally, if more device handles are created during the binding, these handles will also be checked to see if a matching driver can bind to these devices as well. The process is repeated until no more drivers are able to connect to any devices. However, without the option, the newly created device handles will not be further bound to any drivers.

-c Connect console devices found in the EFI global variables (see UEFI specification, Chapter 3).

DeviceHandle Device handle (a hexadecimal number). If not specified, then all device handles will be connected.

DriverHandle Driver handle (a hexadecimal number). If not specified, then all matching drivers will be bound to the specified device. If specified, then this driver will have the highest priority.

cp or copy

This command copies one or more source files or directories to a destination. If the source is a directory, the -r flag must be specified. If -r is specified, then the source directory will be recursively copied to the destination (which means that all subdirectories will be copied). If a destination is not specified, then the current working directory is assumed to be the destination.

```
cp [-r] [-q] src [src...] [dst]
```

src Source file/directory name (wildcards are permitted)

dst Destination file/directory name (wildcards are not permitted). If not specified, then the current working directory is assumed to be the destination. If there are more than one directory specified, then the last is always assumed to be the destination.

-r Recursive copy

-q Quiet copy (no prompt)

date

This command displays and/or sets the current date for the system. If no parameters are used, it shows the current date. If a valid month, day, and year are provided, then the system's date will be updated.

```
date [mm/dd/[yy]yy][-sfo]
```

mm Month of the date to be set (1-12)

dd Day of the date to be set (1-31)

yy/yyyy Year of the date to be set. If only two digits, then 9x = 199x, otherwise 20xx.

-sfo Standard-format output (see UEFI Shell Specification for latest details).

dblk

This command displays the contents of one or more blocks from a block device. `lba` and `blocks` should be typed in hexidecimal value. If `lba` is not specified, block #0 is assumed. If `blocks` is not specified, then only 1 block will be displayed. The maximum number of blocks that can be displayed at one time is 0x10.

```
dblk device [lba] [blocks] [-b]
```

device Block device name

lba Index of the first block to be displayed (a hexadecimal number). The default is 0.

blocks Number of blocks to be displayed (a hexadecimal number). The default is 0. If larger than 0x10, then only 0x10 are displayed.

-b Display one screen at a time.

del or rm

This command deletes one or more files or directories. If the target is a directory, it deletes the directory, including all its subdirectories. It is not allowed to redirect a file whose parent directory (or the file itself) is being deleted.

```
rm [-q] file/directory [file/directory ...]
```

-q Quiet mode; does not prompt user for a confirmation

file File name (wildcards are permitted)

directory Directory name (wildcards are permitted)

devices

The command prints a list of devices that are being managed by drivers that follow the UEFI Driver Model. When specifying no parameters, the command displays all devices that are managed by UEFI Driver model compliant drivers.

```
devices [-b] [-l XXX] [-sfo]
```

-b Display one screen at a time

-l XXX Display devices using the specified ISO 639-2 language

-sfo Turn on standard formatted output (see UEFI Shell Specification for latest details).

devtree

This command prints a tree of devices that are being managed by drivers that follow the UEFI Driver Model. By default, the devices are printed in device names that are retrieved from the Component Name Protocol. If the option –d is specified, the device paths are printed instead.

```
devtree [-b] [-d] [-l XXX] [DeviceHandle]
```

DeviceHandle Display device tree below a certain handle

-b Display one screen at a time

-d Display device tree using device paths

-l Display device tree using the specified language

dh

This command displays the device handles in the EFI environment. If the dh command is used with a specific handle number, the details of all the protocols that are associated with that device handle are displayed. Otherwise, the -p option can be used to list the device handles that contain a specific protocol. If neither –p or handle is specified, then all handles are displayed.

```
dh [-l <lang>] [handle | -p <prot_id>] [-d] [-v] [-sfo]
```

handle Specific handle to dump information about (a hexadecimal number). If not present, then all information will be dumped.

-p Dumps all handles of a protocol specified by the GUID.

-d Dumps UEFI Driver Model-related information.

-l Dumps information using the language codes, as described in Appendix M of the UEFI specification.

-v, -verbose Dumps verbose information about a specific handle.

-sfo Displays data in the standard formatted output (see UEFI Shell Specification for latest details)

dir *or* ls

This command lists directory contents or file information. If no file name or directory name is specified, then the current working directory is assumed.

```
ls [-r] [-a[attrib]][-sfo][file]
```

-r Displays recursively (including subdirectories)

-a Display only those files with the attributes that follow. If no attributes are listed, then all files will be listed. If –a is not specified, then all nonsystem and nonhidden files will be listed. The attributes (attrib) may be one or more of the following: a – archive, s – system, h - hidden, r - read-only, or d - directory

file Name of file/directory (wildcards are permitted)

-sfo Display information in Standard Formatted Output (see UEFI Shell Specification for latest details)

disconnect

This command disconnects one or more drivers from the specified devices. If the -r option is used, all drivers are disconnected from all devices in the system.

```
disconnect DeviceHandle [DriverHandle [ChildHandle]]
```

DeviceHandle Device handle (a hexadecimal number). If not specified, then disconnect DriverHandle.

DriverHandle Driver handle (a hexadecimal number)

ChildHandle Child handle of a device (a hexadecimal number). If not specified, then all child handles of DeviceHandle will be disconnected.

-r Disconnect all drivers from all devices.

dmem

This command displays the contents of system memory or device memory. The `address` and `size` parameters should be typed in hexidecimal value. If `address` is not specified, then the contents of the EFI System Table are displayed. Otherwise, memory starting at `address` is displayed. The `size` parameter specifies the number of bytes to display. If `size` is not specified, then it defaults to 512 bytes. If `MMIO` is not specified, then main system memory is displayed. Otherwise, device memory is displayed through the use of the EFI_PCI_ROOT_BRIDGE_IO_PROTOCOL.

dmem [-b] [address] [size] [-MMIO]

> `address` Starting address in hexadecimal format
>
> `size` Number of bytes to display in hexadecimal format
>
> `-b` Display one screen at a time
>
> `-MMIO` Forces address cycles to the PCI bus

dmpstore

This command is used to manage the UEFI NVRAM variables.

dmpstore [-b] [-d] [-all | ([variable] [—guid guid])]

dmpstore [-all | ([variable] [—guid guid])] -s file

dmpstore [-all | ([variable] [—guid guid])] -l file

> `-b` Display one screen at a time
>
> `variable` Specifies the name of the variable name.
>
> `-guid` Specifies the GUID of the variables to be displayed. The GUID has the standard text format. If guid is not specified and —all is not specified, then the EFI_GLOBAL_VARIABLE GUID is assumed.
>
> `-all` Indicates that all variables should be dumped, including those with a different GUID that EFI_GLOBAL_VARIABLE.
>
> `-d` Delete variables
>
> `-s` Save variables to file
>
> `-l` Load and set variables from file

drivers

This command displays a list of information for drivers that follow the UEFI Driver Model in the UEFI environment.

```
drivers [-l XXX] [-sfo]
```

-l Displays drivers using the language code XXX, which has the format specified by Appendix M of the UEFI specification.

-sfo Displays data in the Standard Formatted Output (see UEFI Shell Specification for latest details)

drvcfg

This command invokes the platform's Configuration infrastructure. The the values for the Type parameter are descrived below. Other values depend on the driver's implementation.

```
drvcfg [-l XXX] [-c] [-f <Type>|-v|-s] [DriverHandle
[DeviceHandle [ChildHandle]]] [-i filename] [-o filename]
```

Type The type of default configuration options to force on the controller.

0 - Standard defaults

1 - Manufacturing defaults

2 - Safe defaults

4000–FFFF - Custom defaults

DriverHandle The handle of the driver to configure

DeviceHandle The handle of a device that DriverHandle is managing

ChildHandle The handle of a device that is a child of DeviceHandle

-c Configure all child devices

-l Configure using the ISO 3066 language specified by XXX

-f Force defaults

-v Validate options

-s Set options

-I Receive configuration updates from an input file

-o Export the settings of the specified driver instance to a file

drvdiag

This command invokes the Driver Diagnostics Protocol.

```
drvdiag [-c] [-l XXX] [-s|-e|-m] [DriverHandle
[DeviceHandle [ChildHandle]]]
```

DriverHandle The handle of the driver to diagnose

DeviceHandle The handle of a device that DriverHandle is managing.

ChildHandle The handle of a device that is a child of Device-Handle

-c Diagnose all child devices

-l Diagnose using the ISO 639-2 language specified by XXX

-s Run diagnostics in standard mode

-e Run diagnostics in extended mode

-m Run diagnostics in manufacturing mode

echo

The first form of this command controls whether or not script commands are displayed as they are read from the script file. If no argument is given, the current "on" or "off" status is displayed. The second form prints the given message to the display.

```
echo [-on|-off]
```

```
echo [message]
```

message Message to display

-on Enables display when reading commands from script files

-off Disables display when reading commands from script files

edit

This command allows a file to be edited using a full screen editor. The editor supports both UCS-2 and ASCII file types.

edit [file]

> file Name of file to be edited. If none is specified, then an empty file is created with a default file name.

eficompress

This command is used to compress a file using EFI Compression Algorithm and write the compressed form out to a new file.

eficompress infile outfile

> infile Filename for uncompressed input file
>
> outfile Filename for compressed output file

efidecompress

This command is used to decompress a file using the EFI Decompression Algorithm and write the decompressed form out to a new file.

efidecompress infile outfile

> infile Filename for compressed input file
>
> outfile Filename for decompressed output file

exit

This command exits the UEFI Shell or, if /b is specified, the current script.

exit [/b] [exit-code]

> /b Indicates that only the current UEFI Shell script should be terminated. Ignored if not used within a script.
>
> exit-code If exiting a UEFI Shell script, the value placed into the environment variable lasterror. If exiting an instance of the UEFI Shell, the value returned to the caller. If not specified, then 0 is returned.

for

The `for` command executes one or more commands for each item in a set of items. The set may be text strings or file names or a mixture of both, separated by spaces (if not in a quotation). If the length of an element in the set is between 0 and 256, and if the string contains wildcards, the string is treated as a file name containing wildcards, and be expanded before command is executed. This command may only be used in scripts.

If after expansion no such files are found, the literal string itself is kept. The `indexvar` variable is any alphabet character from "a" to "z" or "A" to "Z", and they are case-sensitive. It should not be a digit (0–9) because `%digit` will be interpreted as a positional argument on the command line that launches the script. The namespace for index variables is separate from that for environment variables, so if `indexvar` has the same name as an existing environment variable, the environment variable will remain unchanged by the `for` loop.

Each command is executed once for each item in the set, with any occurrence of `%indexvar` in the command replacing with the current item. In the second format of `for ... endfor` statement, `indexvar` will be assigned a value from `start` to `end` with an interval of `step`. `start` and `end` can be any integer whose length is less than 7 digits excluding sign, and it can also applied to `step` with one exception of zero. `step` is optional, if `step` is not specified it will be automatically determined by following rule, if `start` ≤ `end` then `step` = 1, otherwise `step` = -1. `start`, `end` and `step` are divided by space.

```
for %indexvar in set
  command [arguments]
  [command [arguments]]
  ...
endfor


for %indexvar run (start end [step])
  command [arguments]
  [command [arguments]]
  ...
endfor
```

getmtc

This command displays the current monotonic counter value. The lower 32 bits increment every time this command is executed. Every time the system is reset, the upper 32 bits are incremented and the lower 32 bits are reset to 0.

```
getmtc
```

goto

The goto command directs script file execution to the line in the script file after the given label. The command is not supported from the interactive shell. A label is a line beginning with a colon (:). It can either appear after the goto command, or before the goto command. The search for label is done forward in the script file, from the current file position. If the end of the file is reached, the search resumes at the top of the file and continues until label is found or the starting point is reached. If label is not found, the script process terminates and an error message is displayed. If a label is encountered but no goto command is executed, the label lines are ignored.

```
goto
```

guid

This command displays a list of all the GUIDs that have been registered with the UEFI environment. This command displays only GUIDs that were known by the UEFI codebase at the time it was built. GUIDs that are not in the original core build will show up as an Unknown Device.

```
guid [-b]
```

> -b Display one screen at a time.

help

The help command displays information about one or more shell commands. If no other options are specified, each command is displayed along with a brief description of its function.

The help text is gathered from UCS-2 text files found in the directory where the shell or shell command executable was located. The files have the name `command-name.man`, where `command-name` is the name of the shell command. The files follow a subset of the MAN page format, as described below.

The manual page files are standard text files with title and section heading information embedded using commands which begin with a "." (period character). The following two macros are supported:

`.TH command-name 0 "short-description"`

> `Title header` When printing multipage help, this appears at the top of each page.

`.SH section-name`

> `Sub-header` Specifies one of several standard sub-headings. The following is a list of the section names:

> `NAME` The name of the function or command, along with a one-line summary.

> `SYNOPISIS` Usage of the command.

> `DESCRIPTION` General description.

> `OPTIONS` Description of all options and parameters.

> `RETURN VALUES` Values returned.

> `ENVIRONMENT VARIABLES` Environment variables used.

> `FILES` Files associated with the subject.

> `EXAMPLES` Examples and suggestions.

> `ERRORS` Errors reported by the command.

> `STANDARDS` Conformance to applicable standards.

> `BUGS` Errors and caveats.

> `CATEGORY` The comma-delimited list of categories to which this command belongs. Category names must follow normal file naming conventions. Category names that begin with "_" will not be used in the specification.

> `other` Other sections added by the help author.

```
help [cmd | pattern | special] [-usage] [-verbose]
[-section sectionname][-b]
```

cmd Command to display help about.

pattern Pattern that describes the commands to be displayed.

special Displays a list of the special characters used in the shell command line.

-usage Display the usage information for the command. The same as specifying —section:NAME and —section:SYNOPSIS

-section sectionname Display the specified section of the help information.

hexedit

This command allows a file, block device, or memory region to be edited. The region being edited is displayed as hexadecimal bytes, and the contents can be modified and saved. The following example shows typical output for help on this command.

```
hexedit [[-f] filename| [-d diskname offset size] | [-m ad-
dress size]]
```

-f Name of file to edit.

-d Disk block to edit:

DiskName - Name of disk to edit (for example fs0)

Offset - Starting block number (beginning from 0)

Size - Number of blocks to be edited

-m Memory region to edit:

Address - Starting 32-bit memory address (beginning from 0)

Size - Size of memory region to be edited in bytes

if

The if command executes one or more commands before the else or endif commands, if the specified condition is true; otherwise commands between else (if present) and endif are executed.

In the first usage of `if`, the `exist` condition is true when the file specified by `filename` exists. The `filename` argument may include device and path information. Also wildcard expansion is supported by this form. If more than one file matches the wildcard pattern, the condition evaluates to TRUE.

In the second usage, the `string1 == string2` condition is true if the two strings are identical. Here the comparison can be case-sensitive or case-insensitive; it depends on the optional switch `/i`. If `/i` is specified, it compares strings in the case-insensitive manner; otherwise, it compares strings in the case-sensitive manner.

In the third usage, general purpose comparison is supported using expressions optionally separated by `and` or `or`. Since < and > are used for redirection, the expressions use common two character (FORTRAN) abbreviations for the operators (augmented with unsigned equivalents):

```
if [not] exist filename then

    command [arguments]

    [command [arguments]]

    …

    [else

    command [arguments]

    [command [arguments]]

    …

    ]

    endif


if [/i] [not] string1 == string2 then

    command [arguments]

    [command [arguments]]

    …

    [else

    command [arguments]

    [command [arguments]]

    …

    ]

endif
```

```
if [/i][/s] ConditionalExpression then
    command [arguments]
    [command [arguments]]
    ...
    [else
    command [arguments]
    [command [arguments]]
    ...
    ]
endif
```

ConditionalExpression Conditional expression, as described in the section "Expressions" below.

/s forces string comparisons.

/i forces case-insensitive string comparisons.

By default, comparisons are done numerically if the strings on both sides of the operator are numbers and in case sensitive character sort order otherwise. Spaces separate the operators from operands. The /s and /i apply to the entire line and must appear at the start of the line (just after the if itself). When performing comparisons, the Unicode Byte Ordering Character is ignored at the beginning of any argument.

Expressions

Conditional expressions are evaluated strictly from left to right. Complex conditionals requiring precedence may be implemented as nested if commands.

The expressions in the third usage have the following syntax:

```
conditional-expression := expression | expression and ex-
pression | expression or expression

expression  :=  expr | not expr

expr := item binop item | boolfunc(string)
```

```
item := mapfunc(string) | string

mapfunc  := efierror | pierror | oemerror

boolfunc := isint | exists | available | profile

binop :=   gt | lt | eq | ne | ge | le | == | ugt | ult |
uge | ule
```

For the comparisons, the operators are defined as:

gt Greater than

ugt Unsigned Greater than

lt Less than

ult Unsigned Less than

ge Greater than or equal

uge Unsigned greater than or equal

le Less than or equal

ule Unsigned less than or equal

ne Not equal

eq Equals (semantically equivalent to ==)

== Equals (semantically equivalent to eq)

The error mapping functions referenced in *item* are used to convert integers into UEFI, PI or OEM error codes, as defined by Appendix D of the UEFI specification. The following are the defined functions:

UefiError Sets top nibble of parameter to 0100 binary (0x8)

PiError Sets top nibble of parameter to 1010 binary (0xA)

OemError Sets top nibble of parameter to 1100 binary (0xC)

For example, to check for write protect (UEFI error #8):

```
if %lasterror% == UefiError(8) then
```

The Boolean functions are defined as:

IsInt Evaluates to true if the parameter string that follows is a number (as defined below) and false otherwise.

Exists Evaluates to true if the file specified by string exists is in the current working directory or false if not.

Available Evaluates to true if the file specified by string is in the current working directory or current path.

Profile Determines whether the parameter string matches one of the profile names in the profiles environment variable.

ifconfig

This command is used to modify the default IP address for the UEFI IP4 Network Stack.

```
ifConfig [-?] [-c [Name]] [-l [Name]] [-s <Name> dhcp |
<static <IP> <SubnetMask> <Gateway>> [permanent]]
```

Name Adapter name, such as eth0

-c [Name] Clear the configuration for all or specified interface, and the network stack for related interface will fall back to the DHCP as default.

-l [Name] List the configuration for all or the specified interface.

-s < Name> static <IP> <SubnetMask> <GatewayMask> [permanent] Use static IP4 address configuration for all or specified interface. If permanent is not present, the configuration is one-time only, otherwise this configuration request will survive a network stack reload.

-s <Name> dhcp [permanent] Use DHCP4 to request the IP4 address configuration dynamically for all interface or specified interface. If permanent is not present, the configuration is one-time only, otherwise this configuration request will survive a network stack reload.

IP IP4 address in four integer values (each between 0-255). i.e., 192.168.0.1

`SubnetMask` Subnet mask in four integer values (each between 0-255), i.e., 255.255.255.0

`GatewayMask` Default gateway in four integer values (each between 0-255), such as 192.168.0.1

ipconfig

This command displays or modifies the IP configuration of `EFI_PXE_BASE_CODE_PROTOCOL`. If no parameter is specified in the command line, it just displays the IP configuration of `EFI_PXE_BASE_CODE_PROTOCOL`. If `IpAddress` or `NetMask` is specified, the according configuration of `EFI_PXE_BASE_CODE_PROTOCOL` will be changed.

`ipconfig [-r]|[-b] [-c Instance] [IpAddress [-m NetMask]]`

`-r` Restart the PXE base code and DHCP settings.

`-b` Display one screen at a time.

`-c, -controller` Specify the 0-based handle of the `EFI_SIMPLE_NETWORK_PROTOCOL` instance to use.

`IpAddress` IP address in a.b.c.d format.

`-m, -mask` Network mask in 255.255.255.0 format.

load

This command loads a driver into memory. It can load multiple files at one time, and the file name supports wildcards. If the `-nc` flag is not specified, this command will try to connect the driver to a proper device; it may also cause already loaded drivers be connected to their corresponding devices.

`load [-nc] file [file...]`

`-nc` Load the driver, but do not connect the driver.

`File` File that contains the image of the UEFI driver (wildcards are permitted).

loadpcirom

This command is used to load PCI option ROM images into memory for execution. The file can contain legacy images and multiple PE32 images, in which case all PE32 images will be loaded.

```
loadpcirom [-nc] romfile [romfile...]
```

-nc Load the ROM image but do not connect the driver.

romfile PCI option ROM image file (wildcards are permitted).

map

This command creates a mapping between a user-defined name and a device. The most common use of this command is to create the mapped name for devices that support a file system protocol. Once these mappings are created, the names can be used with all the file manipulation commands.

```
map [-d <sname>]
```

```
map [[-r][-v][-c][-f][-u][-t <type[,type…]>][sname]]
```

```
map [sname handle | mapping]
```

sname Mapping name.

handle The number of the EFI handle, which is the same as the value displayed from the dh command.

mapping The device's mapped name. Use this parameter to assign a new mapping to a device. The mapping must end with a ":" (colon).

-t Shows the device mappings, filtered according to the device type. The supported types are fp (floppy), hd (hard disk), and cd (CD-ROM). Types can be combined by putting a comma between two types. Spaces are not allowed between types.

-d Deletes a mapping.

-r Resets to default mappings.

-v Lists verbose information about all mappings.

-c Shows the consistent mapping.

-f Shows the normal mapping.

-u This option will add mappings for newly-installed devices and remove mappings for uninstalled devices but will not change the mappings of existing devices. The user-defined mappings are also preserved.

-sfo Output in Standard Formatted Output. See the UEFI Shell Specification for the latest details.

md *or* mkdir

This command creates one or more new directories. If dir includes nested directories, then parent directories will be created before child directories. If the directory already exists, then the command will exit with an error.

```
mkdir dir [dir...]
```

dir Name of directory or directories to be created. Wildcards are not allowed.

memmap

This command displays the memory map that is maintained by the EFI environment. The EFI environment keeps track all the physical memory in the system and how it is currently being used. The EFI Specification defines a set of Memory Type Descriptors. Please see the EFI Specification for a description of how each of these memory types is used.

```
memmap [-b] [-sfo]
```

-b Display one screen at a time.

-sfo Output in Standard Formatted Output. See the UEFI Shell Specification for the latest details.

mm

This command allows the user to display or modify I/O register, memory contents, or PCI configuration space.

```
mm address [value] [-w 1|2|4|8] [-MEM | -MMIO | -IO | -PCI
| -PCIE] [-n]
```

address Starting address.

value The value to write. If not specified, then the current value will be displayed.

-MEM Memory Address type.

-IO I/O Address type

-PCI PCI Configuration Space. The address will have the format 0x000000ssbbddffrr, where ss = Segment, bb = Bus, dd = Device, ff = Function and rr = Register. This is the same format used in the PCI command.

-PCIE PCI Express Configuration Space. The address will have the format 0x0000000ssbbddffrrr, where ss = Segment, bb = Bus, dd = Device, ff = Function and rrr = Register.

-w Access Width, in bytes. 1 = byte, 2 = 2 bytes, 4 = 4 bytes, 8 = 8 bytes. If not specified, then 1 is assumed.

-n Noninteractive mode.

mode

This command is used to change the display mode for the console output device. When this command is used without any parameters, it shows the list of modes that the standard output device currently supports.

```
mode [col row]
```

row Number of rows.

col Number of columns.

mv

Destination file/directory name (wildcards are permitted). If not specified, then the current working directory is assumed to be the destination. If there is more than one argument on the command line, the last one will always be considered the destination.

```
mv src [src...] [dst]
```

src Source file/directory name (wildcards are permitted)

dst Destination file/directory name (wildcards are permitted). If not specified, then the current working directory is assumed to be the destination. If there is more than one argument on the command line, the last one will always be considered the destination.

openinfo

This command is used to display the open protocols on a given handle.

`openinfo Handle [-b]`

Handle Display open protocol information for specified handle.

-b Display one screen at a time.

parse

This command enables the parsing of data from a file that contains data output from a command having used the —sfo parameter. Since the standard formatted output has a well known means of parsing, this command is intended to be used as a simplified means of having scripts consume such constructed output files and use this retrieved data in logic of the scripts being written for the UEFI Shell.

`parse filename tablename column [-i <Instance>] [-s <Instance>]`

filename Source file name.

tablename The name of the table being parsed.

column The one-based column index to use to determine which value from a particular record to parse.

-i <Instance> Start parsing with the nth instance of specified tablename, after the specified instance of ShellCommand. If not present, then all instances will be returned.

-s <Instance> Start parsing with the nth instance of the ShellCommand table. If not present, then 1 is assumed.

pause

The pause command prints a message to the display and then suspends script file execution and waits for keyboard input. Pressing any key resumes execution, except for q or Q. If q or Q is pressed, script processing terminates; otherwise execution continues with the next line after the pause command.

```
pause [-q]
```

> -q Hide the pause message.

pci

This command will display all the PCI devices found in the system. It can also display the configuration space of PCI device according to specified bus (Bus), device (Dev), and function (Func) addresses. If the function address is not specified, it will default to 0. The —i option is used to display verbose information for the specified PCI device. The PCI configuration space for the device will be dumped with a detailed interpretation. If no parameters are specified all PCI devices will be listed.

```
pci [Bus Dev [Func] [-s Seg] [-i]]
```

> Bus Bus number.
>
> Dev Device number.
>
> Func Function number.
>
> -s Optional segment number Seg specified.
>
> -i Information interpreted.

ping

This command uses the ICMPv4 ECHO_REQUEST datagram to elicit ECHO_REPLY from a host.

```
Ping [-n count] [-l size] TargetIp
```

> -n Number of echo request datagram to be sent.
>
> -l Size of data buffer in echo request datagram.
>
> TargetIp IPv4 address of the target machine.

reconnect

This command reconnects drivers to the specific device. It first disconnects the specified driver from the specified device and then connects the driver to the device recursively. If the -r option is used, all drivers are reconnected to all devices. Any drivers that are bound to any devices will be disconnected first and then connected recursively. See the `connect` and `disconnect` commands for more details.

```
reconnect DeviceHandle [DriverHandle [ChildHandle]]
```

```
reconnect -r
```

> `DeviceHandle` Device handle (a hexadecimal number).
>
> `DriverHandle` Driver handle (a hexadecimal number). If not specified, all drivers on the specified device will be reconnected.
>
> `ChildHandle` Child handle of device (a hexadecimal number). If not specified, then all child handles of the specified device will be reconnected.
>
> -r Reconnect drivers to all devices.

reset

This command resets the system. The default is to perform a cold reset unless the -w parameter is specified. If the reset string is specified, then it is passed into the `Reset()` function, so the system can know the reason for the system reset.

```
reset [-w [string]]
```

```
reset [-s [string]]
```

```
reset [-c [string]]
```

> -s Performs a shutdown.
>
> -w Performs a warm boot.
>
> -c Performs a cold boot.
>
> `string` String to be passed to reset service.

sermode

This command displays or sets baud rate, parity attribute, data bits, and stop bits of serial ports. If no attributes are specified, then the current settings are displayed. If no handle is specified, then all serial ports are displayed.

```
sermode [handle [baudrate parity databits stopbits]]
```

handle Device handle for a serial port in hexadecimal. The dh command can be used to retrieve the right handle.

baudrate Baud rate for specified serial port. The following values are supported: 50, 75, 110, 150, 300, 600, 1200, 1800, 2000, 2400, 3600, 4800, 7200, 9600 (default), 19200, 38400, 57600, 115200, 230400, and 460800. All other values will be converted to the next highest setting.

parity Parity bit settings for specified serial port. Any one of the following settings can be used:

d - Default parity

n - No parity

e - Even parity

o - Odd parity

m - Mark parity

s - Space parity

databits Data bits for the specified serial port. The following settings are supported: 4, 7, 8 (default). All other settings are invalid.

stopbits Stop bits for the specified serial port. The following settings are supported:

0 (0 stop bits - default setting)

1 (1 stop bit)

2 (2 stop bits)

15 (1.5 stop bits)

set

This command is used to maintain the UEFI Shell environment variables. The set command will set the environment variable that is specified by sname to value. This command can be used to create a new environment variable or to modify an existing environment variable. If the set command is used without any parameters, then all the environment variables are displayed.

```
set [-v] [sname [value]]
```

```
set [-d <sname>]
```

> -d Deletes the environment variable.
>
> -v Volatile variable.
>
> sname Environment variable name.
>
> value Environment variable value.

setsize

This command adjusts the size of a particular target file. When adjusting the size of a file, it should be noted that this command automatically truncates or extends the size of a file based on the passed-in parameters. If the file does not exist, it will be created.

```
setsize size file [file...]
```

> file The file or files that will have their size adjusted.
>
> size The desired size of the file once it is adjusted. Setting the size smaller than the actual data contained in this file truncates this data.

setvar

This command changes the UEFI variable specified by name and guid. If = is specified, but data is not, the variable is deleted, if it exists. If = is not specified, then the current variable contents are displayed. If =data is specified, then the variable's value is changed to the value specified by data.

```
setvar variable-name [—quid quid][-bs][-rs][-nv] [=data]
```

`variable-name` The name of the UEFI variable to modify or display.

`-guid` Specifies the GUID of the UEFI variable to modify or display. If not present, then the GUID `EFI_GLOBAL_VARIABLE` is assumed, as defined in the UEFI specification.

`-bs` Indicates that the variable is a boot variable. Should only be present for new variables, otherwise it is ignored.

`-rt` Indicates that the variable is a runtime variable. Should only be present for new variables, otherwise it is ignored.

`-nv` Indicates that the variable is nonvolatile. If not present, then the variable is assumed to be volatile. Should only be present for new variables, otherwise it is ignored.

`=data` New data for the variable. If there is nothing after the "=" then the variable is deleted. If = is not present, then the current value of the variable is dumped as hexidecimal bytes. The data may consist of zero or more of the following:

xx[xx]: Hexadecimal bytes

"ascii-string": ASCII string with no null-terminator

L"UCS2-string": UCS-2 encoded string with no null-terminator

`--device` Device path text format, as specified by EFI Device Path Display Format Overview section of the UEFI 2.1 specification.

shift

The `shift` command shifts the contents of a UEFI Shell script's positional parameters so that %1 is discarded, %2 is copied to %1, %3 is copied to %2, %4 is copied to %3, and so on. This allows UEFI Shell scripts to process script parameters from left to right. The `shift` command is available only in UEFI Shell scripts.

```
shift
```

smbiosview

This command displays the SMBIOS information. Users can display the information of SMBIOS structures specified by type or handle.

```
smbiosview [-t SmbiosType]|[-h SmbiosHandle]|[-s]|[-a]
```

-t Display all structures of SmbiosType. The following values are supported:

0 - BIOS Information

1 - System Information

3 - System Enclosure

4 - Processor Information

5 - Memory Controller Information

6 - Memory Module Information

7 - Cache Information

8 - Port Connector Information

9 - System Slots

10 - On Board Devices Information

15 - System Event Log

16 - Physical Memory Array

17 - Memory Device

18 - 32-bit Memory Error Information

19 - Memory Array Mapped Address

20 - Memory Device Mapped Address

21 - Built-in Pointing Device

22 - Portable Battery

34 - Management Device

37 - Memory Channel

38 - IPMI Device Information

39 - System Power Supply

-h Display the structure of SmbiosHandle, the unique 16-bit value assigned to each SMBIOS structure. SmbiosHandle can be specified in either decimal or hexadecimal format. Use the 0x prefix for hexadecimal values.

-s Display statistics table.

-a Display all information.

stall

This command would be used to establish a timed stall of operations during a script.

```
stall time
```

time The number of microseconds for the processor to stall.

time

This command displays or sets the current time for the system. If no parameters are used, it shows the current time. If valid hours, minutes, and seconds are provided, then the system's time is updated.

```
time [hh:mm[:ss]] [-tz tz] [-d dl]
```

hh New hour (0–23) (required).

mm New minute (0–59) (required).

ss New second (0–59) If not specified, then zero is used.

-tz Time zone adjustment, measured in minutes offset from GMT. Valid values can be between –1440 and 1440 or 2047. If not present or set to 2047, time is interpreted as local time.

-d Indicates that time is not affected by daylight savings time (0), time is affected by daylight savings time but time has not been adjusted (1), or time is affected by daylight savings time and has been adjusted (3). All other values are invalid. If no value follows –d, then the current daylight savings time is displayed.

time

This command displays and sets the current time zone for the system. If no parameters are used, it shows the current time zone. If a valid `hh:mm` parameter is provided, then the system's time zone information is updated.

```
timezone [-s hh:mm | -l] [-b] [-f]
```

> `-s` Set time zone associated with `hh:mm` offset from GMT.
>
> `-l` Display list of all time zones.
>
> `-b` Display one screen at a time.
>
> `-f` Display full information for specified time zone.

touch

This command updates the time and date on the file that is specified by the file parameter to the current time and date.

```
touch [-r] file [file …]
```

> `file` The name or pattern of the file or directory. There can be multiple files on the command line.
>
> `-r` Recurse into subdirectories.

type

This command sends the contents of a file to the standard output device. If no options are used, then the command attempts to automatically detect the file type. If it fails, then UCS-2 is presumed.

```
type [-a|-u] file [file...]
```

> `file` Name of the file to display.
>
> `-a` Display the file as if it is encoded as 8-bit ASCII.
>
> `-u` Displays the file as if it were encoded as UCS-2 Unicode.

unload

This command unloads a driver image that was already loaded and that supports the unloading option in the `EFT_LOADED_IMAGE_PROTOCOL` protocol.

```
unload [-n] [-v|-verbose] Handle
```

> -n Skips all prompts during unloading, so that it can be used in a script file.
>
> -v, -verbose Dump verbose status information before the image is unloaded.
>
> `Handle` Handle of driver to unload, always taken as hexadecimal number.

ver

This command displays the version information for this EFI Firmware or the version information for the UEFI Shell itself. The information is retrieved through the EFI System Table or the Shell image.

```
ver [-s|-terse]
```

> -s Displays only the UEFI Shell version.
>
> -terse Abbreviated version display

vol

This command displays the volume information for the file system specified by `fs`. If `fs` is not specified, the current file system is used. If -n is specified, then the volume label for `fs` will be set to `VolumeLabel`. The maximum length for `VolumeLabel` is 11 characters.

```
vol [fs] [-n <VolumeLabel>]

vol [fs] [-d]
```

> `fs` The name of the file system.

`VolumeLabel` The name of the file system. The following characters cannot be used:

`% ^ * + = [ ] | : ; " < > ? /`

No spaces are allowed in the volume label.

`-d` Empty volume label.

Appendix C

Programming Reference

This appendix gives guidance on the programming environment associated with the UEFI Shell. The UEFI Shell provides programmatic interfaces that are not part of the main UEFI specification. The data in this reference should provide some insight into the programmatic interactions that are possible. This appendix is intended to be a useful summary of the UEFI Shell programming environment. However, if more details are required, refer to the UEFI Shell Specification.

Script-based Programming

Even though Appendix B is really intended as the enumeration of all of the shell commands that can be executed by a script, a few aspects of the scripting environment require additional explanation beyond the descriptions of the commands themselves. These topics include:

- Parameter passing
- Redirection and piping
- Return codes
- Environment variables

Parameter Passing

Positional parameters are the first ten arguments (%0–%9) passed from the command line into a UEFI Shell script. The first parameter after the UEFI Shell script name becomes %1, the second %2, the third %3, and so on. The argument %0 is the full path name of the script itself.

When executing the UEFI Shell script, the %n is replaced by the corresponding argument on the command line that invoked the script. If a positional parameter is referenced in the UEFI Shell script but that parameter was not present, then an empty string is substituted.

When passing parameters to commands, the associated commands might at times accept parameters with wildcards in them. The most common use of such wildcards is in reference to file names. The asterisk (*) and question mark (?) are often used for filename expansion. The asterisk would be used in a case where one is searching for 0 or more characters in a filename. For example, the reference to a filename of "*.*" would be one searching for any valid file names with any valid extension. This typically means "give me everything." The question mark is intended to be used when looking to match exactly one character in a given filename. An example of this would be "?I?.TXT" where items that might match this sequence would be JIM.TXT and KIM.TXT.

Redirection and Piping

Depending on the background of the reader, mixing the terms redirection and piping may not seem natural. For purposes of this section, let us explicitly define the terms:

■ *Redirection* – The ability to redirect the output of an application or command to file or an environment variable. This also includes the ability to use the content of a file or an environment variable as the standard input to an application or command.

■ *Command Piping* – The ability to channel the output of an application or command and feed the data to the standard input of another program.

Redirection

When using output redirection, there are several options available for both the source of the data as well as the output of the data. The command syntax for output redirection is:

■ *Command [options] > Target* – Redirect the output of a command to a target. This will create a new *Target* and will overwrite any pre-existing item of the same name.

■ *Command [options] >> Target* – Append the output of a command to the *Target* location.

It should be noted that the aforementioned *Target* location can be either a traditional file on some nonvolatile media or it can be a volatile environment variable. The latter is introduced to support the operation of scripting logic even in a read-only type of environment. Table C.1 summarizes the redirection character sequences.

Table C.1 Output Redirection Support

	Unicode	ASCII	Unicode Variable	ASCII Variable
Standard Output	>	>a	>v	>av
Standard Error	2>	2>a	2>v	2>av
Standard Output - Append	>>	>>a	>>v	>>av
Standard Error - Append	2>>	2>>a	2>>v	2>>av

When using input redirection, the content of a file or environment variable is read and used as the standard input to an application or shell command. The command syntax for input redirection is:

■ *Command [options] < Source* – Use the *Source* as the standard input for the *Command*.

Table C.2 summarizes the input redirection character sequences.

Table C.2 Input Redirection Support

	Unicode	ASCII	Unicode Variable	ASCII Variable
Sequence	<	<a	<v	<av

Command Piping

By using the pipe (|) character, a data channel is formed that takes the standard Unicode output of a file and feeds the data as standard input to another program. The format for this support is as follows:

■ *Command [options] | Command*

This capability is found in most modern shells and since many common utilities presume the use of pipe operations, this enables maximal environment compatibility for those who port their favorite utilities to this environment. Table C.3 summarizes command piping support.

Table C.3 Command Piping Support

Character Sequence	Description
		Pipe output of a command to another program in UCS-2 format.
|a	Pipe output of a command to another program in ASCII format.

Return Codes

During the execution of most shell commands, a return status is given when that command completes execution. In the UEFI Shell specification, there is a SHELL_STATUS set of return codes used by shell commands.

The `lasterror` shell variable allows scripts to test the results of the most recently executed command using the `if` command. This variable is maintained by the shell, is read-only, and cannot be modified by command `set`. An example of a script testing to see if a command succeeded would be:

```
PROGRAM.EFI
if %lasterror% == 0 then goto success
echo PROGRAM.EFI had an error
:success
echo PROGRAM.EFI succeeded
```

Environment Variables

Environment variables are variables that can hold the user-specified contents and can be employed on the command line or in scripts. Each environment variable has a case-sensitive name (a C-style identifier) and a string value. Environment variables can be either volatile (they will lose their value on reset or power-off) or nonvolatile (they will maintain their value across reset or power-off).

Environment variables can be used on the command line by using `%variable-name%` where `variable-name` is the environment variable's name. Variable substitution is not recursive. Environment variables can also be retrieved by a UEFI Shell command by using the `GetEnv()` function.

Environment variables can be displayed or changed using the `set` shell command. They can also be changed by a UEFI Shell command using the `SetEnv()` function. Table C.4 lists the environment variables that have special meaning to the UEFI Shell. Each variable is defined to be Volatile (V) or Nonvolatile (NV) as well as having Read-Only (RO) or Read-Write (RW) attributes associated with it:

Table C.4 Shell Environment Variables with Special Meaning

Variable	V/NV RO/RW	Description
Cwd	V/RO	The current working directory, including the current working file system.
Lasterror	V/RO	Last returned error from a UEFI Shell command or batch script
path	V/RW	The UEFI Shell has a default volatile environment variable path, which contains the default path that UEFI Shell will search if necessary. When user wants to launch an UEFI application, UEFI Shell will first try to search the current directory if it exists, and then search the path list sequentially. If the application is found in one of the paths, it will stop searching and execute that application. If the application is not found in all the paths, UEFI Shell will report the application is not found.
Profiles	NV/RO	The list of UEFI Shell command profiles supported by the shell. Each profile name may only contain alphanumeric characters or the "_" character. Profile names are semicolon (";") delimited.
Shellsupport	V/RO	Reflects the current support level enabled by the currently running shell environment. The contents of the variable will reflect the text-based numeric version in the form that looks like: 3 This variable is produced by the shell itself and is intended as read-only, any attempt to modify the contents will be ignored.
uefishellversion	V/RO	Reflects the revision of the UEFI Shell specification which the shell supports. The contents are formatted as text: 2.00
Uefiversion	V/RO	Reflects the revision of the UEFI specification which the underlying firmware supports. The contents will look like this: 2.10

Non-Script-based Programming

While the users of shell environments may often focus on the shell commands and scripts, a wide variety of programmatic interfaces are available in the shell environment. In most cases, this kind of infrastructure comes into play when a user wants to create a shell extension (such as a new shell command). One should realize that the UEFI Shell environment is provided by a UEFI application that complies with the UEFI specification. This means that the return codes and underlying system services are at least partially composed of UEFI service calls and conventions. There are however two main protocols (programmatic services) that are introduced by the UEFI Shell environment:

- Shell Protocol
- Shell Parameters Protocol

Shell Protocol

Table C.5 summarizes the functions of the EFI_SHELL_PROTOCOL whose purpose is to provide shell services to UEFI applications. This protocol is the workhorse of the UEFI Shell environment and is used to provide abstractions to services that facilitate the interaction with the underlying UEFI services as well as shell features.

Table C.5 Shell Protocol Functions

Function	Description
BatchIsActive	This function tells whether any script files are currently being processed
CloseFile	This function closes a specified file handle. All "dirty" cached file data is flushed to the device, and the file is closed. In all cases the handle is closed.
CreateFile	This function creates an empty new file or directory with the specified attributes and returns the new file's handle.
DeleteFile	This function closes and deletes a file. In all cases the file handle is closed.
DeleteFileByName	This function deletes the file specified by the file handle.
DisablePageBreak	This function disables the page break output mode.
EnablePageBreak	This function enables the page break output mode.

Table C.5 Shell Protocol Functions (continued)

Function	Description
Execute	This function creates a nested instance of the shell and executes the specified command with the specified environment.
FindFiles	This function searches for all files and directories which match the specified file pattern. The file pattern can contain wild-card characters.
FindFilesInDir	This function returns all files in a specified directory.
FlushFile	This function flushes all modified data associated with a file to a device.
FreeFileList	This function cleans up the file list and any related data structures. It has no impact on the files themselves.
GetCurDir	This function returns the current directory on a device.
GetDeviceName	This function gets the user-readable name of the device specified by the device handle.
GetDevicePathFromFilePath	This function gets the device path associated with a mapping.
GetDevicePathFromMap	This function converts a file system style name to a device path, by replacing any mapping references to the associated device path.
GetEnv	This function returns the current value of the specified environment variable.
GetFileInfo	This function allocates a buffer to store the file's information. It's the caller's responsibility to free the buffer.
GetFilePathFromDevicePath	This function converts a device path to a file system path by replacing part, or all, of the device path with the file-system mapping.
GetFilePosition	This function returns the current file position for the file handle.
GetFileSize	This function returns the size of the specified file.
GetHelpText	This function returns the help information for the specified command.
GetMapFromDevicePath	This function returns the mapping which corresponds to a particular device path.
GetPageBreak	User can use this function to determine current page break mode.

Table C.5 Shell Protocol Functions (contiunued)

Function	Description
IsRootShell	This function informs the user whether the active shell is the root shell.
OpenFileByName	This function opens the specified file and returns a file handle.
OpenFileList	This function opens the files that match the path pattern specified.
OpenRoot	This function opens the root directory of a device and returns a file handle to it.
OpenRootByHandle	This function returns the root directory of a file system on a particular handle.
ReadFile	This function reads the requested number of bytes from the file at the file's current position and returns them in a buffer.
RemoveDupInFileList	This function deletes the duplicate files in the given file list.
SetAlias	This function adds or removes the alias for a specific shell command.
SetCurDir	This function changes the current directory on a device.
SetEnv	This function changes the current value of the specified environment variable.
SetFileInfo	This function sets the file information of an opened file handle.
SetFilePosition	This function sets the current read/write file position for the handle to the position supplied.
SetMap	This function creates, updates, or deletes a mapping between a device and a device path.
WriteFile	This function writes the specified number of bytes to the file at the current file position. The current file position is also advanced by the actual number of bytes written.
ExecutionBreak	Event signaled by the UEFI Shell when the user presses Ctrl-C to indicate that the current UEFI Shell command execution should be interrupted.
MajorVersion	The major version of the shell environment.
MinorVersion	The minor version of the shell environment.

Shell Parameters Protocol

Table C.6 summarizes the functions of the EFI_SHELL_PARAMETERS_
PROTOCOL whose purpose is to handle the shell application's arguments.
This protocol handles state information associated with the command line as
well as the current input, output, and error consoles.

Table C.6   Shell Parameters Protocol Functions

Parameter	Description
Argv	Points to an Argc-element array of points to null-terminated strings containing the command-line parameters. The first entry in the array is always the full file path of the executable. Any quotation marks that were used to preserve whitespace have been removed.
Argc	The number of elements in the Argv array.
StdIn	The file handle for the standard input for this executable. This may be different from the ConInHandle in the EFI_SYSTEM_TABLE.
StdOut	The file handle for the standard output for this executable. This may be different from the ConOutHandle in the EFI_SYSTEM_TABLE.
StdErr	The file handle for the standard error output for this executable. This may be different from the StdErrHandle in the EFI_SYSTEM_TABLE.

UEFI Shell Library

T his appendix provides an annotated reference for the standard macros, functions, and data structures in the UEFI Shell Library. This library is designed to provide a broad range of services for using the UEFI and UEFI Shell APIs, in addition to common functions related to strings, files, and so on.

Macros

This section describes all of the macros provided in the UEFI Shell Developer Kit Library.

EFI_APPLICATION_ENTRY_POINT

This macro declares the entry point of a UEFI Shell application.

Prototype

```
#define EFI_APPLICATION_ENTRY_POINT(x)
```

Parameters

x - The name of the UEFI Shell application entry point.

Description

This macro is used to declare the UEFI application entry point.

EFI_PROPER_VERSION

This macro detects whether the current UEFI implementation is at least the specified major and minor version.

Prototype

```
#define EFI_PROPER_VERSION(revision_low,revision_high)
```

Parameters

revision_low - The current UEFI implementation should have a minor revision of at least this value. To check for compliance with the UEFI 2.0 specification, this should be 0. For the UEFI 2.10 specification, this should be 10.

revision_high - The current UEFI implementation should have a minor revision of at least this value. This is typically set to 99.

Description

This macro returns TRUE if the current UEFI implementation has a major revision of 2 and a minor revision greater than or equal to revision_low and less than or equal to revision_high. For example:

```
if (!EFI_PROPER_VERSION (10, 99)) {
  Print ("Unsupported UEFI version. Must greater than
2.10.\n");
  return SHELL_UNSUPPORTED;
}
```

EFI_SHELL_APP_INIT

This macro performs standard UEFI Shell application initialization.

Prototype

```
#define EFI_SHELL_APP_INIT(x,y)
```

Parameters

x - The image handle of the UEFI Shell application.

y - The pointer to the EFI system table.

Description

This macro calls the standard library initialization function, which sets up the global variables (such as gBS and gRT) and initializes the internal library data structures.

Functions

This section describes all of the functions in the UEFI Shell Developer Kit Shell library.

File I/O Functions

The UEFI Shell Library provides a set of functions that operate on file I/O. Table D.1 lists the file I/O support functions that are described in the following sections. For more information about EFI_FILE_INFO and EFI_FILE please refer to the UEFI specification.

Table D.1   File I/O Functions

Function Name	Function Description
LibGetFileInfo	Gets the file information from an open file handle and stores it in a buffer allocated from pool.
LibSetFileInfo	Sets the file information to an open file handle.
LibOpenFile	Opens a file.
LibOpenFileByName	Opens a file by the file name.
LibCreateDirectory	Creates a directory by the directory name.
LibReadFile	Reads data from the file.
LibWriteFile	Writes data to the file.
LibCloseFile	Closes the file handle.
LibDeleteFile	Closes and deletes the file handle.
LibSetPosition	Sets a file's current position.
LibGetPosition	Gets a file's current position.
LibFlushFile	Flushes data back to the file handle.
LibFindFirstFile	Gets the first file in a directory.
LibFindNextFile	Gets the next file in a directory.
LibGetFileSize	Gets the size of a file.
LibFileDevicePath	Allocates a device path for a file and appends it to an existing device path.

Memory Functions

The UEFI Shell Library provides a set of functions that operate on buffers in memory. Buffers can either be allocated on the stack, as global variables, or from the memory pool. To prevent memory leaks, it is the caller's responsibility to maintain buffers allocated from pool. This means that the caller must free a buffer when that buffer is no longer needed. Table D.2 contains the list of memory support functions that are described in the following sections.

Table D.2 Memory Functions

Function Name	Function Description
SetMem	Fills a buffer with a value.
CopyMem	Copies the contents of one buffer to another buffer.
CompareMem	Compares the contents of two buffers.
AllocatePool	Allocates a buffer from pool.
FreePool	Frees a previously allocated buffer.
AllocateZeroPool	Allocates pool memory and initializes the memory to zeros.

Text I/O Functions

The text I/O functions of the UEFI Shell Library listed in Table D.3 provide a simple means to get input and output from a console device. Both of the active console-in and console-out devices can be located in the UEFI system table.

Many of the output functions use a format string to describe how to format the output of variable arguments. The format string consists of normal text and argument descriptors. There are no restrictions for how the normal text and argument descriptors can be mixed. Each argument descriptor is of the form "%w.lF", where "w" is an optional integer value that represents the argument width parameter, "l" is an optional integer value that represents the field width parameter, and "F" is a set of optional field modifiers and the data type of the argument to print. See the section "Format Strings" later in this appendix for a list of the optional field modifiers and arguments types.

Table D.3 Text I/O Functions

Function Name	Function Description
Input	Inputs a string at the current cursor location using the console-in and console-out devices.
Output	Sends a string to the console-out device at the current cursor location.
Print	Sends a formatted string to the console-out device at the current cursor location.
PrintAt	Sends a formatted string to the specified location on the console-out device.
Sprint	Sends a formatted string to the specified buffer.

Spin Lock Functions

The lock functions in the UEFI Shell Library are listed in Table D.4. Spin locks are used to protect data structures that may be updated by more than one processor at a time or by a single processor that may update the same data structure while running at several different priority levels. A spin lock is stored in a FLOCK data structure, defined in the "Data Structures" section later in this appendix.

Table D.4 Spin Lock Functions

Function Name	Function Description
InitializeLock	Initialize a spin lock.
AcquireLock	Acquire a spin lock.
ReleaseLock	Release a spin lock.

Device Path Functions

Table D.5 lists the support functions for creating and maintaining device path data structures.

Table D.5 Device Path Functions

Function Name	Function Description
DevicePathFromHandle	Retrieves the device path from a specified handle.
DevicePathInstance	Retrieves the next device path instance from a device path.
AppendDevicePath	Appends a device path to all the instances of another device path.
DevicePathSize	Returns the size of a device path in bytes.
UnpackDevicePath	Naturally aligns all the nodes in a device path.

Shell API Functions

The UEFI Shell Library provides a set of functions that access the shell environment. Table D.6 contains the list of shell interface support functions that are described in the following sections.

Table D.6 UEFI Shell API Functions

Function Name	Function Description
GetExecutionBreak	Gets the enable status of the execution break flag.
ShellGetEnv	Gets the environment variable.
ShellGetMap	Gets the device path from the mapping name.
ShellExecute	Causes the shell to parse and execute the command line.
ShellCurDir	Gets the current directory on the device.
EnablePageBreak	Enables the page break output mode.
DisablePageBreak	Disables the page break output mode.
GetPageBreak	Gets the enable status of the page break output mode.
ShellMetaFileArg	Opens the files that match the path specified.
ShellMetaFileArgNoWildCard	Opens the files that match the path specified without wild card.
ShellFreeFileList	Frees the file list that created by ShellMetaFileArg.
ShellInitHandleEnumerator	Initializes the handle enumerator.
ShellNextHandle	Gets the next handle.
ShellSkipHandle	Skips to the next nth handle.
ShellResetHandleEnumerator	Resets the handle enumerator to the given value.
ShellCloseHandleEnumerator	Closes the handle enumerator.
ShellGetHandleNum	Gets the handle numbers in the system.

AcquireLock()

This function acquires ownership of a lock.

Prototype

```
VOID
AcquireLock (
  IN FLOCK *Lock
  );
```

Parameters

Lock - A pointer to the lock to acquire.

Description

This function raises the system's current task priority level to the task priority level of the mutual exclusion lock. Then, it acquires ownership of the lock.

Status Codes Returned

None

AllocatePool()

This function allocates a buffer from memory with type `PoolAllocation-Type`.

Prototype
```
VOID *
AllocatePool (
  IN UINTN Size
  );
```

Parameters

`Size` - The size of the buffer to allocate from pool.

Description

This function attempts to allocate `Size` bytes from memory with type `PoolAllocationType`.

   If the memory allocation fails, NULL is returned. Otherwise a pointer to the allocated buffer is returned. Here `PoolAllocationType` is defined as `EfiBootServicesData`.

Status Codes Returned

≠NULL - Allocation succeeded and the base pointer is returned.

NULL - Allocation failed.

AllocateZeroPool()

This function allocates pool memory and initializes the memory to zeros.

Prototype

```
VOID *
AllocateZeroPool (
  IN UINTN Size
  );
```

Parameters

`Size` - Size in bytes of the pool being requested.

Description

This function attempts to allocate `Size` bytes from memory with type `PoolAllocationType` and initialize the memory area with zero. If the memory allocation fails, NULL is returned; otherwise a pointer to the allocated buffer is returned. Here `PoolAllocationType` is defined as `EfiBootServicesData.`

Status Codes Returned

≠NULL - The pointer to the memory space that the requested number of bytes were allocated.

NULL - The pool requested could not be allocated.

AppendDevicePath()

This function is used to append a device path to all the instances in another device path.

Prototype

```
EFI_DEVICE_PATH *
AppendDevicePath (
  IN EFI_DEVICE_PATH *Src1,
  IN EFI_DEVICE_PATH *Src2
  );
```

Parameters

Src1 - A pointer to a device path data structure.

Src2 - A pointer to a device path data structure.

Description

This function appends the device path Src2 to every device path instance in Src1. A pointer to the new device path is returned. NULL is returned if space for the new device path could not be allocated from pool. It is up to the caller to free the memory used by Src1 and Src2 if they are no longer needed.

Status Codes Returned

≠NULL - A pointer to the new appended device path.

NULL - The space for the new device path could not be allocated from pool.

Atoi()

This function converts a decimal formatted string to a value.

Prototype

```
UINTN
Atoi (
  IN CHAR16 *str
  );
```

Parameters

Str - A pointer to a null-terminated string.

Description

This function converts the decimal formatted string str into an unsigned integer and returns that integer. Any preceding white space character in str is ignored. The input string is a sequence of characters that can be interpreted as a numerical value of the specified type.

The function stops reading the input string at the first character that it cannot recognize as part of a number and returns the unsigned integer that has been converted. This character may be the null character terminating the string. If no character is converted, then 0 will be returned.

The `str` argument has the following form: [`whitespace`] [`digits`], where `digits` are one or more decimal digits. This function can only convert the string within the range of 0 to (`UINTN-1`). If the value is out of range, then (`UINTN-1`) will be returned.

Status Codes Returned

≥0 - A `UINTN` number that the string `str` expresses.

CompareMem()

This function compares the contents of two buffers.

Prototype

```
INTN
CompareMem (
  IN VOID   *Dest,
  IN VOID   *Src,
  IN UINTN  Len
  );
```

Parameters

`Dest` - Pointer to the buffer to compare.

`Src` - Pointer to the buffer to compare.

`Len` - Number of bytes to compare.

Description

This function compares `Len` bytes of `Src` to Len bytes of `Dest`. If the two buffers are identical for `Len` bytes, then 0 is returned. Otherwise, the difference between the first two mismatched bytes is returned. A positive return number indicates the first unmatched byte in `Dest` is greater than the corresponding byte in `Src`, while a negative return number indicates the first unmatched byte in `Src` is greater than the corresponding byte in `Dest`.

Status Codes Returned

0 - Dest is identical to Src for Len bytes.

>0 - Dest is not identical to Src for Len bytes

CopyMem()

This function copies the contents of one buffer to another buffer.

Prototype

```
VOID
CopyMem (
   IN VOID   *Dest,
   IN VOID   *Src,
   IN UINTN  Len
   );
```

Parameters

Dest - Pointer to the destination buffer of the memory copy.

Src - Pointer to the source buffer of the memory copy.

Len - Number of bytes to copy from *Src* to *Dest*.

Description

This function copies bytes from the buffer *Src* to the buffer *Dest*. It can deal with the case of the source and destination buffers overlapping. The caller should ensure *Dest* is large enough to hold bytes of *Src*; otherwise, a buffer overflow may occur.

Status Codes Returned

None

DevicePathFromHandle()

This function retrieves the device path for the specified handle.

Prototype

```
EFI_DEVICE_PATH *
DevicePathFromHandle (
  IN EFI_HANDLE Handle
  );
```

Parameters

`Handle` - A handle to retrieve the device path.

Description

This function retrieves the device path for a handle specified by `Handle`. If `Handle` is valid, then a pointer to the device path is returned. The caller should not attempt to free the returned pointer.

When using this function, the user must guarantee that the `Handle` is valid.

Status Codes Returned

≠NULL - The pointer to the memory space that contain the requested device path.

NULL - The `Handle` is invalid or no devices on it.

DevicePathInstance()

This function retrieves the next device path instance from a device path data structure.

Prototype

```
EFI_DEVICE_PATH *
DevicePathInstance (
  IN OUT EFI_DEVICE_PATH **DevicePath,
  OUT    UINTN            *Size
  );
```

Parameters

DevicePath - A pointer to a device path data structure.

Size - A pointer to the size of a device path instance in bytes.

Description

This function is used to parse device path instances from the device path *DevicePath*. This function returns a pointer to the current device path instance. In addition, it returns the size in bytes of the current device path instance in *Size*, and a pointer to the next device path instance in *DevicePath*. If there are no more device path instances in *DevicePath*, then *DevicePath* will be set to NULL.

Status Codes Returned

≠NULL - A pointer to the next device path instance in DevicePath.

NULL - There are no more device path instances in DevicePath.

DevicePathSize()

This function returns the size of a device path in bytes.

Prototype
```
UINTN
DevicePathSize (
  IN EFI_DEVICE_PATH *DevPath
  );
```

Parameters

DevPath - A pointer to a device path data structure.

Description

This function determines the size of a data path data structure in bytes. This size is returned. When using this function, the user must guarantee that the *DevPath* is valid.

Status Codes Returned

≥0 - The size of the device path `DevPath`.

DisablePageBreak()

This function disables the page break output mode.

Prototype
```
VOID
DisablePageBreak (
  VOID
  );
```

Parameters

None

Description

This function disables the page break interruptions when more than a page of data is being output.

Status Codes Returned

None

EnablePageBreak()

This function enables the page break output mode.

Prototype
```
VOID
EnablePageBreak (
  IN INT32    StartRow,
  IN BOOLEAN AutoWrap
  );
```

Parameters

`StartRow` - The start row number.

`AutoWrap` - To wrap a line is to ensure that a word isn't split apart by having reached the end of the line and will instead be printed on the subsequent line. If TRUE, the function will automatically wrap the line. If FALSE, it will not wrap the line.

Description

This function enables the page break output mode. The *StartRow* sets the rows in a page.

Status Codes Returned

None

FreePool()

This function releases a previously allocated buffer.

Prototype
```
VOID
FreePool (
  IN VOID *Pointer
  );
```

Parameters

`Pointer` - A pointer to the buffer to be freed.

Description

This function frees the buffer that has been previously allocated with `AllocatePool()`. The freed memory is returned to the available pool. The *Pointer* must be a pointer returned by `AllocatePool()` in the previous calling. If the *Pointer* has been freed or is not a pointer allocated by `AllocatePool()`, an exception may be generated.

Status Codes Returned

None

GetExecutionBreak()

This function gets the enable status of the execution break flag.

Prototype
```
BOOLEAN
GetExecutionBreak (
  VOID
  );
```

Parameters

None

Description

This function can be used to implement a break in the application. Applications use this function to receive the break signal sent from the system.

Status Codes Returned

TRUE - Enable.

FALSE - Disable.

GetPageBreak()

This function gets the enable status of the page break output mode.

Prototype
```
BOOLEAN
GetPageBreak (
  VOID
  );
```

Parameters

None

Description

The user can determine the current page break mode with this function.

Status Codes Returned

TRUE - The page break output mode is enabled.

FALSE - The page break output mode is disabled.

InitializeLock()

This function initializes a basic mutual exclusion lock.

Prototype

```
VOID
InitializeLock (
  IN OUT FLOCK    *Lock,
  IN      EFI_TPL Priority
  );
```

Parameters

Lock - A pointer to the lock data structure to initialize.

Priority - The task priority level of the lock.

Description

This function initializes a basic mutual exclusion lock. Each lock provides mutual exclusion access at its task priority level. Since there is no preemption or multiprocessor support in UEFI, acquiring the lock only consists of rising to the locks TPL.

Status Codes Returned

None

Input()

This function reads a string from the system console in device at the current cursor location.

Prototype
```
VOID
Input (
  IN  CHAR16 *Prompt OPTIONAL,
  OUT CHAR16 *InStr,
  IN  UINTN  StrLen
  );
```

Parameters

`Prompt` - A pointer to a string.

`InStr` - A pointer to the string used to store the string read from the console-in device.

`StrLen` - The maximum length of the string to read from the console-in device.

Description

If *Prompt* is not NULL, then *Prompt* is displayed on the console-out device. Then, characters are read from the console-in device and displayed on the console-out device. In addition, these characters are stored in *InStr* until either a "\n" or a "\r" character is received. If the Backspace key is pressed, then the last character in *InStr* is removed, and the display is updated to show that the character has been erased. If more than *StrLen* characters are received, then the extra characters are ignored.

Status Codes Returned

None

LibDevicePathToStr()

This function converts a device path data structure into a printable null-terminated string.

Prototype

```
CHAR16 *
LibDevicePathToStr (
  IN EFI_DEVICE_PATH_PROTOCOL *DevPath
  );
```

Parameters

`DevPath` - A pointer to a device path data structure.

Description

This function converts a device path data structure into a null-terminated string. The memory for the string is allocated from the pool, and a pointer to the string is returned. The format of the device path is described in Chapter 9 of the UEFI specification.

Status Codes Returned

≥0 - A string that the `DevPath` expresses.

LibCreateDirectory()

This function creates a directory of the directory names.

Prototype

```
EFI_STATUS
LibCreateDiectory(
  IN  CHAR16           *DirName,
  OUT EFI_FILE_HANDLE *FileHandle
  );
```

Parameters

`DirName` - A pointer to the directory name.

`FileHandle` - A pointer to the opened directory handle.

Description

If return is EFI_SUCCESS, the *FileHandle* is the directory's handle; otherwise, the *FileHandle* is NULL. If the file already exists, this function opens this directory.

Status Codes Returned

EFI_SUCCESS - The file was opened.

EFI_INVALID_PARAMETER - One of the parameters has an invalid value.

EFI_UNSUPPORTED – The file path could not be opened.

EFI_NOT_FOUND - The specified file could not be found on the device or the file system could not be found on the device.

EFI_NO_MEDIA - The device has no media.

EFI_MEDIA_CHANGED - The device has a different medium in it or the medium is no longer supported.

EFI_DEVICE_ERROR - The device reported an error or cannot get the file path according to the *DirName*.

EFI_VOLUME_CORRUPTED - The file system structures are corrupted.

EFI_WRITE_PROTECTED - An attempt was made to create a file, or to open a file for writing, when the media is write-protected.

EFI_ACCESS_DENIED - The service denied access to the file.

EFI_OUT_OF_RESOURCES - Not enough resources were available to open the file.

EFI_VOLUME_FULL - The volume is full.

LibCloseFile()

This function closes the file handle.

Prototype
```
EFI_STATUS
LibCloseFile (
  IN EFI_FILE_HANDLE FileHandle
  );
```

Parameters

FileHandle - The file handle to be closed.

Description

This function closes a specified file handle. All "dirty" cached file data is flushed to the device and the file is closed. In all cases the handle is closed.

Status Codes Returned

EFI_SUCCESS - The file was closed successfully.

LibDeleteFile()

This function closes and deletes the file handle.

Prototype

```
EFI_STATUS
LibDeleteFile (
  IN EFI_FILE_HANDLE FileHandle
  );
```

Parameters

FileHandle - The file handle to delete.

Description

This function closes and deletes a file. In all cases the file handle is closed. If the file cannot be deleted, the warning code EFI_WARN_DELETE_FAILURE is returned, but the handle is still closed.

Status Codes Returned

EFI_SUCCESS - The file was closed and deleted, and the handle was closed.
    EFI_WARN_DELETE_FAILURE - The handle was closed but the file was not deleted.

LibFileDevicePath()

This function allocates a device path for a file.

Prototype

```
EFI_DEVICE_PATH_PROTOCOL *
LibFileDevicePath (
  IN EFI_HANDLE  Device OPTIONAL,
  IN CHAR16      *FileName
  );
```

Parameters

Device - A pointer to a device handle.

FileName - A pointer to a null-terminated string.

Description

If *Device* is not a valid device handle, then a device path for the file specified by *FileName* is allocated and returned. This function allocates a buffer to store the device path. It is the caller's responsibility to free the buffer allocated by LibFileDevicePath().

Status Codes Returned

≠NULL - Device path successfully created.

NULL - Cannot create path.

LibFindFirstFile()

This function gets the first file in a directory.

Prototype

```
EFI_STATUS
LibFindFirstFile(
  IN  EFI_FILE_HANDLE DirHandle,
  OUT EFI_FILE_INFO   *Buffer
  );
```

Parameters

`DirHandle` - The handle of the directory to search in.

`Buffer` - The pointer to the buffer containing the first file's info.

Description

This function opens a directory and gets the first file's information in the directory. Caller can use `LibFindNextFile()` to get other files.

Status Codes Returned

`EFI_SUCCESS` - Found the first file.

`EFI_NOT_FOUND` - Cannot find the directory.

`EFI_NO_MEDIA` - The device has no media.

`EFI_DEVICE_ERROR` - The device reported an error.

`EFI_VOLUME_CORRUPTED` - The file system structures are corrupted.

LibFindNextFile()

This function gets the next file in a directory.

Prototype

```
EFI_STATUS
LibFindNextFile(
  IN  EFI_FILE_HANDLE  DirHandle,
  OUT EFI_FILE_INFO    *Buffer,
  OUT BOOLEAN          *NoFile
  );
```

Parameters

`DirHandle` - The handle of the directory to search in.

`Buffer` - A pointer to the buffer containing the file information.

`NoFile` - Determines whether any files exist.

Description

To use this function, caller must call the `LibFindFirstFile()` to get the first file, and then use this function get other files. This function can be called for several times to get each file's information in the directory. If the call of `LibFindNextFile()` got the last file in the directory, the next call of this function has no file to get. *NoFile* will be set to TRUE and the data in *Buffer* is meaningless.

Status Codes Returned

`EFI_SUCCESS` - Found the next file.

`EFI_NO_MEDIA` - The device has no media.

`EFI_DEVICE_ERROR` - The device reported an error.

`EFI_VOLUME_CORRUPTED` - The file system structures are corrupted.

LibFlushFile()

This function flushes data back to a device

Prototype

```
EFI_STATUS
LibFlushFile (
  IN EFI_FILE_HANDLE FileHandle
  );
```

Parameters

`FileHandle` - The file handle to flush.

Description

This function flushes all modified data associated with a file to a device.

Status Codes Returned

`EFI_SUCCESS` - The data was flushed.

`EFI_NO_MEDIA` - The device has no media.

EFI_DEVICE_ERROR - The device reported an error.

EFI_VOLUME_CORRUPTED - The file system structures are corrupted.

EFI_WRITE_PROTECTED - The file or medium is write-protected.

EFI_ACCESS_DENIED - The file was opened for read-only access.

EFI_VOLUME_FULL - The volume is full.

LibGetFileInfo()

This function gets the file information from an open file handle and stores it in a buffer allocated from the pool.

Prototype

```
EFI_FILE_INFO *
LibGetFileInfo (
  IN EFI_FILE_HANDLE FileHandle
  );
```

Parameters

FileHandle - A file handle.

Description

This function allocates a buffer to store the file's information. It is the caller's responsibility to free the buffer allocated by LibGetFileInfo().

Status Codes Returned

≠NULL - A pointer to a buffer with file information.

NULL - Cannot get the file information.

LibGetFileSize()

This function gets the size of a file.

Prototype

```
EFI_STATUS
LibGetFileSize(
  IN  EFI_FILE_HANDLE FileHandle,
  OUT UINT64          *Size
  );
```

Parameters

FileHandle - The handle of the file.

Size - The size of this file.

Description

This function extracts the file size information from the *FileHandle*'s EFI_FILE_INFO data.

Status Codes Returned

EFI_SUCCESS - Got the file's size.

EFI_DEVICE_ERROR - Cannot access the file.

LibGetPosition()

This function gets a file's current position

Prototype

```
EFI_STATUS
LibGetPosition (
  IN  EFI_FILE_HANDLE FileHandle,
  OUT UINT64          *Position
  );
```

Parameters

`FileHandle` - The file handle on which to get the current position.

`Position` - Byte position from the start of the file

Description

This function returns the current file position for the file handle. For directories, the current file position has no meaning outside of the file system driver and as such the operation is not supported.

An error is returned if *FileHandle* is a directory.

Status Codes Returned

`EFI_SUCCESS` - Data was accessed.

`EFI_UNSUPPORTED` - The request is not valid on open directories.

LibInitializeShellApplication()

This function initializes the UEFI Shell execution environment for the application.

Prototype

```
EFI_STATUS
LibInitializeShellApplication (
  IN EFI_HANDLE        ImageHandle,
  IN EFI_SYSTEM_TABLE *SystemTable
  );
```

Parameters

`ImageHandle` - A handle of an image that is initializing the library

`SystemTable` - A pointer to EFI system table

Description

This function must be called at the very beginning of an application to enable the use of all the other library functions. If this function fails, the application will exit to the shell.

Status Codes Returned

EFI_SUCCESS - Initialize success.

LibOpenFile()

This function opens a file or a directory.

Prototype

```
EFI_STATUS
LibOpenFile(
  IN OUT EFI_DEVICE_PATH_PROTOCOL **FilePath,
  OUT    EFI_HANDLE                *DeviceHandle,
  OUT    EFI_FILE_HANDLE           *FileHandle,
  IN     UINT64                    OpenMode,
  IN     UINT64                    Attributes
  );
```

Parameters

FilePath - On input, a pointer to the file path. On output, the file path pointer is modified to point to the remaining part of the file path.

DeviceHandle - A pointer to the file system device handle.

FileHandle - A pointer to the opened file handle.

OpenMode - File open mode.

Attributes - The file's *File* attributes.

Description25

This function opens a file with the open mode according to the file path. The *Attributes* is valid only for EFI_FILE_MODE_CREATE.

Status Codes Returned

EFI_SUCCESS - The file was opened.

EFI_INVALID_PARAMETER - One of the parameters has an invalid value.

EFI_UNSUPPORTED - Could not open the file path.

EFI_NOT_FOUND - The specified file could not be found on the device or the file system could not be found on the device.

EFI_NO_MEDIA - The device has no medium.

EFI_MEDIA_CHANGED - The device has a different medium in it or the medium is no longer supported.

EFI_DEVICE_ERROR - The device reported an error.

EFI_VOLUME_CORRUPTED - The file system structures are corrupted.

EFI_WRITE_PROTECTED - An attempt was made to create a file, or to open a file for writing, when the media is write-protected.

EFI_ACCESS_DENIED - The service denied access to the file.

EFI_OUT_OF_RESOURCES - Not enough resources were available to open the file.

EFI_VOLUME_FULL - The volume is full.

LibOpenFileByName()

This function opens a file or a directory by file name.

Prototype

```
EFI_STATUS
LibOpenFileByName(
  IN  CHAR16          *FileName,
  OUT EFI_FILE_HANDLE *FileHandle,
  IN  UINT64          OpenMode,
  IN  UINT64          Attributes
  );
```

Parameters

FileName - A pointer to the file name.

FileHandle - A pointer to the opened file handle.

OpenMode - File open mode.

Attributes - The file's *File* attributes.

Description

If return is `EFI_SUCCESS`, the *FileHandle* is the opened file's handle; otherwise, the *FileHandle* is NULL. The *Attributes* is valid only for `EFI_FILE_MODE_CREATE`.

Status Codes Returned

`EFI_SUCCESS` - The file was opened.

`EFI_INVALID_PARAMETER` - One of the parameters has an invalid value.

`EFI_UNSUPPORTED` - Could not open the file path.

`EFI_NOT_FOUND` - The specified file could not be found on the device or the file system could not be found on the device.

`EFI_NO_MEDIA` - The device has no medium.

`EFI_MEDIA_CHANGED` - The device has a different medium in it or the medium is no longer supported.

`EFI_DEVICE_ERROR` - The device reported an error or cannot get the file path according to the *FileName*.

`EFI_VOLUME_CORRUPTED` - The file system structures are corrupted.

`EFI_WRITE_PROTECTED` - An attempt was made to create a file, or to open a file for writing, when the medium is write-protected.

`EFI_ACCESS_DENIED` - The service denied access to the file.

`EFI_OUT_OF_RESOURCES` - Not enough resources were available to open the file.

`EFI_VOLUME_FULL` - The volume is full.

LibReadFile()

This function reads data from the file.

Prototype

```
EFI_STATUS
LibReadFile (
  IN     EFI_FILE_HANDLE  FileHandle,
  IN OUT UINTN            *ReadSize,
  OUT    VOID             *Buffer
  );
```

Parameters

`FileHandle` - The opened file handle for reading.

`ReadSize` - On input, the size of `Buffer`. On output, the amount of data in `Buffer`. In both cases, the size is measured in bytes.

`Buffer` - The buffer in which data is read.

Description

If *FileHandle* is not a directory, the function reads the requested number of bytes from the file at the file's current position and returns them in *Buffer*. If the read goes beyond the end of the file, the read length is truncated to the end of the file. The file's current position is increased by the number of bytes returned.

If *FileHandle* is a directory, the function reads the directory entry at the file's current position and returns the entry in *Buffer*. If the *Buffer* is not large enough to hold the current directory entry, then `EFI_BUFFER_TOO_SMALL` is returned and the current file position is not updated. *BufferSize* is set to be the size of the buffer needed to read the entry. On success, the current position is updated to the next directory entry. If there are no more directory entries, the read returns a zero-length buffer. `EFI_FILE_INFO` is the structure returned as the directory entry.

Status Codes Returned

EFI_SUCCESS - Data was read.

EFI_NO_MEDIA - The device has no media.

EFI_DEVICE_ERROR - The device reported an error.

EFI_VOLUME_CORRUPTED - The file system structures are corrupted.

EFI_BUFFER_TOO_SMALL - Buffer is too small. *ReadSize* contains required size.

LibSetFileInfo()

This function sets the file information to an opened file handle.

Prototype
```
EFI_STATUS
LibSetFileInfo (
  IN EFI_FILE_HANDLE  FileHandle,
  IN UINTN            BufferSize,
  IN VOID             *Buffer
  );
```

Parameters

FileHandle - A file handle.

BufferSize - The size of the file information.

Buffer - A pointer to the buffer where the file information will be stored.

Description

This function sets information of type EFI_FILE_INFO on the file handle. The data buffer pointer by Buffer must be a structure of type EFI_FILE_INFO.

Status Codes Returned

EFI_SUCCESS - The information was set.

EFI_NO_MEDIA - The device has no medium.

EFI_DEVICE_ERROR - The device reported an error.

EFI_VOLUME_CORRUPTED - The file system structures are corrupted.

EFI_WRITE_PROTECTED - The file or medium is write-protected.

EFI_ACCESS_DENIED - The file was opened with read-only access.

EFI_VOLUME_FULL - The volume is full.

EFI_BAD_BUFFER_SIZE - *BufferSize* is smaller than the size of EFI_
FILE_INFO.

LibSetPosition()

This function sets a file's current position.

Prototype

```
EFI_STATUS
LibSetPosition (
  IN EFI_FILE_HANDLE  FileHandle,
  IN UINT64           Position
  );
```

Parameters

FileHandle - The file handle on which the requested position will be set.

Position - Byte position from the start of the file.

Description

This function sets the current file position for the handle to the position supplied. With the exception of seeking to position *0xFFFFFFFFFFFFFFFF*, only absolute positioning is supported, and seeking past the end of the file is allowed (a subsequent write would grow the file). Seeking to position *0xFFFFFFFFFFFFFFFF* causes the current position to be set to the end of the file.

If *FileHandle* is a directory, the only position that may be set is zero. This has the effect of starting the read process of the directory entries over.

Status Codes Returned

EFI_SUCCESS - Data was written.

EFI_UNSUPPORTED - The seek request for nonzero is not valid on open directories.

LibWriteFile()

This function writes data to the file.

Prototype

```
EFI_STATUS
LibWriteFile(
  IN      EFI_FILE_HANDLE FileHandle,
  IN OUT UINTN *BufferSize,
  OUT     VOID *Buffer
  );
```

Parameters

FileHandle - The opened file handle for writing.

BufferSize - On input, size of *Buffer*. On output, the amount of data in *Buffer*. In both cases, the size is measured in bytes.

Buffer - The buffer in which data is written.

Description

This function writes the specified number of bytes to the file at the current file position. The current file position is advanced the actual number of bytes written, which is returned in *BufferSize*.

Partial writes only occur when a data error has occurred during the write attempt (such as "volume space full"). The file is automatically grown to hold the data if required. Direct writes to opened directories are not supported.

Status Codes Returned

EFI_SUCCESS - Data was written.

EFI_UNSUPPORTED - Writes to an open directory are not supported.

EFI_NO_MEDIA - The device has no media.

EFI_DEVICE_ERROR - The device reported an error.

EFI_VOLUME_CORRUPTED - The file system structures are corrupted.

EFI_WRITE_PROTECTED - The device is write-protected.

EFI_ACCESS_DENIED - The file was open for read only access.

EFI_VOLUME_FULL - The volume is full.

Output()

This function sends a string to the system console-out device at the current cursor location.

Prototype

```
VOID
Output (
  IN CHAR16 *Str
  );
```

Parameters

Str- A pointer to a string.

Description

This function sends the string *Str* to the console-out device specified in the system table.

Status Codes Returned

None

Print

This function prints a formatted string.

Prototype

```
UINTN
Print (
  IN CONST CHAR16 *fmt,
  ...
  );
```

Parameters

fmt- Format string. See Format Strings for more information.

Description

Prints a formatted string to the default console.

Returns

Length of string printed to the console.

PrintAt()

This function sends a formatted string to the console-out device at the specified cursor location.

Prototype

```
UINTN
PrintAt (
  IN UINTN  Column,
  IN UINTN  Row,
  IN CHAR16 *fmt,
  ...
  );
```

Parameters

`Column` - The column number on the console-out device.

`Row` - The row number on the console-out device.

`Fmt` - A pointer to a string containing format information.

`...`- Variable length argument list.

Description

This function uses the format string *fmt* and the variable length argument list to build a formatted string. This formatted string is then sent to the console-out device at the cursor location specified by *Column* and *Row*. The length of the formatted string is returned.

Status Codes Returned

≥0 - The length of the formatted string.

ReleaseLock()

This function releases ownership of a lock.

Prototype

```
VOID
ReleaseLock (
  IN FLOCK *Lock
  );
```

Parameters

`Lock` - A pointer to the lock to release.

Description

This function releases ownership of the mutual exclusion lock and restores the system's task priority level to its previous level.

Status Codes Returned

None

SetMem()

This function fills a buffer with a specified value.

Prototype

```
VOID
SetMem (
  IN OUT VOID    *Buffer,
  IN      UINTN Size,
  IN      UINT8 Value
  );
```

Parameters

Buffer - Pointer to the buffer to fill.

Size - Number of bytes in the buffer to fill.

Value - Value to fill buffer with.

Description

This function fills *Size* bytes of *Buffer* with *Value*.

Status Codes Returned

None

Sprint()

This function sends a formatted string to the specified buffer.

Prototype

```
UINTN
SPrint (
  OUT CHAR16 *Str,
  IN  UINTN StrSize,
  IN  CHAR16 *fmt,
  ...
  );
```

Parameters

`Str` - A pointer to a string.

`StrSize` - The maximum length of the string `Str`.

`Fmt` - A pointer to a string containing format information.

`...` - Variable length argument list.

Description

This function uses the format string `Fmt` and the variable length argument list to build a formatted string. Note that a Null character will be appended automatically after the last character is written. This formatted string, including an additional Null character's size, is no more than `StrSize`.

Status Codes Returned

≥0 - The length of the formatted string.

StrCat()

This function concatenates one string to another string.

Prototype

```
VOID
StrCat (
  IN OUT CHAR16 *Dest,
  IN     CHAR16 *Src
  );
```

Parameters

`Dest` - A pointer to a destination null-terminated string.

`Src` - A pointer to a source null-terminated string.

Description

This function concatenates two strings. The contents of string `Src` are concatenated to the end of string `Dest`. The caller should ensure `Dest` is large enough to hold both strings and a Null terminator; otherwise, a buffer overflow may occur.

Status Codes Returned

None

StrChr()

This function gets a substring start from the specified character. The function is case-sensitive.

Prototype

```
CHAR16 *
StrChr(
  IN CHAR16 *Str,
  IN CHAR16 c
  );
```

Parameters

str - A pointer to a null-terminated string.

c - A character.

Description

If successful, returns the address of the first occurrence of the specified character in the *str*; if not returns NULL.

Status Codes Returned

≠NULL - The substring.

NULL - The substring does not exist.

StrCmp()

This function compares two strings.

Prototype

```
INTN
StrCmp (
  IN CHAR16 *S1,
  IN CHAR16 *S2
  );
```

Parameters

S1 - A pointer to a first null-terminated string.

S2 - A pointer to a second null-terminated string.

Description

This function compares the string *S1* to the string *S2*. If *S1* is identical to *S2*, then 0 is returned. Otherwise, the difference between the first mismatched characters is returned.

Returns

0 - *S1* is identical to *S2*.

≠0 - *S1* is not identical to *S2*.

Strcmpa()

This function compares two ASCII strings. The comparison is case-sensitive.

Prototype

```
UINTN
strcmpa (
  IN CHAR8 *S1,
  IN CHAR8 *S2
  );
```

Parameters

S1 - A pointer to a first null-terminated ASCII string.

S2 - A pointer to a second null-terminated ASCII string.

Description

This function compares the ASCII string *S1* to the ASCII string *S2*. If *S1* is identical to *S2*, then 0 is returned.

Status Codes Returned

0 - *S1* is identical to *S2*.

≠0 - *S1* is not identical to *S2*.

StrCpy()

This function copies one string to another string.

Prototype

```
VOID
StrCpy (
  OUT CHAR16 *Dest,
  IN  CHAR16 *Src
  );
```

Parameters

Dest - A pointer to a destination null-terminated string.

Src - A pointer to a source null-terminated string.

Description

This function copies the contents of the string *Src* to the string *Dest*. The caller should ensure *Dest* is large enough to hold the whole *Src*; otherwise, a buffer overflow may occur.

Status Codes Returned

None

StriCmp()

This function compares two strings. The comparison is case-insensitive.

Prototype

```
INTN
StriCmp (
  IN CHAR16  *S1,
  IN CHAR16  *S2
  );
```

Parameters

S1 - A pointer to a first null-terminated string.

S2 - A pointer to a second null-terminated string.

Description

This function compares the string $S1$ to the string $S2$. If $S1$ is identical to $S2$ case-insensitively, then 0 is returned. Otherwise, the difference between the first mismatched characters is returned.

Status Codes Returned

0 - $S1$ is identical to $S2$.

≠0 - $S1$ is not identical to $S2$.

StrDuplicate()

This function duplicates a string.

Prototype

```
CHAR16*
StrDuplicate (
  IN CHAR16  *Str
  );
```

Parameters

`Str` - A pointer to a null-terminated string.

Description

This function returns the copy of a string. It is the caller's responsibility to free the returned string.

Status Codes Returned

≠NULL - A pointer to the new string.

NULL - Cannot allocate memory for new string.

StrLen()

This function determines the length of a string.

Prototype

```
UINTN
StrLen (
  IN CHAR16 *S1
);
```

Parameters

`S1` - A pointer to a null-terminated string.

Description

Returns the number of characters in the string $S1$, excluding the Null terminator.

Status Codes Returned

≥0 - The length of string $S1$.

Strlena()

This function returns the length of an ASCII string.

Prototype

```
UINTN
Strlena (
  IN CHAR8  *S1
  );
```

Parameters

S1 - A pointer to a null-terminated ASCII string.

Description

This function returns the length of an ASCII string, excluding the Null terminator.

Status Codes Returned

≥0 - The length of the ASCII string *S1*.

StrLwr()

This function converts all the characters in a string to lowercase characters.

Prototype

```
VOID
StrLwr (
  IN OUT CHAR16  *Str
  );
```

Parameters

Str - A pointer to a null-terminated string.

Description

This function converts all the characters in the string *Str* to lowercase characters.

Status Codes Returned

None

StrnCmp()

This function compares a portion of two strings. The comparison is case-sensitive.

Prototype

```
INTN
StrnCmp (
  IN CHAR16 *S1,
  IN CHAR16 *S2,
  IN UINTN Len
  );
```

Parameters

S1 - A pointer to a first null-terminated string.

S2 - A pointer to a second null-terminated string.

Len - Number of characters to compare.

Description

This function compares characters from *S1* to characters from *S2*. If all characters from *S1* and *S2* are identical, then 0 is returned. Otherwise, the difference between the first mismatched characters is returned.

Status Codes Returned

0 - *S1* is identical to *S2*.

≠0 - *S1* is not identical to *S2*.

Strncmpa()

This function compares a portion of two ASCII strings. The comparison is case-sensitive.

Prototype

```
UINTN
Strcmpa (
  IN CHAR8  *S1,
  IN CHAR8  *S2,
  IN UINTN  len
  );
```

Parameters

S1 - A pointer to a first null-terminated ASCII string.

S2 - A pointer to a second null-terminated ASCII string.

Len - The length of the portion of string that will be compared.

Description

This function compares the ASCII string *S1* to the ASCII string *S2*; at most, the first characters in *S1* and *S2* will be compared.

Status Codes Returned

0 - The first characters in *S1* and are identical.

≠0 - *S1* is not identical to *S2*.

StrSize()

This function returns the size of a string in bytes including the NULL terminator.

Prototype

```
UINTN
StrSize (
  IN CHAR16 *S1
  );
```

Parameters

S1 - A pointer to a null-terminated string.

Description

This function returns the size of a string in bytes including the NULL terminator.

Status Codes Returned

≥0 - The size of string *S1*.

StrStr()

This function gets the index of the first occurrence of the specified pattern in the string. The function is case-sensitive.

Prototype

```
UINTN
StrStr (
  IN CHAR16 *Str,
  IN CHAR16 *Pat
  );
```

Parameters

Str - A pointer to a null-terminated string.

Pat - A pointer to a null-terminated string.

Description

If found, the `Pat` in the `Str` returns the first position (starting from 1) of the `Pat`'s occurrence; if not found it returns 0.

Status Codes Returned

0 - Not found.

>0 - The index is (return value − 1).

StrSubCmp()

This function performs a substring search in a null-terminated strings. The search is case-sensitive.

Prototype
```
BOOLEAN
StrSubCmp (
   IN CHAR16 *S1,
   IN CHAR16 *S2,
   IN UINTN  len
   );
```

Parameters

`S1` - A pointer to a null-terminated substring to be searched for.

`S2` - A pointer to a null-terminated string to be searched in.

`Len` - Comparison size.

Description

This function searches substring `S1` in string `S2` case sensitively. If `S1` is found in `S2` it returns TRUE, otherwise FALSE.

Status Codes Returned

TRUE - Found `S1` in `S2`.

FALSE - Cannot find `S1` in `S2`.

StrTrim()

This function removes (trims) specified leading and trailing characters from a string.

Prototype
```
VOID
StrTrim (
  IN OUT CHAR16 *Str,
  IN     CHAR16 c
  );
```

Parameters

Str - Pointer to the null-terminated string to be trimmed. On return, *Str* will hold the trimmed string.

c - Character that will be trimmed from *Str*.

Description

The string pointed to by *Str* will be modified on return if there are leading and/or ending characters of *c*.

Status Codes Returned

None

StrUpr()

This function converts all the characters in a string to uppercase characters.

Prototype
```
VOID
StrUpr (
  IN OUT CHAR16 *Str
  );
```

Parameters

Str - A pointer to a null-terminated string.

Description

This function converts all the characters in the string *Str* to uppercase characters.

Status Codes Returned

None

UnpackDevicePath()

This function unpacks a device path data structure so that all the nodes of a device path are naturally aligned.

Prototype

```
EFI_DEVICE_PATH *
UnpackDevicePath (
  IN EFI_DEVICE_PATH *DevPath
  );
```

Parameters

DevPath - A pointer to a device path data structure.

Description

This function allocates space for a new copy of the device path *DevPath*. The new copy of *DevPath* is modified so that every node of the device path is naturally aligned. If the memory for the device path is successfully allocated, then a pointer to the new device path is returned. Otherwise, NULL is returned.

When using this function, the user must guarantee that the *DevPath* is valid. It is the caller's responsibility to free the memory used by the new device path if it is no longer needed.

Status Codes Returned

≠NULL - A pointer to the new device path.

NULL - The space for the new device path could not be allocated from pool.

Xtoi()

This function converts a hexadecimal formatted string to a value.

Prototype

```
UINTN
Xtoi (
  IN CHAR16 *str
  );
```

Parameters

str - A pointer to a null-terminated string.

Description

This function converts the hexadecimal formatted string *str* into an unsigned integer and returns that integer. Any preceding white space character in *str* is ignored. The input string is a sequence of characters that can be interpreted as a hexadecimal value of the specified type.

The function stops reading the input string at the first character that it cannot recognize as part of a number and returns the unsigned integer that has been converted. This character may be the Null character terminating the string. If no character is converted, then 0 will be returned.

The *str* argument has the following form: [*whitespace*] [0x] [*characters*], where *characters* are one or more hexadecimal characters ("0"—"9", "a"–"f", "A"–"F"). This function can only convert the string within the range of 0 to *(UINTN-1)*. If the value is out of range, then *(UINTN-1)* will be returned.

Status Codes Returned

≥0 A UINTN number that the string *str* expresses.

ShellCloseHandleEnumerator()

This function closes the handle enumerator.

Prototype
```
VOID
ShellCloseHandleEnumerator (
  VOID
  );
```

Parameters

None

Description

This function releases the resource used to access the system handle.

Status Codes Returned

None

ShellCurDir()

This function gets the current directory on the device.

Prototype
```
CHAR16 *
ShellCurDir (
  IN CHAR16 *DeviceName OPTIONAL
  );
```

Parameters

DeviceName - The device's name.

Description

If the *DeviceName* is NULL, it returns the current device's current directory name. If the *DeviceName* is not NULL, it returns the directory name specified by *DeviceName*'s current name.

Status Codes Returned

!=NULL - The current directory.

NULL - Current directory does not exist.

ShellExecute()

This function causes the shell to parse and execute the command line.

Prototype

```
EFI_STATUS
ShellExecute (
  IN EFI_HANDLE   ImageHandle,
  IN CHAR16       *CmdLine,
  IN BOOLEAN      Output
  );
```

Parameters

ImageHandle - A handle of an image that is initializing the library.

CmdLine - Command line.

Output - If TRUE, it will output the result. If FALSE, it will not output the result.

Description

This function executes a shell command or launches an application.

Status Codes Returned

EFI_SUCCESS - The command executed successfully.

EFI_INVALID_PARAMETER - The parameters are invalid.

EFI_OUT_OF_RESOURCES - Out of resources.

ShellFileMetaArg()

This function opens the files that match the path specified.

Prototype

```
EFI_STATUS
ShellFileMetaArg (
  IN      CHAR16          *Arg,
  IN OUT  EFI_LIST_ENTRY  *ListHead
  );
```

Parameters

`Arg` - A pointer to the path string.

`ListHead` - A list of files that match the specified path.

Description

This function uses the Arg pointer to open all the matching files. Each matched file has a `SHELL_FILE_ARG` structure to record the file information. These structures are placed on the list $ListHead$. Users can get the `SHELL_FILE_ARG` structures from $ListHead$ to access each file.

   This function supports wildcards.

Status Codes Returned

`EFI_SUCCESS` - The file list was successfully created.

Other EFI Status Codes - Cannot create the file list.

ShellFileMetaArgNoWildCard()

This function opens the files that match the path specified without wild card.

Prototype

```
EFI_STATUS
ShellFileMetaArgNoWildCard (
  IN     CHAR16         *Arg,
  IN OUT EFI_LIST_ENTRY *ListHead
  );
```

Parameters

`Arg` - A pointer to the path.

`ListHead` - A list of files that match the specified path.

Description

This function is the same as the function `ShellFileMetaArg()`, but does not support wildcards.

Status Codes Returned

`EFI_SUCCESS` - The file list was successfully created.

Other EFI Status Codes - Cannot create the file list.

ShellFreeFileList()

This function frees the file list that was created by `ShellMetaFileArg()` or `ShellMetaFileArgNoWildCard()`.

Prototype

```
EFI_STATUS
ShellFreeFileList (
  IN OUT EFI_LIST_ENTRY *ListHead
  );
```

Parameters

`ListHead` - The list created by `ShellMetaFileArg()` or `ShellMeta-FileArgNoWildCard()`.

Description

This function cleans up the files represented by the file list. It will close the opened files in the list and free the associated resources.

Status Codes Returned

`EFI_SUCCESS` - The file list was successfully freed.

ShellGetEnv()

This function gets the environment variable.

Prototype

```
CHAR16 *
ShellGetEnv (
  IN CHAR16 *Name
  );
```

Parameters

`Name` - A pointer to the environment variable name.

Description

This function gets the environment variable set by the command `set`. To set a variable, use the command `set`.

Status Codes Returned

≠NULL - The environment variable's value.

NULL - The environment variable does not exist.

ShellGetHandleNum()

This function gets the handle number in the system.

Prototype

```
UINTN
ShellGetHandleNum(
  VOID
  );
```

Parameters

None

Description

The `ShellGetHandleNum()` function gets the handle number in the system.

Status Codes Returned

≥0 - The handle number in the system.

ShellGetMap()

This function gets the device path from the mapping name.

Prototype

```
EFI_DEVICE_PATH_PROTOCOL*
ShellGetMap (
  IN CHAR16 *Name
  );
```

Parameters

`Name` - A pointer to the mapping name.

Description

This function gets the device path's mapping name. The user can employ the command map to set a new mapping name to a device.

Status Codes Returned

!=NULL - The device path of the mapping name.

NULL - The mapping name does not exist.

ShellInitHandleEnumerator()

This function initializes the handle enumerator.

Prototype
```
VOID
ShellInitHandleEnumerator (
  VOID
  );
```

Parameters

None

Description

The UEFI Shell library provides serial functions to enable users to access the handle in the system. To use these functions, the user must call this function first to initialize the environment.

Status Codes Returned

None

ShellNextHandle()

This function gets the next handle.

Prototype
```
EFI_STATUS
ShellNextHandle (
  OUT EFI_HANDLE **Handle
  );
```

Parameters

Handle - A pointer to the pointer to an EFI handle.

Description

This function returns the current handle in the handle table and moves the enumerator to the next handle.

Status Codes Returned

EFI_SUCCESS - Got the next handle; enumerator moved to next handle.

EFI_NOT_FOUND - Cannot get the next handle.

ShellResetHandleEnumerator()

This function resets the handle enumerator.

Prototype
```
VOID
ShellResetHandleEnumerator (
 VOID
 );
```

Parameters

None

Description

This function sets the enumerator to zero.

Status Codes Returned

None

ShellSkipHandle()

This function skips to the next *n*th handle.

Prototype

```
EFI_STATUS
ShellSkipHandle (
   IN UINTN NumSkip
   );
```

Parameters

`NumSkip` - The handle number to skip.

Description

This function moves the enumerator to the next *n*th handle.

Status Codes Returned

`EFI_SUCCESS` - Skipped to the next nth handle.

`EFI_ACCESS_DENIED` - Cannot access the next nth handle.

Data Structures

The following are data structures used in the UEFI Shell Library.

Format Strings

Format strings are normal strings with placeholders for runtime values. The placeholders are prefixed with the % (percent) character. The characters that follow the % character determine the type and format of the data to be displayed and have the following format:

```
%w.lF
```

Where *w* is the width, *l* is the field width and *F* is the format. The width *w* can be any one of the following:

0 – Pad with zeroes

- (Hyphen) - Left justify (default is right justify)

, -- Add commas to the field

* -- Width provided on the stack

The field width l, if present, indicates that the value is 64-bits. The format F can be one of the following:

a - ASCII string

s - Unicode string

X - fixed 8-byte value in hexadecimal

x - hexadecimal value

d - value as decimal

c - Unicode character

t - EFI time structure

g - Pointer to GUID

r - EFI status code (result code)

% - Print a %

Spin Locks

Prototype

```
typedef struct _FLOCK {
  EFI_TPL  Tpl;
  EFI_TPL  OwnerTpl;
  UINTN    Lock;
} FLOCK;
```

Glossary

agent An EFI component that can consume a protocol in the handle database.

agent handle A term used by some of the UFI Driver Model–related services in the UEFI specification to represent an image handle, a driver handle, or a driver image handle.

alias The concept of having alternate names for shell commands. A very common alias would be to associate the LS command with the dir command.

Bootable Image Services A term used collectively to describe the Block I/O Protocol, Disk I/O Protocol, Simple File System Protocol, and Load File Protocol.

bus controller handle Managed by a bus driver or a hybrid driver that produces child handles. The term bus does not necessarily match the hardware topology, but in this book is used from the software perspective, and the production of the software construct—which is called a child handle—is the only distinction between a controller handle and a bus controller handle.

bus driver Nearly identical to a device driver except that it creates child handles. The main objectives of the bus driver are to initialize the bus controller, to determine how many children to create, to allocate resources and create a child handle for one or more child controllers, to install an I/O protocol on the child handle that abstracts the I/O operations that the controller supports (such as the PCI I/O Protocol or the USB I/O Protocol), if the child handle represents a physical device, to then install a Device Path Protocol, and to load drivers from option ROMs if present. (To date, the PCI bus driver is the only bus driver that loads from option ROMs.)

child handle A type of controller handle that is created by a bus driver or a hybrid driver. The distinction between a child handle and a controller handle depends on the perspective of the driver that is using the handle. A handle would be a child handle from a bus driver's perspective, and that same handle may be a controller handle from a device driver's perspective.

controller handle A handle that represents a physical device, and that therefore must support the Device Path Protocol. If the handle represents a virtual device, then it must not support the Device Path Protocol. In addition, a device handle must support one or more additional I/O protocols that are used to abstract access to that device.

cwd The shell environment variable used to determine what the current working directory is.

device handle Used interchangeably with controller handle.

driver handle Supports the Driver Binding Protocol. May optionally support the Driver Configuration Protocol, the Driver Diagnostics Protocol, and the Component Name Protocol.

driver image handle The intersection of image handles and driver handles. Supports both the Loaded Image Protocol and the Driver Binding Protocol. May optionally support the Driver Configuration Protocol, the Driver Diagnostics Protocol, and the Component Name Protocol.

DUET The Developer's UEFI Emulation (DUET). DUET is designed to provide a UEFI environment on a non-UEFI pre-boot system. This is achieved by creating an UEFI file image for a bootable device, and then 'booting" that image as a legacy boot.

HII The human interface infrastructure (HII). This is defined in the UEFI specification and is often considered the basis of the UEFI configuration infrastructure.

hybrid driver A hybrid driver has features of both a device driver and a bus driver. The main distinction between a device driver and a bus driver is that a bus driver creates child handles and a device driver does not create any child handles. In addition, a bus driver is allowed only to install produced protocols on the newly created child handles. A hybrid driver creates new child handles, installs produced protocols on the child handles, and installs produced protocols onto the bus controller handle.

image handle Supports the Loaded Image Protocol.

lasterror The shell environment variable that describes what the last error that was returned by a shell command or script.

Network Services Refers to Network Interface Identifier Protocol, Simple Network Protocol, and PXE Base Code Protocol.

path The shell environment variable which contains the default path which the shell will search when attempting to launch a script or application.

PCI Services Refers to PCI Root Bridge I/O Protocol, PCI I/O Protocol, and Device I/O Protocol.

physical controller handle A controller handle that represents a physical device that must support the Device Path Protocol.

profiles The shell environment variable that determines what the current command profiles the running UEFI Shell supports.

protocol An interface exposed by a UEFI software component. Much of the UEFI specification covers a variety of different protocols, as does the UEFI Shell specification.

provisioning The act of configuring the operating system or providing a new operating system.

Programmatic Shell Environment This environment is guaranteed to remain available regardless of what underlying Shell level is supported by a platform that purports to support the UEFI Shell. It is composed of the calling interfaces that shell applications can use.

Script Shell Environment This environment is the one that supports the launching and interpreting of shell scripts. The biggest variation that one might witness between shell support levels is the enumeration of commands that are supported in a given support level.

shellsupport A shell environment variable that can be used by shell applications as well as shell scripts to determine what the underlying UEFI Shell's function support is.

USB Services refers to the USB Host Controller Protocol and USB I/O Protocol.

Index

X

Continuing Education is Essential

It's a challenge we all face – keeping pace with constant change in information technology. Whether our formal training was recent or long ago, we must all find time to keep ourselves educated and up to date in spite of the daily time pressures of our profession.

Intel produces technical books to help the industry learn about the latest technologies. The focus of these publications spans the basic motivation and origin for a technology through its practical application.

Right books, right time, from the experts

These technical books are planned to synchronize with roadmaps for technology and platforms, in order to give the industry a head-start. They provide new insights, in an engineer-to-engineer voice, from named experts. Sharing proven insights and design methods is intended to make it more practical for you to embrace the latest technology with greater design freedom and reduced risks.

I encourage you to take full advantage of Intel Press books as a way to dive deeper into the latest technologies, as you plan and develop your next generation products. They are an essential tool for every practicing engineer or programmer. I hope you will make them a part of your continuing education tool box.

Sincerely,

Justin Rattner
Senior Fellow and Chief Technology Officer
Intel Corporation

Turn the page to learn about titles
from Intel Press for system developers

Dynamics of a Trusted Platform
A Building Block Approach
By David Grawrock
ISBN 978-1-934053-08-9

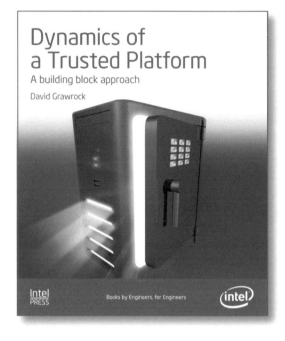

In Dynamics of a Trusted Platform David Grawrock has updated his highly popular Intel Safer Computing Initiative with new topics covering the latest developments in secure computing. The reader is introduced to the concept of Trusted Computing and the building block approach to designing security into PC platforms. The Intel® Trusted Execution Technology† (Intel® TXT) is one of those building blocks that can be used to create a trusted platform by integrating new security features and capabilities into the processor, chipset, and other platform components.

 "The chapters on Anatomy of an Attack and System Protection present useful, practical information that will help familiarize a person with the impacts of protection (or lack thereof) of system components and resources. Treatment of the topic of measurement is particularly useful for system designers and programmers." *- Amy C Nelson, Dell, Inc*

"David finds analogies in everyday life to clearly explain many of the concepts in this book. I would highly recommended Dynamics of a Trusted Platform for researchers, architects, and designers who are serious about trusted computing." *- Dr. Sigrid Gürgens Fraunhofer Institute for Secure Information Technology (SIT)*

"The opportunity now exists to start building trusted systems, making this book very timely. It would be foolhardy to start without a thorough understanding of the concepts; and this is what Dynamics of a Trusted Platform gives you. The building blocks described here are certainly able to imbue the infrastructure with a higher level of trustworthiness, and we may all look forward to the many benefits flowing from that." *- Andrew Martin Director, Oxford University Software Engineering Centre*

Applied Virtualization Technology
Usage Models for IT Professionals and Software Developers

By Sean Campbell and Michael Jeronimo
ISBN 978-0-976483-26-6

Server and desktop virtualization is one of the more significant technologies to impact computing in the last few years, promising the benefits of infrastructure consolidation, lower costs, increased security, ease of management, and greater employee productivity.

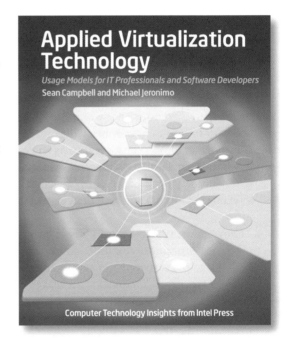

Using virtualization technology, one computer system can operate as multiple "virtual" systems. The convergence of affordable, powerful platforms and robust scalable virtualization solutions is spurring many technologists to examine the broad range of uses for virtualization. In addition, a set of processor and I/O enhancements to Intel server and client platforms, known as Intel® Virtualization Technology (Intel® VT), can further improve the performance and robustness of current software virtualization solutions.

This book takes a user-centered view and describes virtualization usage models for IT professionals, software developers, and software quality assurance staff. The book helps you plan the introduction of virtualization solutions into your environment and thereby reap the benefits of this emerging technology.

Highlights include
- The challenges of current virtualization solutions
- In-depth examination of three software-based virtualization products
- Usage models that enable greater IT agility and cost savings
- Usage models for enhancing software development and QA environments
- Maximizing utilization and increasing flexibility of computing resources
- Reaping the security benefits of computer virtualization
- Distribution and deployment strategies for virtualization solutions

Energy Efficiency for Information Technology

How to Reduce Power Consumption in Servers and Data Centers
By David Grawrock
ISBN 978-1-934053-08-9

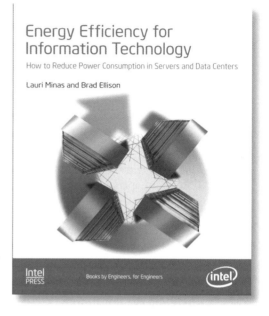

Minimizing power consumption is one of the primary technical challenges that today's IT organizations face. In Energy Efficiency for Information Technology, Lauri Minas and Brad Ellison point out, that the overall consumption of electrical power by data centers can be reduced by understanding the several sources of power consumption and minimizing each one. Drawing on their engineering experience within Intel Corporation and with the industry, they break down power consumption into its constituent parts and explain each in a bottom-up fashion. With energy consumption well defined, Minas and Ellison systematically provide guidance for minimizing each draw on electrical power.

"Throughout my global travels, I hear increasing concern for the issues of power consumption by data centers, both due to the costs and also harm to the planet. *Energy Efficiency for Information Technology* addresses a critical issue for IT suppliers and consumers alike." Vernon Turner, Senior Vice President & General Manager, Enterprise Computing, Network, Consumer, and Infrastructure, IDC

"In *Energy Efficiency for Information Technology* Minas and Ellison underscore the magnitude of increases in power consumption, they systematically suggest ways to minimize consumption and provide checklists and assessments tables that are particularly useful to gather or summarize the right information for the planning. This is a multidimensional book that addresses a serious challenge to IT departments around the globe."
YY Chow, Managing Director, Systems and Securities Services, Mitsubishi-UFJ Securities

"*Energy Efficiency for Information Technology* is a remarkable compilation of cutting edge technical knowledge for addressing the critical issue of power and cooling in data centers. It shows how your data center can compute more but cost less, while also reducing energy use and environmental impacts".
Jonathan Koomey, Ph.D., Project Scientist, Lawrence Berkeley National Laboratory

"Lauri Minas and Brad Ellison have written an important book that explains how diligent IT professionals can maximize the productivity of their data centers while minimizing power costs. These Intel engineers speak from experience and with authority. Anyone seriously interested in the greening of IT should read *Energy Efficiency for Information Technology*." Lorie Wigle, President, Climate Servers Computing Initiative.

Service Oriented Architecture Demystified
A pragmatic approach to SOA for the IT executives
By Girish Juneja, Blake Dournaee, Joe Natoli, and Steve Birkel
ISBN 978-1-934053-02-7

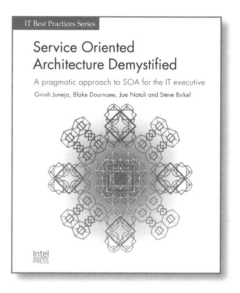

The authors of this definitive book on SOA debunk the myths and demonstrate through examples from different vertical industries how a "crawl, walk, run" approach to deployment of SOA in an IT environment can lead to a successful return on investment.

One popular argument states that SOA is not a technology per se, but that it stands alone and can be implemented using a wide range of technologies. The authors believe that this definition, while attractive and elegant, doesn't necessarily pass pragmatic muster.

Service Oriented Architecture Demystified describes both the technical and organizational impacts of adopting SOA and the pursuant challenges. The authors demonstrate through real life deployments why and how different industry sectors are adopting SOA, the challenges they face, the advantages they have realized, and how they have (or have not) addressed the issues emerging from their adoption of SOA. This book strikes a careful balance between describing SOA as an enabler of business processes and presenting SOA as a blueprint for the design of software systems in general. Throughout the book, the authors attempt to cater to both technical and organizational viewpoints, and show how both are very different in terms of why SOA is useful. The IT software architect sees SOA as a business process enabler and the CTO sees SOA as a technology trend with powerful paradigms for software development and software integration.

SOA can be characterized in terms of different vertical markets. For each such market, achieving SOA means something different and involves different transformational shifts. The vertical markets covered include healthcare, government, manufacturing, finance, and telecommunications. SOA considerations are quite different across these vertical markets, and in some cases, the required organizational shifts and technology shifts are highly divergent and context dependent.

Whether you are a CTO, CIO, IT manager, or IT architect, this book provides you with the means to analyze the readiness of your internal IT organization and with technologies to adopt a service oriented approach to IT.

The Business Value of Virtual Service Oriented Grids

Strategic Insights for Enterprise Decision Makers

By Enrique Castro-leon, Jackson He, Mark Chang and Parviz Peiravi
ISBN 978-1-934053-10-2

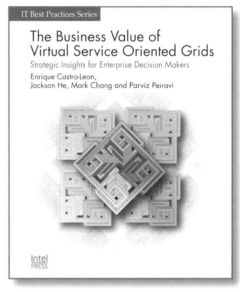

"In this book the authors track the trends, create new rules based on new realities, and establish new market models. With virtual service-oriented grids, the sky is the limit," writes Wei-jen Lee, a University of Texas – Arlington professor, about *The Business Value of Virtual Service Oriented Grids*, a new book published by Intel. The application of service-oriented architecture (SOA) for business will interest application developers looking for the latest advances in technology and ideas on how to utilize those advances to keep up in a global economy. *The Business Value of Virtual Service Oriented Grids* provides a framework that describes how the convergence of three well-known technologies are defining a new information technology model that will fundamentally change the way we do business. The first step, say the authors, is the development of new applications for the consumer market. However, even bigger is the development of new applications in a federated fashion using services modules called *servicelets*. These federated or composite applications can be built in a fraction of the time it takes to develop traditional applications. This new environment will lower the bar for applications development, opening opportunities for thousands of smaller players worldwide.

"We live in exponential times. . . . The economy is now thoroughly global. The Internet has replaced many of the middle layers of business, has enabled many to work from home or from a small company, and is revolutionizing the retail industries." writes Portland State University professor Gerald Sheble.

"The advent of SOA is going to impact information processing and computer services on a scale not previously envisioned." The speed-up in application development and integration will accelerate the deployment of IT capabilities, which in turn will have a consequential effect on the organization's business agility. Corporate decision makers will enjoy the ability to pick and choose among capital and operations expenses to suit their organization's business goals. The book describes the business trends within which this convergence is taking place and provides insight on how these changes can affect your business. It clearly explains the interplay between technology, architectural considerations, and standards with illustrative examples. Finally, the book tells you how your organization can benefit from *servicelets*, alerts you about integration pitfalls, and describes approaches for putting together your technology adoption strategy for building your virtual SOA environment using *servicelets*.

About Intel Press

Intel Press is the authoritative source of timely, technical books
to help software and hardware developers speed up their development
process. We collaborate only with leading industry experts to deliver
reliable, first-to-market information about the latest
technologies, processes, and strategies.

Our products are planned with the help of many people in the developer
community and we encourage you to consider becoming a customer advisor.
If you would like to help us and gain additional advance insight to the latest
technologies, we encourage you to consider the Intel Press Customer
Advisor Program. You can register here:

www.intel.com/intelpress/register.htm

For information about bulk orders or corporate sales, please send e-mail to:
bulkbooksales@intel.com

Other Developer Resources from Intel

At these Web sites you can also find valuable technical information and
resources for developers:

www.intel.com/technology/rr	Recommended reading list for books of interest to developers
www.intel.com/technology/itj	Intel Technology Journal
developer.intel.com	General information for developers
www.intel.com/software	content, tools, training, and the Intel Early Access Program for software developers
www.intel.com/software/products	Programming tools to help you develop high-performance applications
www.intel.com/netcomms	Solutions and resources for networking and communications
www.intel.com/idf	Worldwide technical conference, the Intel Developer Forum

6180-0185-3482-0829

If serial number is missing, please send an
e-mail to Intel Press at intelpress@intel.com

IMPORTANT

You can access the companion Web site for this book on
the Internet at:

www.intel.com/intelpress/eshl

Use the serial number located in the upper portion of
this page to register your book and access additional
material, including the Digital Edition of the book.